Lacan and Other Heresies

This volume gathers together the recent writings of the analysts and members of the Freudian School of Melbourne and the Belgian analyst Christian Fierens, displaying the ongoing interrogation by the School of Lacanian psychoanalysis into its history, theories and practices.

Within the framework of Lacan's interventions in Freudian psychoanalysis, the book in particular highlights Lacan's inventions in theoretical discourse and clinical practice, including the no-sexual relation, the discursive structures of language, the school, the cartel and the pass. Theoretical shibboleths such as the Oedipus complex are questioned, while the historical writings of Sabina Spielrein are read and interpreted anew. Chapters also engage with the psychoanalysis of children, the questions posed by the psychoses to psychoanalysis and the intersection of creativity and the arts in new and original ways.

Bringing together a range of expert contributions, this text will be an illuminating resource for scholars and practitioners of psychoanalysis.

Linda Clifton is an analyst and former director of the Freudian School of Melbourne, founded in Melbourne, Australia, in 1977. Taking its direction from the writings of Freud and Lacan, the School pursues the investigation and transmission of psychoanalysis and the training of Lacanian analysts.

"Orthodoxy may be a lethal poison for theoretical and practical psychoanalysis, but all that is unorthodox is not for all that heretical. This book delineates the subtle game Lacan has played with these crisscross lines. Was Lacan himself an 'heretic'? Is *RSI* a true 'heresy'? What is the status of the assertion that *there is no sexual relation* in the Freudian field?

Through very different approaches, the consistency of analytic knowledge is questioned here. How can the transmission of psychoanalysis occur within the framework of a school? How does the Oedipus complex work? What about the totemic father? The approach to these questions reflects the singularity of the Freudian School of Melbourne, its way of welcoming knowledge from abroad and building original (but not so heretical) perspectives on psychoanalysis".

—**Guy Le Gaufey**, *French psychoanalyst, former member of the École freudienne de Paris, co-founder of the first French Lacanian Revue Littoral and former director of the École lacanienne de psychanalyse.*

Papers of the Freudian School of Melbourne
Series Editor: Linda Clifton

Other titles in the series:

Invention in the Real: Papers of the Freudian School of Melbourne, Volume 24
edited by Linda Clifton

Since Lacan: Papers of the Freudian School of Melbourne, Volume 25
edited by Linda Clifton

Lacan and Other Heresies: Lacanian Psychoanalytic Writings
Papers of the Freudian School of Melbourne, Volume 26
edited by Linda Clifton

Lacan and Other Heresies

Lacanian Psychoanalytic Writings

Edited by Linda Clifton

LONDON AND NEW YORK

First published 2022
by Routledge
2 Park Square, Milton Park, Abingdon, Oxon OX14 4RN

and by Routledge
605 Third Avenue, New York, NY 10158

Routledge is an imprint of the Taylor & Francis Group, an informa business

© 2022 selection and editorial matter, Linda Clifton; individual chapters, the contributors

The right of Linda Clifton to be identified as the author of the editorial material, and of the authors for their individual chapters, has been asserted in accordance with sections 77 and 78 of the Copyright, Designs and Patents Act 1988.

All rights reserved. No part of this book may be reprinted or reproduced or utilised in any form or by any electronic, mechanical, or other means, now known or hereafter invented, including photocopying and recording, or in any information storage or retrieval system, without permission in writing from the publishers.

Trademark notice: Product or corporate names may be trademarks or registered trademarks, and are used only for identification and explanation without intent to infringe.

British Library Cataloguing-in-Publication Data
A catalogue record for this book is available from the British Library

Library of Congress Cataloging-in-Publication Data
A catalog record for this book has been requested

ISBN: 978-1-032-08058-1 (hbk)
ISBN: 978-1-032-07611-9 (pbk)
ISBN: 978-1-003-21272-0 (ebk)

DOI: 10.4324/9781003212720

Typeset in Times New Roman
by Apex CoVantage, LLC

Contents

About the editor and contributors	x
Logos	xiii

PART I

Lacan beyond Oedipus. The inexistence of the sexual relation — 1

1 Heresy: choose it or lose it — 3
MALCOLM MORGAN

2 Let no one enter here who does not believe in Oedipus — 12
DAVID PEREIRA

3 S-exploitation — 19
RODNEY KLEIMAN

PART II

Christian Fierens – Melbourne seminars — 25

4 Introduction — 27
MICHAEL GERARD PLASTOW

5 How to do something with only the saying — 29
CHRISTIAN FIERENS

6 "I think" in the psychoanalytic discourse or *Cogito* and the psychoanalytic discourse — 38
CHRISTIAN FIERENS

viii   Contents

 7 The failure of the phallus: what is to be done with sexuation?   50
CHRISTIAN FIERENS

 8 Interpretation with-out meaning   61
CHRISTIAN FIERENS

PART III
Lacan's inventions – the school, the cartel and the pass   71

 9 Psychoanalysis or . . . psychoanalysts?   73
DAVID PEREIRA

10 On the necessity of becoming dissolute   81
MEGAN WILLIAMS

11 Writing out of school   90
PETER GUNN

PART IV
Psychoanalysis and the child   101

12 Antigonal   103
MICHAEL CURRIE

13 Falling into silence   110
MICHAEL GERARD PLASTOW

14 The words "Papa" and "Mama": from the cave of language   116
DEBBIE PLASTOW

PART V
Intersections: painting, writing and psychoanalysis   127

15 Between destruction and becoming: Sabina Spielrein   129
MICHAEL GERARD PLASTOW

16 To put one's name to what is not a thought . . .   137
MEGAN WILLIAMS

Contents ix

17 **The painter's saying** 149
MICHAEL CURRIE

18 **The image that binds** 155
TINE NØRREGAARD

19 **On the edge of the abyss** 165
HELEN DELL

PART VI
Spaces of madness 173

20 **A speaker's corner** 175
JONATHAN KETTLE

21 **Close to the wild child** 182
PETER GUNN

Index 199

About the editor and contributors

Linda Clifton is an analyst and former Director of the Freudian School of Melbourne who has edited the three previous volumes of the *Papers of the Freudian School of Melbourne – Writing the Symptom, Invention in the Real* and *Since Lacan*. Linda works as a psychoanalyst in private practice.

Michael Currie is an analyst member of the Freudian School of Melbourne who practices privately in Melbourne. He also consults part-time to child and adult public mental health services. From 2002 to 2010, he founded and worked in a public outpatient psychoanalysis clinic at the Centre for Psychotherapy in New South Wales. He has written two books on the treatment of aggression in children and adolescents, published by Melbourne University Press.

Helen Dell is a member of the Freudian School of Melbourne. She also works as a research fellow in English and Theatre Studies at the University of Melbourne, researching and writing on medieval song and on "medievalism", a fascination for the medieval that often takes a musical turn. Her PhD thesis was published as a book, *Desire by Gender* and *Genre in Trouvère Song*. More recently, she has co-edited with Helen Hickey an essay collection on music and death – *Singing Death: Reflections on Music and Mortality* – published by Routledge in 2017. In her research, she is particularly concerned with the connections between psychoanalysis and creativity.

Christian Fierens is a psychoanalyst who has practiced for more than 30 years in Tervuren, Belgium. He gave a series of public lectures as a guest of the Freudian School of Melbourne in 2015 and again in 2019. He is also a psychiatrist, as well as a psychologist with a PhD on the question of psychosis in Freud's work. He has published a number of books on Freudian and Lacanian psychoanalysis, most recently *Lecture du Sinthome [A Reading of the Sinthome]* (Érès, 2018).

Peter Gunn is a Lacanian analyst in private practice in Melbourne. He has a continuing interest in madness and in keeping psychoanalysis open to interrogation from that outside discourse, as well as from other modes of production, including art and literature.

Jonathan Kettle works in private analytic practice and also teaches at a psychology training institute. He is a member of the Freudian School of Melbourne.

Rodney Kleiman is a psychoanalyst. He is an analyst of the school and co-director of the Freudian School of Melbourne. Originally trained as a psychiatrist, he now works predominantly in private practice with an ongoing appointment as consultant with mental health services. He has published numerous articles in the *Papers of the Freudian School of Melbourne* and is a regular presenter at seminars and psychoanalytic conferences. He has a particular interest in the questions posed by psychosis and its potential treatment.

Malcolm Morgan works as a psychoanalyst. He participates in the seminars of, and receives supervision for his clinical work from, the Freudian School of Melbourne. He also works as a luthier, making classical, flamenco and acoustic guitars.

Tine Nørregaard is a psychoanalyst in private practice in Melbourne and an analyst member of the Freudian School of Melbourne. She has written numerous articles on psychoanalysis both in English and in Danish, as well as translated psychoanalytic articles from French to English. Some of her articles are published in the *Papers of the Freudian School of Melbourne* and in *Écritique*, the newsletter of the school, of which she was also a co-editor from 2000 to 2003. From 2007 to 2016, she co-convened the seminar "Psychoanalysis and the Child" with Michael Gerard Plastow. In the past, she has been an associate lecturer at both the Institute of Clinical Psychology and the Department of Philosophy, Education and Rhetoric at the University of Copenhagen.

David Pereira is a psychoanalyst in private practice in Melbourne, Australia, where he is an analyst of the school and is currently a director of the Freudian School of Melbourne. He has written numerous articles on theoretical and clinical psychoanalysis published in both the *Papers of the Freudian School of Melbourne* and elsewhere, and was formerly consultant psychoanalyst with the Alfred Hospital Child and Adolescent Mental Health Service and Senior Clinician with the Department of Child Psychotherapy at the Royal Children's Hospital, Melbourne.

Debbie Plastow is a member of the Freudian School of Melbourne, School of Lacanian Psychoanalysis. She works in private practice (speech pathology and psychoanalysis) in Carlton, and as a speech pathologist at the Austin Child Inpatient Unit.

Michael Gerard Plastow is a psychoanalyst in private practice in Melbourne; he is an Analyst of the Freudian School of Melbourne and the School of Lacanian Psychoanalysis. He works in the public sector as a child psychiatrist at the Alfred Child and Youth Mental Health Service. He convenes a seminar on "The Child, the Adult and the Subject of Psychoanalysis". He is the author of *What is a Child?: Childhood, Psychoanalysis, and Discourse* (Karnac, 2014), and *Sabina Spielrein and the Poetry of Psychoanalysis: Writing and the End of Analysis* (Routledge, 2019), as well as numerous psychoanalytic papers. He is also translator of a bilingual version of Jacques Lacan's seminar *The Knowledge of the Psychoanalyst* (Association Lacanienne Internationale, 2013), and of Christian Fierens' book *The Soul of Narcissism* (Routledge, 2019).

Megan Williams is a psychoanalyst in private practice in Melbourne and Geelong and is an analyst of the school of the Freudian School of Melbourne. She has been engaged with psychoanalysis for many years, including presenting seminars on many topics and publishing numerous articles and several book chapters. Her PhD thesis examined Freud's and Lacan's writings on anxiety and for 3 years she gave a seminar on the place of the father in psychoanalysis. She is currently doing the groundwork for another seminar to commence in 2021.

Logos

The writing of analysts and members of the Freudian School of Melbourne to be read in this volume is marked at its best by what I will call, following Malcolm Morgan, *sustained heresy*. It is this sustained heresy that also incites invention in their clinical work.

Morgan in *Heresy: choose it or lose it* draws on the proposition of Valentine Cunningham in relation to Western literature that *literacy begets heresy*. This literacy involves a reading *perpetually against the grain of previous readings . . . by readers who see it as their proper business to produce a new, other-wise reading*. It is such a heretical reading in the field of psychoanalysis that has produced this volume.

The writing herein is also inspired by the cross fertilisation made possible by the visit in 2015 of Belgian analyst Christian Fierens to work with the School and to present seminars, which can be read in this volume. Fierens reads and rereads the texts of Freud and Lacan. He reads with an insistent and meticulous attention to logic and structure, out of which he produces, in the light of his own clinical experience, a lapidary teaching that is a privilege to experience.

In his paper *'I think' in the psychoanalytic discourse or Cogito and the psychoanalytic discourse*, Fierens writes that:

> Truth must not be understood as an explication of reality but more so the lack of any convenient explication that drives us to speak.

This lack of a convenient explication of reality is also, I propose, what drives us to write. If there could be said to be a commonality in the papers selected for this volume, it is that all have a certain sense of urgency in pursuit of this truth whose very lack of any convenient explication drives the chase. As such, the papers in this volume are the product of both the now more than 40-year history of the Freudian School of Melbourne and a certain sense of urgency, particular to each writer in relation to psychoanalysis. They invite a reading, a close reading, a rereading, a reading against the grain by readers who see it as their proper business to get some new, some other-wise reading out of the text.

Linda Clifton

Part I

Lacan beyond Oedipus. The inexistence of the sexual relation

Chapter 1

Heresy

Choose it or lose it

Malcolm Morgan

A woman sits in the chair gazing at me.

"I've got a cold", she says cheerily.

I recoil into my chair – I've just got over a cold, and I don't want another.

She notices me recoiling, and says, "You'll have to clean the couch when I leave".

I say, "But it's not a couch, it's a chair".

She says, "Chair, couch, whatever".

I say, "Perhaps it's time for you to move to the couch".

This woman, whom I've met with for many years, says, "I don't think I'm suited to the couch".

The following week, during supervision, I speak about this exchange, framing it as an opportunity, not taken up by my client, when she might have commenced a psychoanalysis. Could I have approached it differently? Should I have pressed the matter more forcefully? And, so on. "What makes you think she's not already in a psychoanalysis?" my supervisor says. I am befuddled by this response. "Well", I say, "In a psychoanalysis the person is supposed to lie on a couch. They don't sit in a chair facing their analyst". My supervisor just shrugs, and says, "She says she's on a couch". I say, laughing, "This is heresy!"

Here is my notion: Sustained heresy is necessary, both for the conduct of each psychoanalysis and as a method of enquiry in psychoanalytic theorising. Without sustained heresy, psychoanalysis inevitably becomes doctrinal. Sustained heresy, however, does not mean fidelity to an originally heretical position – since that is the royal road to established orthodoxy. All the world's major religions commenced their lives as heresies, including what Lacan calls the only true religion – Roman Catholicism. Sustained heresy means achieving and sustaining what I call serial heresy, or heretical promiscuity. Jean Allouch (2007, p. 17) draws attention to this when he observes a homophony between Lacan's then current heresy, RSI, and the sound of the word "heresy".[1]

Orthodoxy begets heresy, and heresy invariably congeals into orthodoxy. It is frequently a bloody affair. Jacques Lacan knew this, and throughout his teaching, not just in RSI, we see the evidence of his attempts to address these twin problems.

DOI: 10.4324/9781003212720-2

His theorising the Pass and preoccupation at the time of RSI with the discourse of psychoanalysis form part of these attempts. At the start of RSI, Lacan makes it clear that his principal focus of the year's work *is* the discourse of psychoanalysis. He needs to "energize his school", he says, and is troubled by what he calls, "other teachings besides mine", *unheimlich* teachings, he calls them, coming from within his school, from people he claims are inadequate to the task of interrogating his discourse. These alternate teachings, he says, display a resistance to the very thing that energizes them – his discourse. Lacan, at this point, sounds fed up with the internal strife within his school. He concludes this first seminar with a question as to whether or not he will continue the following week. Maybe he will take a "year's sabbatical" (Lacan, 1974–1975).[2]

It is possible to hear in these statements the voice of the harried protector of an orthodoxy. But they're not that at all. The question for Lacan is how to weave a path between an encroaching orthodoxy and what the Catholic Church would call Material Heresy – heresy born of ignorance.[3] Lacan says the year's work will test a hypothesis, and this is that one must, as he says, *"play the game according to the structure of a discourse"*. If the game is psychoanalysis, then the discourse that structures the game is the psychoanalytic discourse. There is a real at stake in psychoanalysis that must be first shown, then theorized, "monstrated" and then "de-monstrated", as he puts it in RSI (Lacan, 1974–1975).[4] And, if you don't know how to play that game, if you can't operate within the discourse of psychoanalysis, then you stand outside the discourse, you remain, as he says, un-duped. If you are un-duped, you are unable to participate in, and importantly for my argument, unable to undertake, an interrogation of a discourse. Here is what Lacan says in that year's first seminar. It is important to take this carefully, since I think it is deceptively counter-intuitive.

> [T]hey are not duped, those who don't play the game of a discourse, and thus they find themselves in error. They're not necessarily any the worse for all that. . . . It's just that it would be better if to lay the foundation for a new one (that is a new discourse) starting out from these discourses, one were a little bit duped by them.[5]
>
> (Lacan, 1974–1975)

If you want to play the game, and especially if you want to move from one discourse to another, to "lay the foundation for a new one", you must, first of all be at least a little bit duped by that discourse.

So, heresy is for insiders. You can only become a successful heretic – and success in heresy involves an interrogation from within that lays the foundation for a new discourse – if you are first of all duped, or "bitten" and infected, to use Jean Allouch's (2007, p. 171) word,[6] by the discourse you interrogate. You have to first read something before you can re-read and appropriate it for other purposes. So, one implication of this is that those who snipe from the sidelines have nothing to offer. Pagans – non-believers – are in no position to interrogate a discourse.

Heretics, on the other hand, are neither apostates nor blasphemers, though they are often accused of both. They are whistle blowers for what they call the Truth. And heretical Truth, except I argue in Lacan's case, is invariably spelt with a capital "T". Conventionally, if a heretic survived the promulgation of their heresy, which, once the early Catholic Church had forged its links with the state, was a risky business, they invariably established their own orthodoxy. Think Luther, Henry VIII, Joseph Smith and so on. I am arguing that Lacan attempts to resist this inevitable slide of heresy into orthodoxy – and that his RSI seminar was, at that time, his then current heresy against what he later called in his Caracas Seminar, the Freudian Cause (Lacan, 1980).[7] Causes, Oscar Zentner reminds us in his paper "Lacan, Caracas Station", are always lost causes (Zentner, 2016).[8]

"I am Freudian", says Lacan during his Caracas Seminar in 1980. "This is why it is pertinent to tell you . . . about the debate I have with Freud". Heresy is for insiders. For Lacan, it was necessary to be a Freudian, to choose Freud, to be bitten by Freud, in order to conduct a debate with him. He challenges his audience: "if you want, it's your turn to be Lacanians".[9] It is only from this position of having chosen, and been duped by, the Lacanian cause that his audience might become eligible to conduct their own debate with Lacan – it's the only way to keep the choosing fresh.

Valentine Cunningham, who curiously bears the first name of one of the great Gnostic heretics, Valentinus of Rome, is a professor of English at Corpus Christi College Oxford, so it is safe to say he has made his choice. Cunningham has written a provocative introductory chapter titled *The Necessity of Heresy* to a book called *Figures of Heresy* (Dix & Taylor, 2006).[10] Cunningham's essay is particularly interesting for my argument in that he extends a conceptual bridge between heresy as an exclusively religious concept and secular texts. He argues that Western literature is inspired by, draws upon and extends the great Christian heresies. And he means this more than merely metaphorically. He argues that all the great English writers deeply understood and were concerned about the great heretical themes of the early Christian church. Literature, he says, thrives on heresy. In his argument, heresy becomes a grand creative principle. Reading, re-reading and re-writing are the three R's of Cunningham's analysis of heresy. Literacy begets heresy. Texts are

> not just continually reread, but read perpetually against the grain of previous readings. . . . They're read and re-read by readers who see it as their proper business to get some new, some other-wise, reading out of the text – readers who, disrespectful of earlier readings, are thus eager and committed *formal* heretics.[11]
>
> (Dix & Taylor, 2006)

6 Malcolm Morgan

Like Lacan, Cunningham believes that these secular re-readers are only eligible to write their heresies from within. They are true believers, in their professions, the Academy, the Canon and so on. He quotes Emily Dickinson, herself a heretic Christian, "internal difference", she says, is "Where the meanings, are" (Dix & Taylor, 2006).[12] And eventually, as with many of the early Christian heresies, "offending heretical readings do have a way of getting eventually assimilated and recuperated, re-arriving as neo-orthodoxy" (Dix & Taylor, 2006).[13] How, then, to resist this slide from heresy into orthodoxy?

At the start of the Sinthome, in the year following his RSI seminar, Lacan (1975–1976) claims a kinship with James Joyce as two *haeresis*. He uses the Latin *haeresis*, with its close association with the Greek αίρεσισ, which Cunningham tells us means choice, taking a position or being part of a choosing group or sect (Dix & Taylor, 2006).[14] Lacan is claiming that both he and Joyce are choosers. At this stage of its etymology, *haeresis* had not yet come to mean wrong choice. Additionally, I propose, Lacan is saying that both he and Joyce keep on choosing until their choice is exhausted, or, as he puts it, "is sated".

Lacan says,

> it's a fact that Joyce makes a choice, and in this regard he is, like me, a heretic. For haeresis is precisely what specifies the heretic. One has to choose the path by which to capture the truth.[15]

Lacan specifies Joyce's choice as between what he calls the *Sint'Home* Rule and the *Sinthome roule*.

Sinthome roule – the Rolling *Sinthome* – Heresy

OR

Sint'home rule and what Lacan also calls *Sinthomasaquinas* are ways of describing Joyce's orthodox choice – the Orthodox Sinthome. *Sinthome roule*, the "rolling *sinthome*, on rollers",[16] describes an unstable spinning *sinthome* – Joyce's heretical choice.

So, the Lacanian heretic chooses a path by which to capture the truth. Certainly, not every traditional heretic does this, or at least not in those terms. The traditional heretic has already caught the truth – their truth. The traditional heretic says, "At last, the real truth of the written Word of God is being revealed through me – through us" (Dix & Taylor, 2006).[17] Luther, for instance, concludes his final response to the Catholic Church's repeated demand that he recant his gross error with the famous words. *On this I take my stand. I can do no other. God help me. Amen* (Bettenson, 1963).[18] Luther doesn't say, "I'm on the path to capture the truth, I'll let you know when I've caught it". He says: here is the truth. I nailed it to the front door of the Wittenberg Castle church, and it binds me to this spot. Luther holds fast to his eternal truth, develops a religion based on this truth and before long begins to persecute the next generation of Lutheran heretics who diverge from its teachings. *Haeresis* as choice morphs into orthodoxy, correct choice. They're "doppelgangers",[19] says Cunningham.

It is into this mighty Truth engine that Lacan throws his conceptual spanners. Jean Allouch (2007) observes in his article Lacan Love 11 that the first of these was Lacan's much-quoted aphorism that truth is *mit dire*, only half sayable.[20] The next spanner that Allouch refers to occurs much later, in Seminar 24. Here Lacan invents a neologism that ties the concept of truth to the concept of the variable. What this turns into in English is the *variety* of truth, or the *varity* of truth.[21]

Lacan says in his seminar of April 19, 1977,

> what do so-called statements have to do with a true proposition? We should, as Freud states, try to see what that thing – which functions only by eroding what is supposedly the truth – is founded upon. We should see something being opened to the dimension of *the truth as a variable*: with an elided é.[22]
>
> (Lacan, 1976–1977)

Allouch adds the following explanatory "quasi-linguistic equation" that describes the combination of *vérité* and *variete*, which creates *varity*. The "equation" is:

[*vérité* (truth) + *variété* (variety) = *varité* (varity)].[23]

Lacan's neologism therefore condenses variety and verité to produce a fluctuating truth concept – varity. Truth is a variable, whose value depends on the vagaries of the signifier – an elided é.

Listen to the way that Lacan undercuts the power of truth statements. He starts with "so-called statements", and a seemingly true proposition. "The eternal trinity is consubstantial" – forever True. He next invokes the word of Freud: don't look for, or listen to, "the truth", instead focus on the Freudian Thing that erodes supposable truth. Find out what the Freudian Thing, the unconscious that erodes apparent truth statements, is founded upon. The signifier, as sensed through an elided é. One of Lacan's major heresies is thus embedded in this statement: the unconscious is structured as a language. Enduring truth statements and psychoanalysis are mutually exclusive. Truth is a varity.

So, Lacan is clearly a different kind of heretic. For him, truth is no fixed star. Not an arrival, rather a journeying. Though not journeying towards a specific destination, either, but more a turbulent rolling and spinning around kind of movement. His heresy does not capture the truth. In his poetic introduction to the English preface of the Four Fundamental of Psychoanalysis, he says,

> All I can do is tell the truth. No, that isn't so – I have missed it. There is no truth that, in passing through awareness, does not lie. But one runs after it all the same.[24]
>
> (Lacan, 1979)

For psychoanalysis, then, "the path by which to capture the truth" becomes the path along which "one runs after it all the same". Lacan's heresy runs after the

8 Malcolm Morgan

truth, never capturing it. After linking himself to Joyce as *haeresis*, Lacan tells his audience how to be his kind of a heretical heretic "in the right way", as he ironically puts it. Here, then, is Lacan's orthodoxy on heresy!

> The right way is the one that, when the nature of the sinthome has been recognized, doesn't shrink from using it logically, that is, from using it to the point of reaching its real, at the end of which it is sated.[25]
>
> (Lacan, 1980)

Choose it, use it, then lose it. That's what my paper should have been called. How does one become a heretic "in the right way"? First of all, Lacan says, after the choosing has been achieved, by subjecting it to confirmation. However, Lacan stresses that this is not necessary. "No one is prevented", says Lacan, "from subjecting one's choice to confirmation". And this confirmation allows one to recognize the nature of one's sinthome. Once the nature of one's sinthome has been, as Lacan says, recognized, the right way to sustain one's heretical choosing is to be willing to use it, to follow the logic of the recognized sinthome until it approaches its horizon – what Lacan calls its real. And then one's heretical choice is, as he says, sated. By choosing what he calls the *Sinthome roule*, the spinning wheel sinthome, the rolling sinthome, rather than the Sint'home Rule, the orthodox sinthome that takes its stand, and thus cannot move, one sets in motion a movement along a path to capture a truth that resists capturing.

Lacan doesn't say this, but I think it is at least plausible, given his preoccupations with his school at that time, that subjecting one's choosing to a confirmation involves a psychoanalysis taken to its conclusion. A conclusion that involves heretical re-writing of one's psychoanalysis that is provoked by the Pass. This conclusion leaves a subject little choice thereafter than to use what he has recognized, following the twists and turns of his own *sinthome roule*, as it rolls along pursuing its truth.

I want now to link, in what might be considered a long bow, this choice of *sinthome roule*, what Lacan calls Joyce's rolling sinthome, with another spinning and turning in circles that Lacan refers to in the Seminars of March 8 and 15, 1977. This spinning and turning is his way of explaining an alternate writing of the formula for the discourse of psychoanalysis that surprised both his audience and Lacan himself. I am grateful to Oscar Zentner for writing his paper "Lacan, Caracas Station" (Zentner, 2016), which has enabled me to appropriate, in the heretical sense referred to by Cunningham, some of what I have found there. In the first part of this paper, Zentner addresses what he calls a "lost opportunity" when Lacan, in an apparent mistake, re-wrote his formula for the psychoanalytic discourse on the black board. After beginning to puzzle over what he might find in this new writing, Lacan was promptly brought back to the canonical version of that formula by the intervention of Jacques Allain-Miller. Oscar Zentner argues that had Lacan been left to continue his interrogation of what he had re-written, had he been allowed to follow the twists and turns of his theorising provoked by the sudden appearance of this new formula, to pursue the path of its truth, a new horizon might have opened up that offered something to both his school, which was becoming mired in orthodoxy, "thus becoming a church",[26] and psychoanalysis in general.

In the intervening week between seminars, some people, whose alleged "good intentions" Lacan derides, send him a letter suggesting that his "mistake" during the previous seminar amounted to a "lapsus linguae", a slip of the tongue. Clearly annoyed, Lacan says that his mistake, so-called, was not a lapsus linguae at all, but a writing. He then differentiates between the alleged lapsus linguae and what he calls "gross error".[27] So, not a "lapsus calami" or slip of the pen, as Freud calls it in The Psychopathology of Everyday Life, but a "gross error".[28] Oscar Zentner stresses the point that a lapsus linguae cannot occur in a writing, and that a writing could be developed, in effect re-written. This wasn't what caught my attention, however, in Lacan's response to all those suspicious good intentions. I heard something else in Lacan's insistence on "gross error" in favour of either "lapsus linguae" or indeed "lapsus calami". When you read official Catholic Church responses to the great heresies of the Catholic Church, this is precisely the phrase the church fathers use to denounce these heretics. They have fallen into "gross error".

> Those who hold this opinion are not only in gross error, they even debase the concept of true religion and, little by little, lapse into Naturalism and Atheism.[29]

So, I pose the question as to whether Lacan, as well as insisting that his mistake was a writing, was also reminding anyone who wanted to hear that this mistake was part of his formal heresy, his *sinthome roule*, and that he was not yet finished spinning along his path to capture the truth. Indeed, he makes a point of saying,

> in other words, I am going in circles, spinning around. . . . And this is what happened: the letters written on the blackboard were spinning and tangling me up. . . . I was insisting on this by turning my letters and telling you about the S1 that appeared to assure a S2.[30]

> (Lacan, 1980)

"I was insisting on this". Formal heresy, therefore, rather than material heresy, wilfully chosen heresy rather than accidental heresy. And, as Oscar Zentner points out, Lacan clearly wanted to work his putative mistake. Lacan says,

> I didn't commit this slip completely without reason, and if I certainly pictured the letters turning in the wrong order, I believe that I at least knew what I wanted to say.[31]

> (Lacan, 1980)

10 Malcolm Morgan

Indeed, if we look at the precise moment when he recants, if I may use that provocative word to describe Lacan's response to Miller's injunction, Lacan is already beginning to theorize this latest, surprising re-writing of his discourse of psychoanalysis. We will never know, as Oscar Zentner says, into what "uncharted waters" this re-writing might have taken Lacan, and us.

Notes

1 Allouch refers to the homophony between RSI and *hérésie*, in *Jacques Lacan: His Struggle,* page 17. In: Lacan Love – Melbourne seminars and other works, Edited and with a Foreword by Maria-Inés Rotmiler de Zentner and Oscar Zentner, Lituraterre, Ourimbah, New South Wales, 2007.
2 Jacques Lacan, *The Seminar of Jacques Lacan, R.S.I. (1974–1975)*, translated by Jack Stone, Text established by Jacques-Alain Miller, Seminar of November 19, 1974.
3 The Catholic Church differentiates between formal heresy, those heresies born of sophisticated theological understanding, and material heresy, those born of ignorance, slavishly following an ideology or belief system without understanding. The real threat to the Church was posed by the formal heretics since they inspired others to follow them. Luther, for instance, was a formal heretic, whilst most of his followers would be considered by the Catholic Church as material heretics. Valentine Cunningham, The Necessity of Heresy, In: *Radical Theology in English and American Writing 1800–2000*, Edited by Andrew Dix and Jonathan Taylor. Brighton: Sussex Academic Press, 2006, page 2.
4 Jacques Lacan, *The Seminar of Jacques Lacan, Book 22*. Op. cit., Seminar March 11, 1975.
5 Jacques Lacan, *The Seminar of Jacques Lacan, Book 22*. Op. cit., Seminar November 19, 1974.
6 Jean Allouch, *Lacan Love*. Op. cit., Perturbation in *pernepsy*, page 171.
7 Jacques Lacan, *The Seminar, Caracas, 12th July 1980*. Op. cit., pages 103–106, In: Papers of the Freudian School, 1980, *Homage to Freud/on Perversion*, Edited by Oscar Zentner.
8 Lacan Oscar Zentner, *Caracas Station*. Op. cit., pages 13–31.
9 Jacques Lacan, *The Seminar, Caracas, 12th July 1980*. Op. cit., page 104.
10 Valentine Cunningham, The Necessity of Heresy. Op. cit., pages 1–18.
11 Ibid., page 15.
12 Ibid., page 3.
13 Ibid., page 16, From: *There's a Certain Slant of Light*, 320, Emily Dickinson.
14 Valentine Cunningham, The Necessity of Heresy. Op. cit., page 1.
15 Jacques Lacan, *The Sinthome, Book 23, 1975–1976*, edited by Jacques-Alain Miler, translated by A. R. Price, Seminar of November 18, 1975, page 7.
16 Ibid., page 6. Lacan plays on a number of homophonies associated with the word "sinthome". Joyce, he says, "conjoins" his *sint'home rule*, and *sinthomasaquinas*, as evocations of the pull of Joyce's orthodoxy, with *sinthome roule*, Joyce's *haeresis*. "Both spellings", says Lacan, "concern him".
17 Valentine Cunningham, The Necessity of Heresy. Op. cit., page 4.
18 *Luther's Final Answer, 18th April 1521*, in *Documents of the Christian Church*, Selected & Edited by Henry Bettenson, Oxford University Press, 1963, page 283. Luther's response to Pope Leo X's 1521 *Diet of Worms* which provided a final demand that Luther recant his heresy, prompted Luther final answer which concludes with the words cited. Whilst Luther's response was written entirely in Latin, these final words were written in his mother tongue, German.
19 Valentine Cunningham, The Necessity of Heresy. Op. cit., page 7.

20 Jean Allouch, *Lacan Love*. Op. cit., page 105.
21 Jacques Lacan, *The Seminar of Jacques Lacan*, Book 24, *L'insu que sait de l'une bévue, s'ailéà mourre*, Text established by Jacques-Alain Miller, translated by Dan Collins, Second Corrected Draft, Seminar April 19, 1977, *The Varity of the Symptom*, pages 52 and 54.
22 Ibid., page 52.
23 Jean Allouch, *Lacan Love*. Op. cit., page 106.
24 Jacques Lacan, *The Four Fundamentals of Psychoanalysis*, edited by Jacques-Alain Miller, translated by Alan Sheridan, Penguin Books, GB, 1979, page vii.
25 Jacques Lacan, *The Seminar, Caracas, 12th July 1980*. Op. cit., page 7.
26 Lacan Oscar Zenter, *Caracas Station*. Op. cit., page 16.
27 Jacques Lacan, *The Seminar, Caracas, 12th July 1980*. Op. cit., Seminar 24, Quoted in Oscar Zentner, *Caracas Station*. Op. cit., page 18. Translation by Oscar Zentner.
28 I am grateful to Linda Clifton for drawing my attention to this distinction between lapsus linguae, slip of the tongue, and lapsus calami, slip of the pen. Freud refers to Slips of the Pen in Chapter 6 of *The Psychopathology of Everyday Life*, Volume VI, Standard Edition of the Complete Psychological Works of Sigmund Freud, 1901, translated by J. Strachey, Hogarth Press, London, page 116ff.
29 *The Church's Constant Teaching on our dealings with Non-Catholics*, www.catholicapologetics.info/modernproblems/ecumenism/noncath.htm
30 Jacques Lacan, *The Seminar, Caracas, 12th July 1980*. Op. cit., Seminar 24, Quoted in Lacan Oscar Zentner, *Caracas Station*. Op. cit. Translation by
31 Jacques Lacan, *The Seminar, Caracas, 12th July 1980*. Op. cit., Seminar March 15, 1977, page 43.

References

Allouch, J. (2007) *Lacan Love: Melbourne Seminars and Other Works*. Edited with a foreword by M. I. Rotmiler de Zentner & O. Zentner. Translated by C. Henshaw. Ourimbah, NSW: Bookbound Publishing.

Bettenson, H. (1963) *Documents of the Christian Church*. Oxford: Oxford University Press.

Dix, A., & Taylor, J. (2006) *The Necessity of Heresy, Radical Theology in English and American Writing 1800 2000*. Brighton: Sussex Academic Press.

Freud, S. (1901) *The Psychopathology of Everyday Life, Volume VI, the Standard Edition of the Complete Psychological Works of Sigmund Freud*. Translated by J. Strachey. London: Hogarth Press.

Lacan, J. (1974–1975) *The Seminar of Jacques Lacan, Book 22, R.S.I.* Edited by J. A. Miller. Translated by J. Stone. Unpublished.

Lacan, J. (1975–1976) *The Seminar of Jacques Lacan, Book 23, the Sinthome*. Edited by J. A. Miller. Translated by A. R. Price. Unpublished.

Lacan, J. (1976–1977) *The Seminar of Jacques Lacan, Book 24, L'insu que sait de l'une bévue, s'ailéà mourre*. Edited by J. A. Miller. Translated by D. Collins. Unpublished.

Lacan, J. (1979) *The Four Fundamentals of Psychoanalysis*. Edited by Jacques-Alain Miller. Translated by Alan Sheridan. Penguin Books, GB.

Lacan, J. (1980) The Seminar, Caracas, 12th July 1980. In: *Homage to Freud /On Perversion 1980, Papers of the Freudian School of Melbourne*. Edited by O. Zentner. Melbourne: Freudian School of Melbourne. Vol. 2.

Zentner, O. (2016) Lacan, Caracas Station. In: *Since Lacan, Papers of the Freudian School of Melbourne*. Edited by L. Clifton. London: Karnac Books. Vol. 25.

Chapter 2

Let no one enter here who does not believe in Oedipus

David Pereira

"I have never taken a step in public that did not compromise me; that is my criterion for acting right".[1]

The title of this paper – "Let no one enter here who does not believe in Oedipus" – is very much concerned with the place from which one speaks, and the rightness or otherwise of one's speech and actions, which does not, however, bypass an element of risk. It is borrowed from the pages of *Anti-Oedipus*, a work by Gilles Deleuze and Felix Guattari published in 1972, in which they undertake a critique of the familiarisation of psychoanalysis underwritten by the Oedipus complex.[2] Specifically, the critique made in *Anti-Oedipus* is that psychoanalysis has been prone to familiarising sexuality in reading Freud as binding sexuality to the family, to castration and to sexual difference. The constitution of sexual relations through the wedding of sex to the familial complex is supported and sutured by this mythological argument.

It is not a question here of invoking, as Klein does, the pre-Oedipal, which would nonetheless retain a developmental or structural relation to Oedipus. Indeed, it is in Kleinian psychoanalysis in particular where Deleuze and Guattari read a terrorism of Oedipus: a colonising territorialism in the name of mummy and daddy. It is precisely such a territorialism that creates a theoretical and clinical creep that extends to psychoanalysis at large, and allows the authors of *Anti-Oedipus* to assert with regard to the state of psychoanalysis at the time: "Let no one enter here who does not believe in Oedipus".

Forty-plus years on from this critique, a critique that gathered its momentum from Lacan's own interrogation of psychoanalysis and was given impetus by his subsequent teaching, notwithstanding what might have been his reported personal disaffection for the project, where do we now stand in psychoanalysis with regard to Oedipus?

To begin to address this question, let me share with you a quite recognisable, familiar even, let's say, clinical vignette.

> I can only understand the sufferings of my adult patients in terms of the desires, fictions and anxieties they experienced at the Oedipal stage. And I tell myself that these infantile desires, fictions, and anxieties are still present

DOI: 10.4324/9781003212720-3

Let no one enter here who does not believe in Oedipus 13

today, disguised in the numerous agonies of the patient's neuroses. When, for example, I listen to "Sarah," a twenty-six-year old who is severely anorexic, in my mind I see the little girl that she was and I imagine how she was torn between the desire to be a boy with a "flat" body like that of her brother, the favourite child of the father, and the desire of being a woman loved by the father. Now, it is by addressing myself to this little four-year-old girl within Sarah that I have a chance of influencing the course of her anorexia. When, during a session, I suggest an interpretation, it is Sarah the patient who hears it, but it is the little Sarah who receives it. Which little Sarah? She is the little Oedipal girl that I imagine in my listening and that I suppose to be active in the unconscious of the adult Sarah.[3]

Now, I hope that you will have realised, perhaps even if a little uncomfortably, that this familiar little clinical vignette has a provenance that bypasses my own practice. It belongs to the practice of another analyst: the first psychoanalyst to be inducted, in 1999, into the French Legion of Honour, and in 2004 into the Order of Merit in France. The honour, however, that he considers to be the greatest in his life took place on Monday, May 14, 1979, when Lacan said to him, "Nasio", for that is his name, Juan-David Nasio, "tomorrow you will give my seminar", and he was to speak *ex cathedra* as it were, or as he prefers to indicate it, "standing at the same pulpit from which the master usually spoke . . .".[4]

This little clinical vignette comes from a book published in France in 2005 and in English in 2010, under the title, *Oedipus: The Most Crucial Concept in Psychoanalysis*. In this work, in which Nasio speaks in eulogistic and evangelical terms regarding the Oedipus complex, he does not simply contend that Oedipus is the most crucial of psychoanalytic concepts, but that it is "psychoanalysis itself",[5] since it is "for us psychoanalysts, the model that allows us to understand the adult that we are". A model "that conceives of human beings today on the basis of the Oedipal trial that all children must undergo when they must learn to restrain their desire and temper their pleasure".[6] He must learn to control his or her desires and "adjust them . . . to stop treating his or her parents as sexual objects". To say to his or her "insolent desire: 'Calm down! Behave yourself! Learn to live in society!'"

You will notice the attention that I am drawing to the notion of understanding, which repeats in Nasio's text, together with the restraint that it necessarily brings. These constitute a motif, which recurs throughout the text with a form of a rhetoric of persuasion that positions the Oedipus complex as a "grid" or at other times "prism" – a "theoretical *a priori*",[7] as he defines it, through which one is able to reduce an analysand's saying to a series of familiar statements. Such a grid of understanding *familiarises* the Oedipus sufficiently to have as its outcome, for Nasio, an individual, even a "singular individual".[8]

We ought to be troubled by the fact that the "here" referred to by Deleuze and Guattari in "Let no one enter *here*" is not some dark recess of the IPA which has been impervious to the critique of the Oedipus complex. Rather, it is a narrow psychologistic reading within Lacanianism. Even, as you have heard, quite close to Lacan, which, despite his efforts, proves therefore to not be immune to psychologism under the banner of a reductive Oedipalism.

Nonetheless, we cannot ignore that in addition to the broader *socius*, belief in Oedipus pays the price of entry into a psychologised psychoanalysis, even Lacanian, the French Legion of Honour, the Order of Merit, and even to speak *ex cathedra* from the place of the idealised paternal imago. Membership has its privileges. The price of entry is an identification with a super-egoic mandate encountered as the demand to control, to adjust, to renounce and to consign one's speech, one's "sayings", to a set of "saids" which eulogise and evangelise an Oedipus placed at the vanguard of social and family values. This is the Oedipus invoked by Nasio.

Deleuze and Guattari had, however, already foreshadowed such a failure of their first critique when they noted that it is "Not that Oedipus counts for nothing in our society: we have said repeatedly that Oedipus is demanded, and demanded again and again; and even an attempt as profound as Lacan's at shaking loose from the yoke of Oedipus has been interpreted as an unhoped-for means of making it heavier still"[9] rather than carrying it, as Lacan wanted, "to the point of autocritique".[10]

No doubt Lacan inherited from Freud an Oedipus that normalises in its civilising endeavour. He takes up this inheritance from the very beginning of his teaching and we find it developed from the time of the encyclopaedia article *Family Complexes and the Formation of the Individual* from 1938, and subsequently in the early Seminars. Such an Oedipus exists, and as we have already heard emphasised, in a reading whose demand comes from civilisation itself; submission to it granting access, paying the price of admission, to the best seats in the house. It even organises things rather nicely in the bedroom. The Oedipus complex therefore becomes the "initial cell" of specifically "human relations", a term that Lacan has recourse to in the earlier Seminars.[11] He even ventures forth the idea of Oedipus allowing the human being to establish "the most natural of relations, that between male and female . . .".[12]

Before we rush to the bedroom, however, let's talk, let's chat a little first; that is something which cannot go without saying. This is to say that these specifically "human relations" are a point at which the sexual law in Oedipus is tied to the law of speech; the way in which Oedipus conditions our relationship to enjoyment and to speech.[13] What we ought to note here is the extent to which the normativity of sex is therefore linked to the normativity of speech and language; reduced to the function of a said, a statement.

Lacan's approach to the Oedipus complex at this point invokes these notions of human relations, naturality and normativity, and the fixed and constrained forms of speech, which are their outcome. The law to which the Oedipus complex gives rise is continuous with the law of language as such, to the extent that it "covers the whole field of our experience with its signification";[14] covered or upholstered in a way in which the order of the signifier is quilted, is buttoned down, is wedded in that familiar way, to the order of the signified.

This quilting point, this buttoning point – as an effect of the domesticating and civilizing function of Oedipus understood as the prohibition by the father of maternal incest – ties off and curtails an excess at the level of sex and at the level of speech. Lacan, as Freud before him, however, remained unsatisfied with this yoke of the Oedipus and its rendition of the father as reduced to the function of prohibition of maternal incest.

Let us remind ourselves that it is not that Oedipus, in this culturally normatising form, is of no use; the social value of the prohibition is not to be discounted. It is that it is of no use to psychoanalysts; something which Lacan clearly contends in the seminar of March 11, 1970, 2 years before the publication of *Anti-Oedipus*.[15] In looking for a way out of the impasse of Oedipus reduced to this key to a "normative", "human" and familiarised sexuality and speech whose outcome was an individual, Lacan returned to a piece of lunacy called Freud's invention of the myth of *Totem and Taboo*.[16]

In returning to *Totem and Taboo*, Lacan differentiates the two myths operating in the Oedipus complex. Firstly, Oedipus itself whose dimensions are derived from the Sophoclean drama. This is the normative, culturally appropriated form in which we reassuringly re-encounter the father as the prohibitor of maternal incest. Secondly, the father of *Totem and Taboo* where Freud invokes the existence of this mythical being "whose enjoyment is supposed to be that of all the women".[17] This is the father who is killed by the sons, who subsequently form a pact, which becomes the operation of the Law predicated upon the dead father as the sign of an enjoyment promoted to the rank, Lacan says, of an absolute.[18]

The first is the one that invites our belief – "Let no one enter here who does not *believe* in Oedipus". The second is completely incredible, it is outside the realm of anything which finds reference in our *familiar* experience. It exists in surplus, in excess therefore to the drama of the family figures viewed through the Oedipal prism or grid. Outside of the normalising, civilising Oedipus, one encounters a non-human, non-personable, non-individual *jouissance*.

What is revealed to us with regard to the Oedipus complex is that it is the key to enjoyment, to *jouissance*; in a way, however, which doesn't fall prey to the dominance, as for Nasio, of the function of a sublimating renunciation of the enjoyment of the mother – telling our unruly desires to calm down and to become a respectable member of society. These functions of the Oedipus complex no doubt exist as it is prevalent to the extent, as we noted earlier, that it is central in civilisation. For Lacan, it is not, as we have already noted, that Oedipus is of no use; it is that it is of no use to psychoanalysts in this form of a normative, naturalising constraint.

The neat distribution of murder of the father, on the one hand, and enjoyment of the mother, in both the objective and subjective sense, on the other, elides this question of what to do with a surplus enjoyment, a surplus *jouissance*.[19] It is precisely such a surplus that is veiled in the familiarised Oedipus myth to the extent of making the game of mothers and fathers the only game in town; the game we are all queuing to enter, paying our entry with our belief in the evangelical status of Oedipus. Indeed, neurosis itself becomes inseparable from a flight from this surplus *jouissance*.

The interest of the psychoanalyst is in an enjoyment that is surplus to that constrained within a normatised sexuality given by Oedipus. It concerns the effect of a prohibition that initiates the incitement to an impossible enjoyment placed on the side of the dead father of the primal horde, who is nothing other than the sign of this impossible whose product is not moral constraint but the impossible taunt to "enjoy". Such an enjoyment is clearly situated outside the domain of normal human sexual relations and exceeds the family figures invoked in the Oedipal grid. This surplus becomes the daily problem for the psychoanalyst who does not gain entry to that safe haven of familiarised sexuality guaranteed by the belief in Oedipus and the constraining moral agency which is its precipitate.

To this extent, Oedipus becomes the key to an enjoyment which situates itself outside of human sexual relations; rather, inhabiting speech and language as that through which it finds its realisation. Such surplus enjoyment is something that is only realised in language, incarnated outside of what belongs to the domain of human sexual relations.

From this point, Lacan contends that the Oedipus complex is not therefore what one had thought, but what he says.[20] The emphasis I want to draw attention to is on the "saying" as a persistent de-territorialising of the sign, rather than on the well-quilted terrorism of the "said" as understood. This was something Lacan was particularly addressing around this time, leading to that lecture that acquired the title *L'Etourdit*. There we find the enigmatic enunciation: "That one says remains forgotten behind what is said in what is understood".[21]

We encounter here that possibility of a saying which exists in surplus, in excess to the said, the statement; a saying which draws its funding from this enigmatic figure of the primal father. A saying, a function of speech, therefore that incarnates an impossible enjoyment. It is not, however, in all discourse that such a "saying" can come to exist.[22] Certainly, my argument has been that it cannot exist in that place we enter when we believe in the familiarised Oedipus. There we encounter a form of speech, which eulogises the values of the familiar Oedipus, in which we find a language "understood as a medium of lack and distortion, possibly also as the organ of over-sensitiveness and compensation, of settling claims and therapy . . . barely distinguishable from medium-level depression", as rather nicely penned by the philosopher Peter Sloterdijk in describing the form of eulogising typical of evangelical discourse in which nothing is risked and one is never compromised.[23]

For this reason, as an antidote to the moral cowardice of medium level depression, it is this impossible, Real of *jouissance*, rather than Oedipus as a model of "understanding" human relations, which ought to be privileged by us. The impossible Real of enjoyment located on the far side of Oedipus shows, Lacan contends, what can emerge from language as surplus to normativity and the endorsement of family values.[24] When we do not enter the place guaranteed by belief in Oedipus, the speaker finds a voice, the grain of which compromises his precious individuality, and in so doing renders him worthy of language. This is a point where Sloterdijk, following Nietzsche, argues that existence earns the exultation inherent in a dis-evangelised speaking of language. Dis-evangelism lays bare the force of Oedipus so as to reveal its lunatic, non-human and un-homely side; that of an incitement to an impossible enjoyment which can only be realised in speech and language and constitutes the truth of language; not in its functionality, but the point where it incarnates an enjoyment impossible in the domain of the sexual.

Such a dis-evangelism is what is primarily at stake in an analysis; the possibility of extricating speech from the confines of the familiar as guarantee of individuality, and touching upon this impossible Real which carries itself to the point of an autocritique in the face of the relentless gravity of the Oedipalising tendency. Felix Guattari makes an interesting observation about the method in Lacan's madness in this regard, in asserting that: "he is crazier than most people, and that, in spite of his efforts to 'normalize' everything, he manages to slip, and to slip back into deterritorializing the sign".[25]

Guattari, when he goes on to say that Lacan was an event in his life, differentiates himself from the apologist and eulogist who speaks from the pulpit of the master and wears the familiar medals of his trade. As distinct from the pulpit, the power of the event is to be found in that place of de-familarisation; the dis-evangelism of Oedipus such as to potentiate, as Sloterdijk again so elegantly phrases, the accidental into the destinal. It is that which allows Nietzsche – himself, like Lacan, an event which is a propitious catastrophe in the history of language – to declare himself a dis-evangelist of language; to find the rightness of his action in relentlessly compromising himself and his precious individuality.

Notes

1 Friedrich Nietzsche, Ecce Homo, in *The Anti-Christ, Ecce-Homo, Twilight of the Idols and Other Writings*, Cambridge Texts in the History of Philosophy, Cambridge University Press, New York, 2005, p. 82.
2 Gilles Deleuze and Felix Guattari, *Anti-Oedipus: Capitalism and Schizophrenia*, Penguin Books, New York, 2009.
3 Juan-David Nasio, *Oedipus: The Most Crucial Concept in Psychoanalysis*, SUNY, Albany, NY, 2010, p. 5.
4 Ibid., p. xi.
5 Ibid., p. 4.
6 Ibid., p. 3.
7 Ibid., p. 5.
8 Ibid., p. 48.
9 Gilles Deleuze and Felix Guattari, *Anti-Oedipus: Capitalism and Schizophrenia*. Op. cit., p. 175.
10 Ibid., p. 268.
11 Jacques Lacan, *The Seminar of Jacques Lacan. Book I. Freud's Papers on Technique. 1953–1954*, edited by Jacques-Alain Miller, Cambridge University Press, Cambridge, 1988. Seminar of February 17, 1954.
12 Jacques Lacan, *The Seminar of Jacques Lacan. Book III. The Psychoses. 1955–1956*, edited by Jacques-Alain Miller, W.W. Norton, New York, 1993. Seminar of January 18, 1956.

13 Jacques Lacan, *The Seminar of Jacques Lacan. Book I*. Op. cit., Seminar of February 24, 1954. "All of this process has its point of departure in this initial fresco constituted by significative speech, formulating a fundamental structure which, in the law of speech, humanises man".

14 Jacques Lacan, Function and Field of Speech and Language in Psychoanalysis, in *Écrits: A Selection*, Tavistock, London, 1977, p. 66.

15 Jacques Lacan, *The Seminar of Jacques Lacan. 1969–1970. The Reverse of Psychoanalysis*, translated by Cormac Gallagher from unedited French manuscripts. For private use only. Seminar of March 11, 1970. "I am not at all saying that the Oedipus complex is of no use, or that it has no relationship with what we do. True, it is of no use to psychoanalysts, but since it is not sure that psychoanalysts are psychoanalysts, that proves nothing".

16 Ibid.

17 Jacques Lacan, *The Seminar of Jacques Lacan. 1971. On a Discourse That Might Not Be a Semblance*, translated by Cormac Gallagher from unedited French manuscripts. For private use only. Seminar of January 20, 1971.

18 Ibid. Seminar of June 9, 1971.

19 Jacques Lacan, *The Seminar of Jacques Lacan. 1969–1970. The Reverse of Psychoanalysis*. Op. cit., Seminar of March 11, 1970.

20 Jacques Lacan, L'Etourdit, in *Scilicet, 4*. Paris: Editions du Seuil, 1973. English version translated by Jack Stone. For private circulation, p. 12.

21 Ibid., p. 1.

22 Ibid., p. 16.

23 Peter Sloterdijk, *Nietzsche Apostle*, translated by Steven Corcoran, Semiotext(e), Los Angeles, 2013, p. 11.

24 Jacques Lacan, *The Seminar of Jacques Lacan. Book XIX, 1971–1972*, translated by Cormac Gallagher from unedited French manuscripts. For private use only. Seminar of January 12, 1972.

25 Felix Guattari, Lacan was an Event in My Life, in *Soft Subversions: Texts and Interviews 1977–1985*, translated by Chet Wiener and Emily Wittman, Semiotext(e), Los Angeles, 2007, p. 167.

Chapter 3

S-exploitation

Rodney Kleiman

I am proposing in this paper to take up a short section of the received text of Lacan's seminar titled, *Ou pire, . . . or worse*[1]. Some text, as a useful underpinning, at least I find it so, for something fundamentally important that Lacan said within this seminar, something that he repeatedly said, and that he didn't cease from saying.

The text constitutes only a paragraph or two, from the session delivered on May 17, 1972. We will of course need to consider the context, and this is my attempt to explicate why I think it might constitute something called a key, unlocking one door, out of many possible entry points. It reminds us, or at least it reminds me, of the fact we need to constantly return to the exposition of Lacan's discoveries. His words bear a resonance of the truth, notwithstanding the problematics of what constitutes the truth, in particular by a honing of that truth that we are constantly trying to forget. We constantly manage to forget some of his discoveries, despite continually working on them.

And why not, as even he tried to forget them? Or so he suggests in the introductory pages of this seminar. He states:

"There is no way I cannot do this worse, exactly like everyone else".

And by this worse he refers to,

". . . the trying to get out of the fact, that there is no sexual relation".

Herein is stated the bare truth of his discovery, perhaps his most important for psychoanalysis. There is no sexual relation. Obviously, this is not an easy statement to apprehend, nor comprehend, nor to accept, nor to respond to.

From where did Lacan produce his discoveries such as this one? They were uncovered, he at times confirms, in the context of listening to those who spent some time speaking on his couch. That's where his discoveries presumably still have their currency, not on his couch of course, but on others. Or, moreover, in the consulting rooms of others, where people speak, irrespective of where they are situated with respect to couches or other pieces of furniture.

DOI: 10.4324/9781003212720-4

In these spaces, it's not just simply that men complain of women, and women complain of men, struggling with the impossibilities of relating. They do, of course, complain. But the imperative is not simply to be found in the differences between the sexes and the battles encountered as a consequence of these differences in life, conflicts forever ensuing and ongoing. Beyond the complaints, there are structuring imperatives that it was the genius of Lacan to recognise and articulate according to his capacity for the well said.

From this clinical evidence and experience comes forth Lacan's statement: "There is no sexual relation". This is his discovery, no one else's, at least in terms of saying it so well. For the artists of various persuasions have been saying it, writing it, displaying it, performing it, through the ages, just not so succinctly. It's not really a happy finding nor a "eureka" moment. Eureka jumped from the bathtub and ran naked down the street with Archimedes. He for his effort was rewarded for his discovery, the physics of displacement, by the king's golden prize. Regarding psychoanalysis and the discovery of Lacan, where's the reward?

It might be tempting to stay in the tub and reach for the razor. This would seem, at first glance, a more appropriate response to this truth, if accepted as the truth. And it may indeed be the case that suicidality, in all its guises, is one of the "or worse" responses. The bloody wrist says something other than the truth, it's worse in some ways.

But the truth remains even after you are gone. And so the truth remains as it is, as far as it, the truth can be said or allows itself to be revealed. Since the truth has never been in any haste to reveal itself, unlike Archimedes. It's also quick to cover itself up again . . . with the worse?

The saying he refers to, "there is no sexual relation", is to act as a hub for the considerations of what might be said, even what might be heard. A truth so centrally cast within all our attempts to avoid it, as we proceed with doing the worse of his title, "*ou pire*", or worse.

This discovery of Lacan's is not derived from some logical nor mathematical process which occurs outside the analytic discourse since it is derived from speech: the everyday speech of analysands, to the extent that we always speak the truth . . . without knowing it.

His form of reply to this discovery then utilises the processes and possibilities of philosophy or even a mathematisation, in order to say something about people, men and women.

People talk, they say the worse, since everyone is trying to escape. The better is somewhat less apparent. Is there a "better" counterposed to this worse? Would the truth of the lack of sexual relation be for the better? Presumably so, if there is a better for this worse. But why assume there is a better, when it may all be worse? This question is worth some consideration, and I will return to it later.

Is there a better, can the truth make you better, and if so by what mechanism, or in what manner? Is the truth better than the worse? Is the aim of analysis, with respect to this truth, to get better by way of it?

People do talk. People do talk. About what?

S-exploitation   21

They talk about how they attempt to relate. They attempt to relate, despite the impossibility that language imposes upon their interactions, the limit upon their relating, the absence of the relation which would be sexual.

So, people talk of their relations, relationships, speech replete with tales of failure, frustration, rejection, insecurity, aggression and love. "Is this love?" they ask. Hate is more sure, for there seems no doubt that there is hate. All our inexplicable avoidances, accompanied by wringing of hands, tears and even blood, just keep us talking. Do people talk despite the fact, or consequent upon, the lack of the sexual relation? What burns them up, what boils their soul? What's the tinder for these bonfires of the vanities? What's the tinder for this inferno, the tinder that has always had its mobile facility, long before this kindling found its current application?

What do people think, whilst listening or speaking in analysis, listening to themselves, hearing themselves, listening to others, hearing others? Is the sexual relation always the subject matter? Is the sexual relation, by virtue of its not being, leading us to say . . . the worse, each in our own particular way?

And what of all the single people, those decidedly so? What of the unloved romantics and the never good enough? What are they speaking about? But who is not good enough for whom? Who, to our considerations, is ever good enough? Since, by our definition, they are never good enough to cure a certain distance between one and another.

The decidedly single, for example, those who have chosen not to hobble existence or curtail freedom with the responsibility of answering to another. One may follow one's own singular path, sacrifice: but not the sacrifice of relationship, the constant compromise, the struggle. It's immediately obvious how much can be said to confirm the apparent attractiveness of singleness. The absence of a body, of another, to find in its presence, a problem. But being alone doesn't subtract one from the worse. It's just another answer. Being alone doesn't stop the talk.

So, on any analyst's couch, people are heard speaking, saying . . . the worse, for the sexual relation in lacking, produces within them, all manner of speech when they try to get out of this fact.

May 1972, it's almost half a century ago, so what's become of Lacan's discovery? I have selected the following passage because it seems to explicate something important of what Lacan is saying regarding the lack of the sexual relation. It's a parable, wherein we can grasp the import of his statement, his proposition, from which a very profound truth emanates. It's the deceptively simple tale of the striking worker.

Lacan describes at his seminar the event of a strike occurring that morning. The electricity has gone off, cut off by the strike, consequently in the darkness someone broke a glass of which he was quite fond. He found it difficult to read his notes in the dim light preparing for the seminar. But he's not really upset because the event is nonetheless picturesque.

Lacan says: "A strike is the most social thing in the world, it represents a respect for the social bond which is something fabulous". It's fair to say that a strike is an event of discourse. It is discursive, a message addressed to the oppressors but also engaging others, bystanders, in the struggle. Thus, it is a very social activity. Why do people strike? Because the workers are exploited – by the employers. They are underpaid, undervalued and exploited.

Lacan found it mildly annoying, the electricity cut, and he suggests that others, in particular the wives of the workers, also would be disconcerted by the event. Whilst clearly connected in a different, presumably supportive manner, to the occasion of the worker, her husband, going on strike, she also is nonetheless annoyed whilst going about her morning business.

Lacan goes on,

"The wife of the worker, is called, from the very mouth of the worker, all the same, I associate with some of them, the wife is called a *bourgeoise*".

What's that! The *bourgeoise*, despite their discreet charm, they are generally as a class, designated as the exploiters. And for these exploited men, that is their wife!

It's regarding exploitation that there is a reason for strikes. But where does this domestic exploitation manifest?

He continues, "There are workers, those who are exploited. . . . They prefer that to this sexual exploitation of the bourgeois woman! There you are! That is worse. It is the . . . *Ou pire*".

Now there is a prevalence of commentaries, political certainly, correct and otherwise, the many words denoting the politics of sexuality: sexual politics.

People are exploited. But who is exploiting whom?

Men exploit women, sexualise, objectify and exploit for their own satisfaction. Man is perverse in tendency, according to Lacan, who presumably thus doesn't dispute this status of exploitation, as he in fact emphasises the perversity of man. Man, he states, is restricted from reaching his partner by his perversion as she is only for him the object, *petit a.*

Do women exploit men? The workers seem to think so, according to what they say. If that was not their view then why cast women in the role of the *bourgeoise*. But here Lacan continues to arrive at the important conclusion.

"You cannot say that sexual relationships are only presented in the form of exploitation, it is previous to this. It is because of this that exploitation is organised because there is not even this exploitation".

There is not even this exploitation.

The complaints of exploitation could thus be considered as a ruse, or worse, a covering and concealment of the truth. The sexual relation doesn't exist. How is that truth better than the false conceit of exploitation? I keep asking. . . .

If there were this exploitation, in a previous state, simply an exploiting of one by another, as the pure state of things, would not then this exploitation constitute whatever you might think of it in a judgement of its morality, would it not still constitute a sexual relation? Thank God, it exists after all!

Would people be happier to be truly exploited than to be confronted with what lacks? Don't you think they precisely are already? Is that not already their expressed aspiration?

The workers prefer to find themselves always subjected to exploitation from the *bourgeoise*, the employers on the one hand in the commercial arena, their spouses on the other in the field that could be aspirational regarding the sexual relation. Why does such a preference exist, a preference for feeling exploited?

Why not for the purpose of avoiding the disturbing confrontation with the lack of the sexual relation, which in lacking is primordially not exploitative, since how can it be exploitative if it does not exist? People prefer the semblance of being exploited. A semblance of being is all the being there is for us.

I offer these words of Lacan for consideration about the many ways this idea of exploitation has become prevalent in the discussions about the lack of relation between these two sexes. These two who never can find themselves as productive of One.

It's not apparently politically correct to dispute the original exploitation, but it's not that Lacan is denying exploitation. There is exploitation by men of women, by women of men, by employers of workers, by the rich of the poor, by the powerful of the weak, by the *bourgeoise* of the worker, etcetera. Of course, history and the present give all too numerous examples of the exploitation of one group by another, of one individual by another.

Isn't he proposing that this pressure towards exploitation and its product, either as the beneficiary or as the contributor, as the exploiters and as the exploited, constitutes a response to what lacks? Is he not saying that conceivably this exploitation, as it constitutes "the worse", is the manner, one style by which, men and women, by utilising a "perverse" preference, find a solution to the problem of the lack of sexual relation? I think he is both proposing and stating that, and the argument can be developed further.

If there were a true primordial exploitation, then we would have a sexual relation. Whether it would be for the good or the bad, that being a moral question, could be a judgement upon which each could decide. Ponder the extremity of sadomasochism: the shades of grey, the black and the white. Of sadists and masochists, who is exploiting whom? Whatever the case, it doesn't make for the existence of a sexual relation.

People are obedient. We obey the Other, even the non-existent Other, which exploits us in the manner of a particular sacrifice that each finds themselves predisposed towards.

Repetitive modes of relating to their significant other, which is always in part a form of exploitation. True exploitation of one by another does exist as a possibility, except it's just a fantasy.

Man and woman are only from our psychoanalytic interest simply signifiers, thus indefinable from any external reference. But signifiers are all we have, with which to be, as our being is only through speaking. Which makes for just a seeming to be, as we attempt to be in the pursuit of the sexual relation, at which we cannot arrive.

So, what if through exhausting the terms of reference in an analysis, via speech, some recognition occurs regarding these fantasies of your exploitation? What then becomes of these semblances of the sexual relation, this particular worse, which you have repeated all your life? Through free association, perhaps, it is possible to produce some freedom of association, an association not predicated on being exploited. What if you glimpse something of the full weight of the truth of what lacks, irrefutably lacks?

My earlier questions: Is the truth better than the worse? Is there a better? How does the truth make us better?

Presumably, we have to do something with that truth, or allow the truth to do something with us. May we not even allow it to exploit us, as no one else really can? Mournfully then, to be exploited, by what language asks and demands of us. And what is that, but to keep on speaking?

Note

1 Lacan, J. (1971–1972) *The Seminar of Jacques Lacan. Book XIX. . . . Ou pire, . . . or worse* Translated by C. Gallagher. Unpublished.

Part II

Christian Fierens – Melbourne seminars

Chapter 4

Introduction

Michael Gerard Plastow

The following four seminars, which were presented by Christian Fierens during his visit to the *Freudian School of Melbourne, School of Lacanian Psychoanalysis* in 2015, can be brought together under the rubric "structure in psychoanalysis". The word structure, however, generally implies something fixed or immovable. This is certainly not what Lacan proposes in regard to the psychoanalytic discourse. On the contrary, it is the very absence of stability in the psychoanalytic discourse that provokes what Lacan calls the round of discourses, in other words, the movement from one discourse to another through being confronted with the impossibility of each of the four discourses in turn. To take this from its reverse side, it is, moreover, the very instability of the psychoanalytic discourse that reveals the structure of the four discourses. And what underwrites this lack of stability is that there is, according to Lacan, no sexual relation, leading to a lability in which the subject ex-sists, a lability that may be harnessed as the specific ability of the psychoanalytic subject. This, we might say, is what is demonstrated by Christian Fierens in these four seminars.

The first seminar *How to do something with only the saying*, the saying with which the psychoanalyst works, introduces these themes through its reference to the four fundamental concepts of psychoanalysis, four modalities of psychoanalytic experience each of which is specified by being in motion. Fierens links each of the four fundamental concepts to four forms of equivocation – by virtue of which the words of the analysand may swing in one direction or another – to the four objects in psychoanalysis, the oral, anal, scopic and invocatory objects. One of the striking elements in Fierens' proposition is that each of these objects is a different form of the impossibility of the sexual relation: each manifestation is a way in which the impossible object *a* manifests as an illusion of possibility.

In the second seminar, *"I think" in the psychoanalytic discourse*, he takes up more specifically the four discourses in psychoanalysis as written by Lacan. Here, once again, we find that each discourse specifies a certain possibility of speaking and of listening, which, when pushed to its limit, encounters its own particular form of impossibility of reaching the subject by means of the signifier. It is in demonstrating this impossibility of each discourse in an analysis that this discourse is overturned into the next discourse.

DOI: 10.4324/9781003212720-6

In the third seminar, *The failure of the phallus*, Christian Fierens defines the phallus as the signifier that fills the gap of the absence of sexual relation. Lacan's formulae of sexuation then, in so far as they deal with the phallic function, deal with the different means of plugging the sexual relation. But since any plug reveals itself as deficient, each leak must continually relaunch the analysand's search. Fierens examines the four positions of the formulae of sexuation as so many means of responding to the questions posed by the lack of sexual relation.

Finally, in the fourth seminar, *Interpretation with-out meaning*, Christian Fierens takes up the leakiness of the signifier by reminding us of Freud's story of the man who lent a kettle to his neighbour who brought it back in a damaged condition. The neighbour defended himself, first that he had given it back undamaged; secondly, that the kettle already had a hole in it when he borrowed it; and thirdly, that he had never borrowed it at all. Like the interpretation in psychoanalysis, the neighbour's answer remains an enigma, an enigma that neither solves nor resolves the question. On the contrary, it keeps the question alive: it is continually relaunched in an ongoing questioning. Fierens' interrogation of the topic is relaunched by reference to the three types of equivocation mentioned by Lacan in *L'Étourdit*, the homophonic, the grammatical and the logical. Here, the resources of language, of the signifier, and of logic, allow the question to remain alive so that the interpretation remains outside meaning, and outside the signifier, allowing the subject to be confronted by the real. This real can take the form of the *sinthome*, which may become the subject's very ability to put this lability to use.

Chapter 5

How to do something with only the saying

Christian Fierens

1. The conditions of the saying

What is said is absolutely different from the act of saying. During an interview, you can have a lot of sentences, a lot of communications, a lot of "saids", without having the least access to the very process of the patient's saying. Saying is an event, an encounter that goes far beyond what is said.

How can you get hold of the saying? Silence is golden.

What is silence? What is it to keep silent in order to hold on to the dimension of the saying? To listen without saying a word is not enough to guarantee, to secure the patient's saying. It's not enough, and you can't go on hunting for this saying by asking him to put words to things and to produce more and more sentences. We can't reach the dimension of the saying by this method; on the contrary, more and more information with this overload of saids can be used precisely to avoid the saying.

So let us go back to silence. It's not a pure lack of speech; it's not a closed mouth. It is the foundation of a space for speech. Silence is the building of this space and the condition for every saying.

How can I build a space of silence? What silence is it that gives access to the space of listening itself?

We could start by thinking of a dual relation between an ego and its object, and the communications implicated in this schema.

But the objectivity of the object is not without a *question*, not just that concerning the ego, which reflects the object, but rather a question of a "subject". So, when the said is concerned with the weather, if it is rainy or sunny, it implies not only the possibility of the ego that is thinking about an umbrella, but also the possibility of the rainy or sunny mood of the subject in regard to his whole history.

On the other hand, the ego is not only the mirror of reality. It is nothing without the field of the Other, the big Other, the field of the various discourses in which it found – and in which he finds – its place.

We are inclined to simply think that we are in front of our object, that the adult, the ego, is in front of the child and his object, and he can observe it. But that is not enough. The adult is not outside of the field of the various discourses, which

DOI: 10.4324/9781003212720-7

will always exceed his thoughts. And the child, as our object, is not outside of the question of what is at stake behind this object, the question of him as an unknown subject, a subject that will remain unknown to us.

There is no true silence if we remain within the simple schema of an object in front of the ego, of a child in front of an adult.

The silence is not a hush or a muzzle, an impediment to speak, but, on the contrary, the genuine possibility of speech. We must take care of the silence by bearing in mind the four points previously mentioned regarding silence: the object, but also the underlying and unknown subject, and the ego, but also the underlying and unknown Other.

Required parameters are missing or incorrect

When the space of silence is developed, the saying can find a place; it is welcome, and what occurs in the place of the Other determines the Subject. Speech is no longer reduced to the relation between an object and the ego, or between two persons who are simply communicating about things. There is a place for the event of an encounter, not without the effect of something like hypnosis. The space of silence can be inhabited by a hypnotic passion.

Silence is never fully earned, and neither is the saying. We have to continually re-build silence. But be careful: if we fill it with our suggestion – "in your place, I would do this or that" – then it's clear that the space of silence has disappeared completely. Once again, we have the schema of an object (what is to be done) in front of an ego (who must do it) and we have lost the dimension of saying for the patient.

Let us see what the saying does when the space of silence is spread between these four points.

What does the saying do?

In his book, *How to do Things with Words* (1955), philosopher John Langshaw Austin emphasises that you can do something simply by saying something. These are the performative utterances. For example, if the judge says to the accused, "I condemn you to five years in prison", the accused is convicted in so far as this magistrate is empowered to do such a thing. The same applies to a wedding, a bequest and so on. You say it and it's done, whatever your purpose may be.

But in psychoanalysis, there is no such judge. The analysand and the analyst are not empowered to *do*, to perform things like weddings, bequests and so on (they are supposed to follow the so-called principle of abstinence). So, saying-doing is quite different to the simple saying-doing of the performative utterances, but it is also more general, and dependent on the space of silence.

When the saying is based on this silence, four phenomena necessarily happen for each one: neurosis, psychosis, perversion and so on. But beware: if you are involved in a diagnostic process, perhaps, or probably, you have already lost the

How to do something with only the saying 31

space of silence, or it's quite restricted (once again, you as an ego are in front of the object of your diagnosis), and you will not encounter these four phenomena.

These phenomena are the four fundamental concepts of psychoanalysis: repetition, the unconscious, the drive and transference. Be careful! These "concepts" are not a kind of notion, a kind of bag into which you stick your observations. These are living concepts, and I would like to explain these fundamental concepts not as theoretical concepts, but as *doing* something.

2. The four fundamental experiences of psychoanalysis

Repetition

Repetition is the first degree, the most basic form of doing. If you always do the same thing, then you are doing almost nothing and it's very boring. After very few sessions, everything is said: "I have told you everything about my life. You know everything", the analysand would say. The patient's story can be summarised. And the only issue if we want to continue is to repeat what has already been said. Psychoanalysis begins with this repetition. But why repeat? Or why begin a psychoanalysis that seems very boring? It is very boring if the space of silence is not fully unfolded. When you open out this space, what occurs is that what is repeated is never the same, there is a difference in the repetition. Whatever is repeated – a word, a smile, an interest in a tiny detail (for example an autistic child who is continually looking for cigarette butts) – you must look for the difference in what is repeated. With this difference, you have a signifier: a signifier is something that becomes other, or different, something that is altered or changed, whatever it is. If you can hear this process of becoming through the space of silence, it becomes very interesting and you enter into a living saying. A word, even an important word for the patient, is a signifier only if something is fundamentally changed in it, and through it. For example, the name of the father would be a signifier only if, through it, something is actually changed in it, and if, through it, you can find a new way to be a father, but not to be a father according to classical or analytical theory.

The unconscious

If you keep saying everything that comes to mind, it won't be long before you come to a contradiction. You can't maintain an objective point of view; a universe of discourses appears with a lot of conflicts, contradictions and internal wars. For example, you speak about the great love of your life, but quite soon if you say everything, you speak about what doesn't fit into that schema . . . eventually you come to hate the loved person. Do you love them, or hate them? It's quite bothersome to be caught in this opposition. We wish to escape it and to find a solution to these conflicts. Another example: you dreamt of a certain woman and soon you think to yourself that she is *not* your mother. Of course, she is not your mother, but your thought is about your mother. She is not . . . but she is. . . . There is a conflict between the two positions and you can't decide which is the right one. The interpretation – in the lightning space of the silence – is to hear that there is a conflict about your mother that involves your unconscious, that is, a space of conflicts that are always moving. The second degree of doing is the war, the conflict.

The drive (Trieb – often translated as "instinct")

If you keep saying everything that comes to mind, it won't be long before your body begins to speak. Tears start to flow, or you feel uncomfortable, or you speak about your body, your headaches, your sports or your diseases. You must deal with your body. Following Freud, the drive is the measure of psychic work required to deal with the necessities of the body. These necessities are not simply instincts of self-preservation (hunger, thirst and so on), but also sexual drives and death drives. All this may seem either very practical and without any importance for the inner soul, or very theoretical and without any importance for the concrete life of the patient. So, let us take another example. Somebody arrives too late for his psychoanalytic session because there was a general strike, or some other obstacle. It was physically impossible to arrive sooner; his body couldn't come sooner. Very well, he has a good excuse in the outside world. But it is not finished because there remains the question of a psychic strike in his inner mind; maybe the traffic jam that prevented him arriving sooner is also a psychic jam in his unconscious. The drive is the necessity of dealing with these contingencies of the body. The third degree of doing is the invention that starts with the contingencies of the body to put the soul to work.

Transference

If you keep saying everything that comes to mind, it won't be long before you come to speak about the modalities of the encounter. For example, you'll speak about the person to whom you are speaking, but also of the framework of the setting and also about what is at stake in the space of silence. For example, if the child who is speaking feels that the psychologist is not open-minded enough to understand something, he will conceal this and meanwhile he will continue to think about the psychologist. There is something you are not able to hear; the space of silence is filled in or blocked up by your own person. Of course, he can project feelings of love, hate and so on onto the psychologist, or he can put his confidence in the helping person. This sort of transference is the usual case in every sort of assistance – for the nurse, the doctor, the butcher, the baker and so on. It is the same in regard to feelings of sympathy or antipathy (love or hate). In a psychological situation, you also have this general transference. But there is something quite different and more specific, about precisely this space of silence. The patient has something quite difficult to say; he has to say what is impossible, and then it happens that you – the listener – are always at stake. The fourth degree of doing is to take account of the space of silence.

The conditions of whatever is said

These four concepts are not notions that would describe things. They are things to be done; they are processes. The psychoanalyst – and the psychologist – must follow this path, never dealing with things that are simply given. There is absolutely no reality independent of the space of silence. You can't imagine that there are things, and that you then have to put words to the things, like labels on goods. We never only have things; you have to manufacture them through the space of silence and the process of the four concepts. We never have a child who is so and so; we never have his complaint, his sorrow or his symptom. We always have to make them up, to manufacture them in the space of silence and through the processes of the four fundamental concepts. This is doing something, with only the saying: the conditions of our object are exactly the same as the conditions of the saying of the object. We must break down, destroy, undermine and crush every realism that presupposes that the things were waiting for us, without our own part to play in the silence and in the saying.

But these concepts always seem to return to things. How is it possible to keep them doing, and doing? These concepts, which are in fact experiences in the field of the saying, are not things that can be observed. Each of them functions within itself, which involves a necessary reflection. The concepts are functioning and there is no possibility of overseeing them, of supervising them or of controlling the processes. We are plunged into their movement without any possibility of getting rid of them. We can certainly make up a schema and "return" to the things themselves, but in this way, we don't abolish the functioning of these concepts. It can't be cancelled. With such psychologisation, the processes of the concepts are simply forgotten, but they go on taking us in without our knowledge of them.

So, let's plunge another way with a questioning inherent to equivocation.

3. Four types of equivocation

Is it the same or is it different?

Let us take a tiny thing, say, a drop of water. And then a second drop of water. Are they the same or are they different? You can say that a drop of water is a drop of water and thus they are the same. Or that they are quite different because they are in different places in space. It depends on your point of view. In your mind, they are the same, but in reality they are different. And you can't decide upon your point of view once and for all without losing the working of repetition. Let us take another example of this process of repetition. Freud's daughter left her son alone, and the latter, Freud's grandson, threw a little reel with a thread from his cradle to symbolize the separation from his mother and then pulled the thread to find it again. . . . Was it the reel or the mother? The mother and the reel: are they the same, or are they different? The repetition loses its sense if you choose one of these two possibilities. When we hear an equivocation in what is said, when we reject one of the possibilities, and if we simply clutch at a univocal sense, we lose the process of the repetition.

Is what is said in accordance with reality, or with another said, or, on the contrary, is it quite conflictual?

Obviously, when we take truth as conformity of the said with the thing, we are seeking a perfect concordance. But the said never fits the thing. And truth is always in the act of speech: "I, the truth, speak". Thus, truth always entails the equivocation of the accordance and the conflict. So, when a dreamer says that this person of his dream is not his mother, you can be sure that it is his mother who is at stake, but also that this statement is conflictual. There is both accordance and conflict. We must keep hold of the two sides of this equivocation to go further in the interpretation. And the dreamer must hold on to the two sides of the conflict to go further in his life with his problematic mother.

Is what occurs to somebody to be attributed to his body (the external machinery of the human) or to his mind (the internal machinery of the human)?

Whatever occurs in the field of the human body-and-soul can be exogenous or endogenous. Exo or endo. But once you have chosen one of them and excluded the other, the very work of the drive (*pulsion*) is extinguished. We can't follow the Cartesian differentiation between body and mind because it's a false differentiation. The person we meet is not in this differentiation. On the contrary, if something apparently occurs purely in his body, this always has to do with his mind, and if something apparently occurs purely in his mind, this always has to do with the realisation in his body. We must keep working this interaction between the inside and the outside, since, on the one hand, they are the same, and on the other hand different, but also because on the one hand they are in agreement, and on the other hand in conflict. This is all the more so since the speaker never knows why it occurs to him to say this thing rather than another, or to be too late for his session . . . and this is particularly true for the child who is often able to accuse the adult for his failure.

What is determining in the saying, the analysand or the analyst, the speaker or the listening, the patient or the analyst?

We could say that the speaker (the analysand) brings the stuff of the encounter, and that the listener (the analyst) brings the form of the encounter, that is, the space of silence. In fact, it is not precisely true. The listener is always there with the stuff of his body-and-mind and the speaker is always there in the space of silence that pre-exists any saying. It is not relevant after a good session or a good therapy to say modestly that the listener determined nothing, and that everything

How to do something with only the saying   35

came from the stuff of the speaker. It's more irrelevant still to consider that the psychologist cured the patient. But these questions are not only relevant to the end of the process. On each occasion of the saying, we cannot say what determines the process, the stuff or the form, the analysand or the analyst. And we must remain in this equivocation that involves our listening with our body-and-mind. The analyst is always passive and, at the same time, active. And the same applies to the analysand.

A living equivocation

We have to deal with a general equivocation, not because there are not enough words in our language to express the infinite number of things in the word. That can be true in the space of the infinite number of saids, but it's absolutely not the reason of the equivocation in the saying.

The very reason of this equivocation is to be sought in the doing of the four experiences of psychoanalysis and in the reflection inherent to each of these four concepts. Surely, one can try to disentangle the threads of the equivocation and to find the one unifying thread: "this is so, this is real, and we cannot escape this fact". With this simplification, we obtain a realism and we can say, "the things are the things", or, "a cat is a cat", without equivocation. We can say, "a psychotic is a psychotic", without equivocation. We can say, "I am as I think", without equivocation. With these types of sentences, we have lost the space of silence. We are only on the line between the ego and the object: the cat is an object, the psychotic is an object, and "I am as I think" is an object.

Here we think and go from point to point, so have quite a simple schema. At the starting point, we have a cat. We give treatment to the cat, and finally, we have a treated cat:

However, for the saying, we must think and proceed otherwise. We don't have the object a priori; it comes from another place which we don't know: the subject. We don't have a simple ego; it comes from another place which we don't know: the Other. So, the object for the ego is inserted between two unknown movements:

$$\ldots \to \bullet\bullet \to \ldots$$

This is the reason that we must always keep in touch with the different forms of equivocations and with the impossibility inherent in the object itself.

4. The four forms of impossibility or Lacan's four forms of the object *a*

The function of Lacan's object *a* is to sustain the working process of the saying. The object *a* is not a univocal object, not only because it has four forms, corresponding to the four fundamental concepts of psychoanalysis, but also because, fundamentally, each form of this object is equivocal *in se*. It is an impossible object that appears possible, as we shall see.

The so-called oral object

Within repetition, a lot of things, saids or whatever are repeated. But repetition includes the fact that there is sameness between these different objects, or something that organizes repetition. All the addicts in the word endlessly repeat a series of behaviours, things and so on, which are organized in the hope of finding the lost paradise. Of course, it doesn't exist and it never existed. It is quite impossible, because it is only a product of the imagination, being invented by reason (*ens rationis*) in order to put a sameness, a unity, in repetition. We can imagine this object *a* as the motherly breast, but that is not necessary, and repetition with the different types of addiction doesn't always appear as oral. For example, workaholics don't refer to an oral object but to another paradise at the end of their work. But it's the same structure: the sameness that conveys the repetition of the different works.

The so-called anal object

With the unconscious and conflict, we can build another impossible. With two equal forces, we can build a nothing from movement, provided that we place them in opposite directions. We pull in one direction and together, we push in the opposite direction. We have a conflict, and we have togetherness, an accordance of the conflict with the result of nothing as its effect. This is precisely the mechanism of primal repression: an anti-cathexis against a cathexis. But we can put this forward with simpler examples. If you give a gift, it's very kind, and if you want to get rid of what you give, your gift becomes a waste product . . . and the gift can always be waste, an anal object. But it's not necessarily anal. For example, the anorexic plays with food in order to eat it, as well as to not eat: to eat and to vomit, to love and to loathe. It remains nothing: you give and you take back. It is built up by a double movement of generosity and of privation (*nihil privativum*).

The so-called scopic object: the gaze (regard)

Inside and outside, with the body and mind, we have the possibility of every object in the world and in fantasy. But with this space, let us say our space of silence, we don't yet have an object. It's only the possibility of the appearance of an object. Certainly, this space can be imagined in front of our eyes. . . . [I]t's a scopic object. But the structure of this space depends on constructions of the possibilities of the saying. And it's quite empty. These possibilities go beyond everything that can be seen; it is the mysterious gaze (*regard*) outside the real vision of reality. And it's not only about what can or can't be seen, but also what can or can't be felt, smelt, touched and, last but not least, heard. This object is very important in the field of the saying. As long as we don't reduce it to the scopic field, it's the space within which everything can appear (*ens imaginarium*). This is the topology – empty topology – of our space of silence. In French, it's the *regard*, that is, the gaze . . . but also "the look after". Moreover, the regard is the respect for what has not yet been said (because it was impossible to fulfil the space of silence) and what can be said (that is possible).

The so-called invocatory object

We started with the stuff of the analysand who can find his place in the form of silence offered by the analyst. Here, everything is possible. But this presentation is too easy. We must take into account the following point: this schema is quite impossible; our space of silence doesn't work. This latest form of the Lacan's object *a* insists upon the fact that whatever we found as a schema for our listening structure is not enough. The latest form of object is the negation of the very system of possibilities, of the space of silence; it is the very negation of the scopic object, of the topology (*nihil negativum*). And so we'll have to invent something else on our own account each time we meet, and in regard to the saying that cannot be captured in any form of program.

The ways of the real

We have now to find new ways. The field is open for thought. Beginning from the Cartesian cogito, or with whatever occurs to the ego (he can look in the mirror, or become conscious of himself, and so on), it invents the universe of discourses (and the psychoanalytic discourse, of course). When it starts to explain the world, it invents the phallic function. When it starts to explain everything, it invents the big Other and the interpretation, not without taking account of the general equivocation and of the impossibility of the object.

Reference

Austin, J. L. (1955) *How to do Things with Words*. Edited by J. O. Urmson & M. Sbisà. Oxford: Clarendon Press.

Chapter 6

"I think" in the psychoanalytic discourse or *Cogito* and the psychoanalytic discourse

Christian Fierens

The so-called discourse of the analyst

I am a person, you are people and everybody can decide to speak. Then we'll have the discourse of the person who chooses to speak; if this person is hysterical, we'll have the discourse of the hysteric; if he is a master, we'll have the discourse of the master; if he is an academic, we'll have the discourse of the academic; and if this person is a so-called psychoanalyst, we'll have the discourse of the analyst. But are these differences really the starting point of these discourses? And for the discourse of the analyst: who decided to speak? The analysand or the analyst?

Let us begin with the analyst.

We suppose that the analyst is a savvy person who is shrewdly informed about psychoanalysis; he knows and will act with his knowledge. This knowledge is the very agent or even the very broker of what occurs in the session, in the encounter between the analysand and the analyst, between the patient and the psychologist. The analyst is listening quite carefully to his object, the patient, and he is trying to understand him in the framework of his theoretical knowledge. And if the latter is good enough, he is supposed to succeed in it. This is the first role of the analyst and the schema of this practice is nothing more than the practice of a garage mechanic: his knowledge helps him to work on the object that is defective, to repair it in order to satisfy the driver. This practice is a discourse, and, starting from knowledge, it is an academic discourse; we can try to conceal it, but the discourse of this analyst is in fact a dogmatic discourse or an academic discourse. And the functioning of this discourse misses the point of psychoanalysis.

Academic discourse:

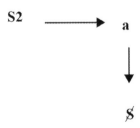

Figure 6.1

DOI: 10.4324/9781003212720-8

But everybody knows that it's better for the clinic to keep an empty place in knowledge, especially in the field of psychology. The analyst must ignore what he knows, Lacan said.[1] Every patient is a new one and we must listen to him as if he were the first one, without any preconceptions. So, the analyst is now starting from a point of view he doesn't know; he is the subject who doesn't know about anything. And this is a sceptical position. The analyst is a blank subject who agrees to be without any knowledge in order to question the symptom or the signifier of the patient. And it is only then that the latter can produce a new knowledge. The patient is thus introduced in the sceptical discourse of the analyst. But the so-called discourse of the analyst is in fact a hysterical discourse: the analyst plays the role of the hysteric in order to put the symptom into question. This is not a monopoly of psychoanalysis. This position of scepticism (or the analyst in a hysterical discourse) is certainly a necessary one for psychoanalysis, but it is not sufficient to sustain the psychoanalytic process.

Hysterical discourse:

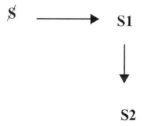

Figure 6.2

Then, following Lacan, we can consider that the analysis consists in putting the signifier to work. So, we can engage the clutch in the process of knowing in order to produce results in the objective world. With the signifier as a semblance, the analyst becomes dynamic; he represents a driving force towards objective results. Perhaps, he becomes a guru. In this schema, the agent of discourse is not precisely the analyst, but it is the signifier itself, the master signifier, and the analyst is the broker of a master discourse. Through the signifier that is supposed to act, the analyst is playing the role of a master. When we are dancing in a roundabout of the three discourses (the academic, the hysteric, the master), we are always under the pressure of a signifier. . . . [I]t's always the same theme of a signifier that is supposed to call the tune. With all these discourses, the analyst soon believes that he must be a master with the signifier. The analyst has taken the role of master: we are in a master discourse.

Discourse of the master:

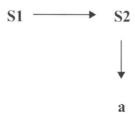

Figure 6.3

Every time the analyst wants to take on a role, the so-called discourse of the analyst is either an academic discourse, a hysterical discourse or a master discourse. It seems that the discourse of the analyst doesn't exist as such; it's only a window dressing, which conceals a quite ordinary discourse.

Can we find a fourth possibility? Far from these suspicious discourses that miss the point of psychoanalysis, we would like to stick to the reality, the "psychic reality" if it exists, or to what is true for the patient, or to what occurs conspicuously in the treatment: dreams, projects or simply what is said and lived by the patient. Then the analyst would be the witness of that reality, in other words, the very listener or the very writer of his patient's story. This last option implies that there is a reality that remains unscathed by the discourses, by the listener or by the analyst, and that it would be possible to expect a complete adequation between reality and what is said. Then the saids could completely tally with reality. That is never the case. We never have this pure reality, this reality without any traces of discourse. But we are always dreaming of this so-called reality. This faith in a pure reality including psychic reality, this realism, is a dream, an illusion or self-delusion, and this is quite opposite to psychoanalysis, as we shall see. So, the fourth discourse, the discourse of the analyst-witness, is surely not adequate for psychoanalysis. Whatever the role of the analyst may be, it doesn't fit the experience itself of psychoanalysis.

Before going further, I hope everyone recognises himself in at least one of these four discourses (academic, hysterical, master and witness), because we are always led astray by at least one of these roles. Even more so by the four, one after the other, all the more so since we cannot escape from the requirement of taking on roles, roles and roles. When we realize – and here "realize" means that we cannot deal with a so-called blank reality – when we realize that we are caught in these four roles without keeping in touch with psychoanalysis, then we are invited to return to the very beginning of the psychoanalytic process: the unconscious that appears to be made up of thoughts, or more precisely, of thinkings. I think, but *what* I think is not an accurate account, neither of what it is nor of what I am. And I think is not just the fact of the analysand; it must be true for the analyst.

So, we must start with the thinking or with the fundamental rule: "Say whatever you think, without making any selection".

Introduction to the Freudian cogito

The subject is not the same as an individual. An individual is "one", without any division. He is what he is. Full stop. He thinks that he is quite as he thinks. "I am as I think" is the most simplistic and the most common form of the cogito; and of course: "I think as I am". One could think that such an individual is paranoid, but it's much simpler and more commonplace: everybody has a tendency to believe that what he thinks is reality, and that he is as he thinks. However, with such a

"I think" in the psychoanalytic discourse   41

position it's quite impossible to start an analysis. The first condition for an analysis – or more generally, to start a genuine encounter between a subject and a listener – is to suppose that he is not what he thinks. Why should he consult you if he already knows who he is and what the problem is?

So, when a psychoanalysis is beginning, one thing that is absolutely excluded is: "I am as I think". One can express it more clearly: "either I don't think or I am not". . . . This is not the same as "either I think or I am", because it's also quite possible that "I don't think and I am not". And this is very important; this principle remains until the end of psychoanalysis and thereafter.

Figure 6.4

We can show it in an image using set theory to distinguish four loci, from which one is absolutely excluded. The field of psychoanalysis is thus reduced to the three remaining loci. We must cope with these three possibilities and with the necessity to exclude the fourth, to achieve the framework of the psychoanalytical discourse.

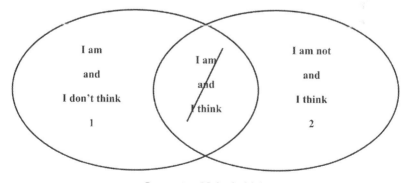

Figure 6.5

42 Christian Fierens

We can provide another schema of these four fundamental points for psychoanalysis (the possibility of three points, plus the exclusion or the impossibility of the fourth):

1. I don't think **and I am**	**0. Either I don't think** **or I am not**
2. I think **and I am not**	**3. I don't think** **and I am not**

Figure 6.6

This diagram gives us precisely the schema of the four places of any discourse with the advantage that we can better understand what is at stake in the places in the discourses:

1. Agent? **Or semblance?**	**0. Other?** **Or enjoyment?**
2. Truth? **...**	**3. Product?** **Or surplus enjoying?**

Figure 6.7

The realistic stuff, or the matters of the discourses

If the condition for psychoanalysis is to give up the position: "I am as I think", this condition is also exactly the same as the general condition for the discourses. With this condition of giving up the idea: "I am as I think", instead of the process of psychoanalysis, it would be easier to start with the simpler discourses where the semblance seems to be an agent: the agent as knowledge (i.e. academic discourse), the agent as subject (i.e. hysterical discourse) and the agent as signifier (i.e. master discourse). But meanwhile, with these different forms of discourse, we are easily brought back to the idea that: "we are as we think", and that the agent of discourse (whatever it is) is speaking to another individual (the Other) who is generating a product. We are plunged into a realistic world where the truth consists only in sticking to the real object about which we are speaking, where the semblance is a real agent, where the enjoyment is reduced to the other individual to whom we are speaking, where the surplus enjoyment is reduced to a real product, that is, an object that can give satisfaction.

"I think" in the psychoanalytic discourse 43

As I first put forward, the so-called discourse of the analyst appears sometimes as an academic discourse, sometimes as a master discourse, or a hysterical discourse, or self, as a realistic discourse. If we want to see the discourse of the analyst as a realistic one, the analyst as agent speaks to the analysand in order to produce a signifier, then the truth of the interpretation can follow to finish the process.

1. Agent	0. Other
a = Analyst	S = Analysand
2. Truth	3. Product
S2 = Interpretation	S1 = Signifier

Figure 6.8

Finally, the interpretation could come back to the analyst: the round would be completed. In doing so, we have perhaps secured the analyst in his position and that can mean a kind of "passe" . . . a bad one.

Discourse of the analyst:

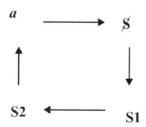

Figure 6.9

However, if we take into account the fact that with this kind of psychoanalysis the interpretation becomes the agent of psychoanalysis, and that the object a becomes the truth of psychoanalysis, we must reverse the positions of object a and knowledge:

Figure 6.10

This realistic discourse of the analyst looks somewhat like a capitalist discourse; it could be named the capitalist discourse of the analyst:

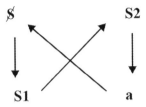

Figure 6.11

Why? What should have been in the place of surplus enjoyment – "I am not and I don't think" – is taken as an objective product. In the capitalist discourse, the surplus enjoyment is taken for mere profit. Similarly, in the realistic discourse of the analyst, the signifier is no longer surplus enjoyment: it is a real linguistic product. It can be pinpointed as a realistic object and you can more or less easily manage to find an interpretation for this signifier in psychic reality.

Why is this possible? Because we have lost the ground of psychoanalysis: "either I do not think, or I am not". The subject who should be in the place of the Other or the analysand is no longer in the equivocation of: "either I do not think, or I am not"; he is an individual.

Finally, with the subject who is taken for an individual, with the objectification of the signifier and through the hermeneutic interpretation, the analyst becomes the truth of a *realistic* discourse of the analyst. But this truth sounds like: I am a psychoanalyst, I am sure of it. . . . I am . . . and henceforth I don't think anymore. . . . And the place of truth is no longer the place of thoughts, but it sticks to reality.

These four elements (analyst, analysand, signifier and interpretation) are merely the realistic matters that fill the empty holes of the four loci of the psychoanalytical cogito. Although these four loci are always more or less filled with such types of material, it's quite important to keep in touch with their previous holes, with the emptiness that is their very reason for existing. These matters never quite fit into the four loci: the analyst is never an object *a*, and the analysand doesn't exist without his first equivocation: "Either I don't think or I am not". The signifier, in order to be a possibility for being and thinking, is precisely outside every being and every thinking, and it can't be pinpointed. Truth must not be understood as an explication of reality but, more so, the lack of any convenient explication which drives us to speak.

How to sustain the empty space of the four loci of the psychoanalytical discourse

It's impossible to dismiss the four elements (analyst, analysand, signifier and interpretation). They are there and they each have their roles. Our

"I think" in the psychoanalytic discourse   45

discourses – psychoanalysis included – are necessarily taken up in the established discourses, even in a realistic discourse. Although we understand the underlying cogito and its four loci underlying each discourse, we must consider that the loci of the discourses are always plugged with realistic objects (an individual subject, a signifier, an object, a knowledge). Furthermore, we are keen to understand these loci as parts of a machine regardless of the difficulties of the cogito, of our being that is in question, and of our unconscious which is always thinking.

How can we deal with such difficulties?

When we are speaking normally, we try to give a coherent account of what is to be said. As far as possible, everything must fit into our discourse and we reject what is inappropriate. Here, in psychoanalysis, we have to retain these inappropriate things that seem dirty, these lacks in comprehension, even these contradictions and this waste that nobody wants. Why cope with all these difficulties? Because we want as far as possible to keep in touch with the aforesaid unconscious that thinks through the holes. Maybe we can speak as easily as a master, as an academic, as a hysteric or as a realist. But at the heart of and in the depth of these discourses, there is a hole or there are holes where we remain without any resources, without any possibility. We can find these holes, these impossibilities. We can do it: it's doable. And that is the very reason for the Lacanian matheme: you can do it without any outside support. (It's true in mathematics that you can resolve a sum without any help from outside and without the recognition from outside; it's the same in psychoanalysis but outside of mathematics: you can do it on your own, that is, in the session, without the help of the outside.) Everybody can take stock of these holes.

The matheme of the impossible

How is this to be done? First of all, we must do what is possible. In fact, we do it when we are plunged quite spontaneously into the academic discourse, into the hysterical discourse, into the master discourse or into the realistic discourse. In the framework of the academic discourse, we must try to involve the object represented by the analysand in our good enough theories. In the framework of the hysterical discourse, we must try to let the subject work to find another explication on his own. In the master discourse, we must try to pinpoint a signifier, whatever it would be, to produce new objects and new objectives for his life. We must try to track the reality although we do know that it doesn't exist as such. But all of these attempts or trials are only the first part of what is doable, the first part of the aforesaid matheme. As a matter of fact, this first part is not really a matheme because it depends on the particular conditions of knowledge, of the subject, of the signifier, of the object. In these matters, we are quite dependent on the outside. It occurs, but not necessarily in this way or that, and we cannot mastermind these contingent events. These are already done or given, but they are not doable as such. And they are just the stuff, the matter – any matter is good – for the matheme.

46   Christian Fierens

Let us move on to the second part. Starting from these possible matters, we can always track the impossibility *within* these possibilities. As we push our discourse as far as possible, we shall always reach a point where it doesn't fit anymore, neither in the framework of thinkings, nor in the framework of beings. But it's difficult to accept this statement of impossibility, and the product of our discourse is then taken only for a plug that conceals the hole of the place where it neither thinks, nor it is. But we can imagine the place where we are totally without any resource of thinking or being; we are lost inside our discourse, whatever it is. And that is always doable.

So, in the academic discourse, when I try to form or produce a subject in the exercise of my knowledge or in the framework of my psychoanalytic theory (academic discourse), it's always a subject without any possibility of inventing or creating something. To tell the truth, it is always a dead subject or at least a completely unemployed subject. Inside the possibility, we can find the impossibility of reaching the acting subject with the signifier.

1. Agent	0. Other
S2 = knowledge	Object *a* (student)
2. Truth	3. Product
S1	S = Subject

Figure 6.12

In the hysterical discourse, when I try to devise a new knowledge, starting from the individual case, it's always a theory that remains outside of the possibility of understanding the truth of the subject, that is, the object to which it sticks in his fantasy. Inside the possibility, we can find the impossibility of reaching the truth of the subject, in other words, his object *a*.

1. Agent	0. Other
Subject	S1 (master signifier)
2. Truth	3. Product
Object *a*	S2 = new theory

Figure 6.13

In the master discourse, when I try to push forward an objective, the effectiveness of my act, I don't find the essence of the object. At best, it's only an approach of what I wanted consciously, a material object that takes the place of my unknown objective. Inside the realisation of the possibility, we can reach the impossibility of masterminding what we want.

1. Agent	0. Other
S1	S2 = the knowledge at work
2. Truth	3. Product
Subject	Object a = objectivity

Figure 6.14

And when we speak of the reality of a patient, his dreams and his life, which is always possible, we can be sure that what we think doesn't fit with the aforesaid reality; there is no reality at all outside of our discourses that always hit against the impossibility.

So, the first step is to accept the possibility: "it is that", whatever the discourse. The second step is to find the impossibility *inside* the aforesaid possibility: "it is not that" (and that is what is always doable, i.e. the matheme). The analyst is always a possible master, a possible hysteric, a possible academic, a possible witness of reality. But in doing so, he is not yet in the psychoanalytic discourse, whatever the effects of his practice might be. Psychoanalysis is only at stake when the second step (i.e. the matheme) begins to work. The only training for psychoanalysis is to try, of course, and then to practise doing this second step, to find the impossibility in the possibility.

We could think that we received the free associations of the patient as a field of infinite possibilities. And so they are. And then we would try to find the impossibilities in the psychic field of the patient. There are a lot of holes in his story, in his past, his present and his future; he cannot do just anything. He is limited. But it would be too easy to fill these holes in the field of the analysand when it is more important to find impossibilities and holes in the movement of psychoanalysis. Certainly, to find and fill the holes regarding the patient seems to be an adequate clinical point of view. But it's a point of view that depends once again on the academic, hysteric or master discourses. And the analyst appears there in the possibility; he appears to be able to mastermind all of these elements.

In answer to *this* possibility, the impossibility is to be found first concerning the aforesaid analyst. Of course, he cannot avoid being trapped in these different discourses that effectively miss the point of psychoanalysis; but when he is speaking or simply thinking, he can and he must hunt for the impossibility inherent to his own discourse, whatever it is.

The impossibility can be of different types: the contradiction or the impossibility of being coherent, the incompleteness or the impossibility of being complete, the impossibility of demonstrating, the impossibility of deciding.

Of course, one can try to find a solution. If there is an incoherence, one can try to find a new argument or a compromise; for Freud, the symptom was essentially a compromise-formation between the preconscious and the unconscious. If there is an incompleteness, one can try to fill in the hole; the fantasy is powerful in creating or recreating a paradise lost. If there is an indemonstrability, one can try to find a more powerful mind that can demonstrate everything, and we shall invent the reality of the big Other that knows and sees everything. But if it is an indecidability, what is to be done? Shall we wait for somebody who will decide for us? Insh'allah? Or will the analyst decide for the analysand?

The four places in the psychoanalytical discourse

Although the fulfilment is always ready-made for each kind of impossibility, the so-called analyst won't surrender to these conveniences, because he will keep the place of the blank hole of the impossibilities behind every plug in the hole. He won't accept to be the compromise, he won't accept to be the paradise, he won't accept to be the demonstration, he won't accept to make the decision. These naysayings before each kind of possibility are the four forms of the so-called object *a* of Lacan. The analyst as person must disappear to allow a place for this object *a*. But, of course, such an object as impossible cannot act or work in common sense; it is only a semblance. Certainly, the patient is always expecting that his so-called analyst would find a compromise and the solution to his problems, that his so-called analyst would give him paradise for the satisfaction of all his drives, that his so-called analyst would explain and demonstrate the means of his psychic apparatus or that he would give him good counsel to decide. But if the analyst complies with these requests, he and his patient are already outside of the analytic discourse.

But what is the aim of this ascetic practice? The first aim is to keep the analysand in the place of the analysand, that is: "either I don't think or I am not". So, he is just *working on*, not in the sense of a *working through* which would lead to a solution of his problems . . . if possible, but *working on* in the sense of sustaining the ground of psychoanalysis and at the same time the ground of discourse and human acts in general. The analysand is then held in the position of questioning the subject and not at all the individual.

What are the consequences of this process? One might anticipate some signifier . . . and so sometimes the analysand and the analyst are looking forward to encountering a marvellous signifier in the style of a "Signorelli" for Freud. But a beautiful signifier, with a multitude of meanings, doesn't occur very often. So much the better. The signifier produced by the analytic discourse is not at all a signifier that must lead to a beautiful interpretation. This kind of signifier is only a plug in the hole of surplus enjoying, in the hole where "neither it thinks, nor it is". This hole is the supreme form of enjoyment, the delightful enjoyment without matter to think or to be. But nevertheless, this surplus enjoying must be imagined; it must be a signifier, and this is the phallus that we shall talk about later. Let's say for the moment that the phallus can play its role only if it is deprived of its imaginary form, only through the form of a minus phi, only through castration. You can't interpret the phallus because it's the very ground of interpretation in general.

The fourth place, truth, doesn't consist in taking account of the different saids and statements in psychoanalysis. On the contrary, the hole in the knowledge, the impossibility of getting a big Other that would supervise all the matter, is the condition for the exercise of truth: "I, the truth, speak". And that is the practice of psychoanalysis: to speak without any supervision or control from an outside, and giving each discourse the movement to change, create and invent.

The assurance of the psychoanalytical discourse

Would it be sufficient to create, to invent, in order to be in the psychoanalytic discourse? It is not so easy because we are trapped in the matter that constitutes the very stuff of psychoanalysis and there is no specific stuff for its discourse. It always borrows its content from another discourse. And so it is very important to differentiate between the process of psychoanalysis and its matter.

Lacan's topology is made for that purpose. The matheme that edicts an "it's not that" in the "it's that" is something like a cut in a surface, and it can change everything when you stitch the two sides of the cut differently, that is, after a twist that gets one face of the surface in continuity with the other. Then you can easily travel from one face of the surface to the other, because they are now the same. This gives you a new field of possibilities and creations.

I said that we would speak without supervision. Isn't there supervision in the field of psychoanalysis? The so-called supervision is only an encounter to be sure that we are still in the matheme, in the maintaining of our discourse, that we aren't lost in another discourse, forgetting the psychoanalytic discourse. The supervisor has nothing to say to the practitioner except to remind him of his duty to keep in touch with the aforesaid matheme. For the rest, the practitioner will invent everything that seems good to him for the development of the *cogito*.

Note

1 *Variantes de la cure-type.*

Chapter 7

The failure of the phallus

What is to be done with sexuation?

Christian Fierens

What is to be done with sexuality – the fact that all of us are born either girl or boy, and that everyone has his own sexual characteristics? Two paths seem possible: either sexuality is to be fully enjoyed, or it is for reproduction. For each of these schemas, we start from a given point (sexuality and its characteristics) and we look forward to reaching another point (i.e. satisfying enjoyment or making a child). We also encounter difficulties or conflicts in the given sexuality, in the symptoms, and then look forward to solving the problems and curing the sane person behind the patient. All these schemas can be represented with an arrow between two points:

(given sexuality) $\bullet \rightarrow \bullet$ (full enjoyment)
(given sexuality) $\bullet \rightarrow \bullet$ (successful reproduction)
(given problems regarding sexuality) $\bullet \rightarrow \bullet$ (recovery of a sane sexuality)

All of these schemas can be understood in the framework of a mathematical function. This leads from a point in a first set to a point in another set. My thesis is that this does not fit into the field of psychoanalysis. We don't have a given sexuality; we have to fabricate it, to create it in our discourses. And that is sexuation.

Lacan said: "there is no sexual relation". Of course, there are sexual relations. But, in these relations, we miss the point at the beginning and we miss the point at the end of the process. It is not just the fact of pathology. At the beginning, human sexuality is never a given; it must be made (that is the process of sexuation). In the end, enjoyment is never fully satisfying (we must deal with one more thing). And reproduction is not the endpoint: we must deal with the child: "What is a child?" asked Plastow (2015). So, we don't have endpoints and we are left with only an arrow. Let us try: this arrow would be the phallus, an arrow or a movement, or even better, a change in the movement, without beginning and without end.

If we begin now from the psychoanalytic discourse, we have a similar situation. With all the possible roles for the analyst, we miss the point: we cannot fulfil any of these roles. And if, with the saids of the analysand, we enter into repetition, into the conflict of the unconscious, into the drive, into the transference, then each time we come up against an impossibility. We don't have the possibility of completing

DOI: 10.4324/9781003212720-9

The failure of the phallus   51

the repetition, of avoiding the contradiction of the unconscious, of demonstrating the functioning of the drive or of deciding the transference. We don't achieve anything in the framework of a classical mathematical function.

In human sexuality and in the psychoanalytic discourse, we inevitably encounter a failure, the impossibility of knowing, the impossibility of resolving the problem. Instead of plugging up these different leaks or impossibilities in sexuality and in the discourses, with explications, interpretations and different meanings, the psychoanalytic discourse must maintain the signifier in the field where each being and each thinking disappears: "I am not and I don't think". Then the signifier 1 is cut off from the signifier 2. The signifier 1 does not lead to sense; from sense we come back to nonsense or to absence.

What does this mean? Let us take a slip of the tongue or a slip of the pen. We have a signifier 1 that does not fit with the general meaning in which it occurs. Of course, we can find an explanation through the so-called unconscious of the patient and we then have a signifier 2. With this, we get a sense or meaning from the slip. This is the classical Freudian interpretation: to make sense of the formations of the unconscious, and we have many examples of this in Freud's early works. But such interpretation does not fit with the mystery of the unconscious and remains a plug in the hole. Of course, we can give such explanations, but, with these, the saying, beginning from where I don't know, the saying is at stake in the unconscious: "the saying remains forgotten behind what is said in what is heard" (Lacan, 2001, p. 449; Gallagher, p. 1).[1]

By emphasizing this saying that is always forgotten, we take account of the psychoanalytic discourse. The given explanations (for example the classical Freudian interpretation: "this person in your dream is your mother") find relations between today's symptoms and the patient's early life. However, these relations or interpretations are always approximations which plug a hole that is impossible to fill. There is no relation. This person in your dream is not your mother and it is inadequate to explain the current symptoms with childhood memories. The classical schema of the function does not fit. Between the points, there is no relation.

But why add "sexual": "There is no *sexual* relation?"

It is not because the patient might or should have to speak a lot about his sexuality. This is not always the case. But whatever is said, it is always said within the interest of the speaker, and this interest is always sexual. Nothing is said without underlying attention, and this attention – conscious or unconscious – is always built upon a sexual interest. And nothing exists outside the framework of our fantasies (refer to Lacan's Schema R).

Attention and interest are sexual, but we don't know where they come from and where they lead. Of course, we would like to stick to an ultimate reality, but we don't have one. Our discourses are based on the fact that we lack any concordance between being and thinking, between being and saying ("I am not or I don't think"). The absence of sexual relation does implicate these impossibilities. And starting out from them is the only way for psychoanalysis to take into account, not common reality, but the Real. But it is insufficient to continue to repeat: "it

52   Christian Fierens

is impossible" or "there is no sexual relation". We must deal not only with these formulae, but with the facts. It is not simply a duty for the psychoanalyst theoretician to explain the formulae. We must take into account the fact of the lack and the general tendency for everyone to make good the lack, the impossibility and then its disappearing. There is always a making good to these lacks. To tell the truth, we never see the impossibility, we never see the absence of sexual relation, we never see the saying itself. We just see the plugs that take the place of the hole or the absence of sexual relation. We saw it in regard to discourse: we don't see the place of surplus enjoyment ("I am not and I don't think"); we see only the concrete product of the discourse.

The general structure is a hole that is always filled with a plug. Whatever the phenomenology of the hole, what is at stake is always the absence of sexual relation. Whatever the plug is, it can always be called the phallus. The general schema supposes a thing, anything, which is always in the place of nothing. Anything in the gap. And, furthermore, the plug must *fully* take the place of the hole to conceal, as much as possible, any trace of lack: the hole appears then as a whole (with a "w").

What is this phallus that makes good the absence of any sexual relation? It can be anything in so far as it can carry out its function of making good. It can be called a signifier because, with this plug, it has found another use, another meaning. Let us suppose that my garden hose is leaking. I fill the hole with *whatever* I find, a bit of my glove, for example. And through this operation, this bit becomes another thing: it acquires another function in filling the gap. It has become a signifier.

The phallus – whatever it might be – is the signifier that fills the gap of the absence of sexual relation. Anything can be the phallus. As for its function, it must have two characteristics. Firstly, it must be an appearance and not a reality, a pure phenomenon detached from a certain reality (the glove is no longer used to protect my hand). Lacan said the phallus appears as "a phanere favoured by its aspect of detachable addition accentuated by its erectility" (Lacan, 2001, p. 456, 2009, p. 8). Secondly, it must be strong enough to *fully* fill the gap of the absence: it must provide a universal, a whole which is able to plug the hole, the inexistence of the sexual relation. Lacan referred to this as: "a trick . . . in the different catches that make discourses of the voracities by which the inexistence of the sexual relation is plugged" (Lacan, 2001, p. 456, 2009, pp. 8–9). The discourses can deal with everything, and everything appears in a discourse. But everything is only what is concealing the gap. Meanwhile, the functioning of the discourses is precisely the functioning of the phallus.

Why then distinguish the discourses and the phallic formulae? The discourses deal with something, not everything, whilst the phallus is always dealing with the hole, the gap and the whole: with everything. We could begin with the male sexual organ. But that is not enough. Starting from this point, we could easily think that it is a matter of describing sexuality, even from a macho point of view, but also from the point of view of the female if we notice that the gap comes before the plug. But then we would think that the phallic function has just one principal use: to treat sexuality. On the contrary, the phallic function must treat anything; it explains

The failure of the phallus   53

the functioning of the mind, of thinking in general, by the filling of the gap. And it is only afterwards that sexuation – I mean the human sexuation – appears as a consequence of the process of thinking or speaking.

Let us start with the child who is asking not just: "why am I born?" or "why am I a boy?", but also "why is there a sunset?", "where does the world come from?", and so on. His questions are not just about his own place in the world or about sexuality, but about everything, about the world itself. Maybe they are sexual questions, but first of all they are cosmological questions and the sexual characteristics come only from the expected answer (it can be fully answered: the world) and from the interests at stake (the interest in the complete answer, where sexuality is at stake). The child is always looking for the ultimate explanation, the explanation of the whole. Of course, the parents fail to give satisfaction to this huge request because this explanation is quite impossible. It is quite the same in psychoanalysis: the analysand and eventually the analyst are always looking for the ultimate explanation, the explanation of the whole, but they always fail to find this ultimate explanation. This questioning is the phallic function as a process: to look for an ultimate answer – let us say an imaginary phallus – without finding the solution. The phallic function is to search without encountering either the beginning or the end of the process. Nevertheless, the questioning remains quite concrete; the child and the analysand are speaking about the sunset or about a dream or whatever, and in this concrete thing the search is relaunched.

We can explain the research of the child and of the analysand. The searching process is not only a single arrow. A first arrow is relaunched with the help of quite a concrete thing, and is followed by a second arrow that sustains the questioning. Let us say that the phallus is the relaunching point of the phallic process (whatever this point is):

$$\ldots \rightarrow \bullet \rightarrow \ldots$$

With the phallic process, we no longer need to see sexuation as a description of human sexuality. Far more fundamentally, sexuation is the process of questioning without finding the ultimate answer, but nevertheless finding an answer that relaunches the question. This particular answer is then, as Lacan says, "the fish that gobbles up what is necessary for the discourses to be able to sustain themselves" (Lacan, 2001, p. 457, 2009, p. 9). The phallus, then, is the signifier of the psychoanalytic discourse. It is the product of the psychoanalytic discourse, but it is not without a great difficulty. We cannot take this signifier as a mere product, but as what is coming in the hollow place of surplus enjoyment or surplus jouissance, that is, where neither it is nor it thinks: "I am not and I do not think". So, we give this point a concrete value. It is a point, it is a product, but we must deny this point the possibility of finding its own aim: we can't find the beginning in a being that does not exist, and we can't find the end in a thinking and its finality.

In so far as the phallus is not an object, but an unfolding of thoughts, we can deal with the thinking of the phallus and its relaunch in two different ways. We

54   Christian Fierens

can stay outside the phallus and we *have* the phallus, we behave in front of the phallus, it determines our behaviour. But we are also plunged in the functioning of the phallus, we *are* in it: it is a question of being the phallus. Lacan says: "There is nothing excessive in regard to what experience provides us, to put under the heading of being or having the phallus . . . the function that supplements or makes good the sexual relation". It would be too easy to say, "having is for men and being is for women". This would be to understand the phallus as a behaviour, a sexual behaviour, as if we could deal with it from the outside without being plunged inside the process of thinking and its impossibility. The phallic function is not a treatment of a given sexuality, but the functioning of the thinking – and the unconscious is made only of thoughts – in so far as it responds to the absence.

Having the phallus, or the first and second phallic formulae (the so-called masculine functions)

The first: I quote Lacan:

> for all x, phi x is satisfied, which can be expressed by a T noting the truth-value. This, expressed in the analytic discourse where the practice is to make sense, "means to say" that every subject as such, because that is what is at stake in this discourse, is inscribed in the phallic function to guard against the absence of the sexual relation (the practice of making sense, is precisely to refer oneself to this absence).
>
> (Lacan, 2001, p. 458, 2009, p. 11)

"Every subject is inscribed in the phallic function", we could hear "every human being is inscribed . . .", but more generally, we should understand "every grammatical subject", whatever you say, could be "inscribed in the phallic function" and "could be expressed by a truth-value". The first formula does not concern sexuality in the first instance, it is just the practice of making sense, and it is the very question of analytic discourse with the signifier 1, S1, as a product leading towards sense. So, it does not mean that every human being first had the penis, following the Freudian conception. It means that we are always making sense, always and everywhere; the discourses are everywhere and reality depends entirely upon the discourses.

The second: If we have the function before us – and this is from the point of view of having the phallus – then we must take into account the person who is considering the function and who, being outside the function, is not functioning. Lacan states that it is: "the case where there exists an x for which phi x, the function, is not satisfied, namely, by not functioning, is in effect excluded" (Lacan, 2001, p. 458, 2009, p. 11). It is the exception that is outside the functioning in order to master it.

This second formula entails the question of the subject, who is abstracted from thoughts. We have the thoughts, and, to be true, all that I think can also be false. At this point, it appears as a mere doubt. Starting from this point, I doubt, Descartes said: "I think therefore I am". This is the ego, but we have seen that it is much

The failure of the phallus   55

more complicated than this. The subject of the doubt must be clarified through the explanation of "I am not or I am not thinking". The question of the subject appears not then as the negation of an objective statement, not in putting a particular object into question, but at the point where the function of giving a statement of facts or a sense is squarely excluded. If the thoughts – the thoughts of the unconscious – are always a relaunching process, there must exist a support for this process, and this point is outside the process. The negation of the second formula does not concern something that is inside "for all, phi x", but is outside phi x, it is the negation of phi x. So, I write a point that supports the process and it is not the arrows, but is outside them:

$$\rightarrow \bullet \rightarrow$$

With this point, the subject seems to get a sense on his own. On the one hand, we have the saids, and they can always be caught in the process of relaunching, within the senses (we can find not only a meaning, but a sense for every formation of the unconscious), within phi x: "for all x, phi x". On the other hand, we have the saying, the subject of enunciation, the subject of saying, and it seems to be a being. With these two sides, we could say that we have two types of men. The first are enrolled in the saids: they do and they are what is said, following the rules of phi x, for all that they do, they think and they are following phi x, for all x, phi x. They are the private soldiers of phi x. The second are outside the throng; each of them has to be chief, the master, the head who supports the functioning of phi x. We could choose between the first ones and the second ones; it seems to be a game of heads or tails – "heads" for the second formula, support of phi of x outside phi of x, and "tails" for the first one inside phi of x. But, in fact, it is impossible to distinguish these two types of men, because each man entails and heads both sides. Whatever his function in society, he is obeying the saids and he puts himself outside to judge the functioning of phi of x. So, the difference between the two formulae does not separate two kinds of individuals, but goes through each person and, furthermore, through each process of thinking.

As we have seen, the psychoanalytic discourse proceeds from the second formula, starting from the subject and his question, from the absence of any sense (the signifier remains in the place of surplus enjoyment or surplus jouissance), from what the saying would be. Would it be better now to promote this second formula, the head: "be an exception", "get rid of common sense", "get rid of the dictates of phi x", "be the Creator" and so on? From this position, the subject could manage the discourses. For example, the analyst – with his different roles, whatever they might be (mastering, waiting, knowing, witnessing the saids of the analysand) – the analyst, I said, could be outside the very process of the analysand. But this position is only a semblance or a semblant. With his roles, he thought that he had the phallus, but he does not possess it. Rather, he is snapped up in the phallic process, which is playing with him like a monster with a little mouse.

These two positions could explain what is at stake in Freudian castration. First the phallic stage: at the beginning of its life, the child has the phallus and is outside the phallus; but taking into account that it is just a semblant, it *can* be lost (for the boy) or it has already been lost (for the girl), that is, the threat of castration or real castration. And the human being is then submitted not only to having the phallus or not, but also to the functioning of the phallus that entails the castration (for all x phi of x).

From a Freudian perspective, the phallus and the phallic process appear as an objective statement and the truth of this statement could be discussed. One could say, for example, that "for all x phi of x" is not true, and then "not all x phi of x". And for the second formula, which is just a semblance, "there exists an x not phi of x" is not true, thus, "there does not exist an x not phi of x". With the antithesis of each of the two first formulae, we would have the third and the fourth ones, the so-called feminine formulae. Be careful: this point of view is wrong. As we shall see, the stakes of the so-called feminine formulae are quite different.

What are the values of these Freudian formulae ("for all x phi of x" and "there exists an x phi of x") and the values of their critical counterpart ("not all phi of x" and "there does not exist an x phi of x")? All of them say, "it is true" or "it is false". But are they themselves true or false?

Starting from the Freudian point of view, which considers sexuality and the phallus as given in reality, they must be true *or* false: it would be sufficient to seek them out in the clinic to decide.

But human sexuality is never a given; the phallic function is never a classical function. The reality of human sexuality is not a part of reality, but the framework of reality in general, because there is no reality without the framework of one's interest in reality, and this interest is always sexual. When we wanted to grasp sexuality, to have the phallus, we simply missed the point. It is quite impossible to get the phallus. It disappears completely. The two Freudian formulae can't obey a logic of "true or false". And the same applies to their critical counterparts.

Nevertheless, we can clearly say that to take these formulae and their counterparts as something objective that could be simply observed from the outside, and to say that they are objectively true or false, is simply false. The Freudian formulae and their criticisms are both wrong.

We cannot possess the phallus; we are plunged in to the phallic process. So, we pass now from having the phallus to being the phallus.

Being the phallus, or the third and fourth phallic formulae (the so-called feminine formulae)

Once again, it is not that the woman would be the phallus for a man or for whatever. Nor that castration would be her starting point.

To be the invisible condition of everything, the sexual interest sustaining all of reality is not a phenomenon. It is not an object that could be observed. It is not an object for science and for mathematics. When Lacan insists in saying that the so-called feminine formulae ("not all phi of x" and "there does not exist an x phi of x") are "not usual in mathematics" (Lacan, 2001, p. 465, 2009, p. 18), he does not mean that it is a little bit odd in the mathematical field. He means that it is outside it, and does not fit into the field of what can be dealt with by mathematics, that is, the field of the object.

The failure of the phallus   57

How can we get out of the mathematical field? How can we leave the field of phenomena, the field of what can be observed? It is not a problem of finding other possibilities. On the contrary, we have to encounter the different forms of impossibility, beginning from the possibilities, the possibilities of repetition, the possibilities of conflict with the unconscious, the possibilities of the drive and the possibilities of transference. Lacan writes: "it is from logic that this discourse (psychoanalytical discourse) touches on the real by encountering it as impossible" (Lacan, 2001, p. 449, 2009, p. 1).

The third formula is the formula of impossibility. It sounds like: "there does not exist an x phi of x". This is not only the dispute with the chief, the exception, as the hysteric can do endlessly; with the hysteric, a master can be superseded by another master and it is only a roundabout of the exceptions. With the third formula, it is the radical impossibility of each point that would be the exception: "there does not exist *any* x phi of x". With this radical lack, the relations are always short lived and unsound. "There is no sexual relationship", sexual because this fundamental lack is related to sexuality as the condition of every reality.

One can certainly justify the functioning of the discourse, the symbolic, the "for all x phi of x" with the exception, with the Name-of-the-Father, with the second formula "there exists an x not phi of x". But this is just a semblance and it is only a particular way of dealing with the lack of sexual relation. This particular way consisted in staying as far as possible outside the process of making good the lack. Now there are other possibilities of making good from within. Starting from what I am (being the phallus), it would be the symptom, not so much as a conflict between contradictory tendencies, but rather, we can understand the symptom as the genuine way of filling the lack of sexual relationship (Lacan writes "sinthome"). And it is much more interesting.

"There does not exist *any* x phi of x" appears then not so much as a negative formula, but as the point that tells us: here is the lack of sexual relationship and it can't be entirely plugged; it is a point that is not sufficient to delete the lack. On the contrary, it indicates the fundamental lack. While the second formula was supposed to give an enclosure for the universal of the phallic function that is inside the fence, here we have an opening and the beacons of the enclosure simply indicate that we can go beyond the enclosure and that there is something else outside the universal enclosed within the fence. Each beacon, then, is the sign of a liberty that trespasses the reasonable reason. It is true that with this beacon, one can grasp a certain universal inside the enclosure, but it is also true that this beacon indicates a field outside.

We can take a symptom as a symbolic product for a conflict that implies the phallic function and castration. In the Freudian sense, it would depend on the Oedipus complex, on the figure of the father, more precisely on the Name-of-the-Father. But it is not just that. It is always an invention, a liberty outside this classical interpretation and outside the determination of life through childhood and so on. And then we encounter the analysand who does not fit into the framework or the classical theory of psychoanalysis. His symptom does not disappear; it becomes the motor of an infinite relaunching.

The fourth formula "not all x phi of x": We might think that the universality of any concept does not fit for the psychic field. When we think in generalities, we always miss the point. So, we should have to radically exclude the "all". If the "not all" had this meaning, it would be exactly the same as the affirmation of "the existence of a subject to say no to the phallic function" (Lacan, 2001, p. 465, 2009, p. 18). But Lacan emphasises that: "this is not the sense of the saying, which is inscribed here" (Lacan, 2001, p. 465, 2009, p. 18). In other words, this is not the sense of the third and the fourth formula. . . . This existence of a particular that says no to the phallic function is just the exception, the second formula. You can always put any universal into question and we would have to promote the particularity of any subject, irreducible to any concept or to any universal. And we may say that we have to examine everything on a case-by-case basis. This is a general precautionary principle, but it is not the sense of the "notall" of the phallic function. It is only the sense of "there exists an x phi of x", the second formula, the formula of the exception, of the chief, of the master, which is at stake in every individual, slaves included.

On the contrary, we have to start from the universal (first formula) to take account of the boundary of this universal (second formula) to see that this boundary is a semblance and it does not exist outside the phallic function (third formula). . . . With this opening, through the gates in the boundary or in the enclosure, through the lack of the Name-of-the-Father, through the sinthome, we have access to another field much more extensive than the "all" of the first formula. The "notall" is not smaller, but much bigger than the "all", which the first formula unified, bigger than the "universal". As Lacan said: the notall "is an all outside universe" (Lacan, 2001, p. 466, 2009, p. 18).

Whether we know it or not, we are plunged into the notall as in a field of invention outside the framework of the universal:

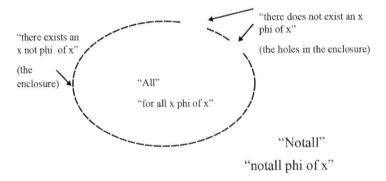

Figure 7.1

The failure of the phallus   59

Thus, it is quite wrong to oppose the two sides of sexuality – the masculine side and the feminine side. The so-called masculine "all" is included in the so-called feminine "notall". And the affirmation of an exception and the negation of the exception are speaking about the same enclosure and its holes. Of course, there is a presentation of these two different sides of the formulae in *Seminar XX, Encore* (Lacan, 1972–1973, p. 73). But Lacan says in a direct manner that this presentation is quite exemplary for producing misunderstandings, misunderstandings that consist mainly in the presentation of the two sides.

If, on the contrary, we understand that the "all" of the universe is inscribed *inside* the "all" of the notall, then it relaunches the sense of the "all phi of x". The universal must be thought of as something that tries to plug or to occupy the space, and it appears then as a plug. A plug for what? For absence, where there is no thinking and no being. Then it appears as a relaunching of the process of thinking. We started from the universal (first formula) to infer from it the exception (second formula); then from this exception as a semblance we encountered the opening of the liberty (third formula); and then the field of the notall (fourth formula). . . . But it is the notall that gives us the sense of the phallus as a function of infinite relaunching, and we start again with the first formula in an endless roundabout of the four formulae of sexuation.

Sexuation is not sexuality. It is more so the roundabout of these four formulae, the very process of thinking going as far as this is unthinkable, outside any universal, which indefinitely relaunches the discourses and the questioning of the subject. We are caught in this process, and it is all that sustains our interest in anything: our "sexual" interest, Freud would have said. Human sexuality must be thought via this interest . . . and it is only afterwards that it appears that some stages of this process are more masculine or more feminine. But to get a truly human sexuality, it is necessary to deal with the impossibility of the exception, of the formula of existence. It is necessary to ask the question of freedom and so to open the field of the unknown, the field of the notall. Human sexuality must pass through feminine sexuation.

And this sexuation is at stake in any psychoanalysis that is able to go beyond the Freudian conception of the phallus as a masculine symbol. The failure of the phallus is the main point – the hole in the fence – which takes us into the field of the notall. That will be the crucial point, to understand interpretation not as a mere meaning – that would always be in the sense of the universal (of the all) – but also beyond and outside of this meaning. An interpretation with-out meaning.

Note

1 "Qu'on dise reste oublié derrrière ce qui se dit dans ce qui s'entend" (2001, p. 449); Translated by C. Gallagher (2009, p. 1) as: "That one might be saying remains forgotten behind what is said in what is heard". Note: the author's translation differs, in some instances, from Gallagher's translation.

References

Plastow, M. G. (2015) *What Is a Child? Childhood, Psychoanalysis, and Discourse*. London: Karnac.

Lacan, J. (1972–1973) *Encore*. Paris: Editions de l'Association Lacanienne Internationale.

Lacan, J. (2001) *L'étourdit* in *Autres Ecrits*. Edited by J.A. Miller. Paris: Éditions du Seuil.

Lacan, J. (2009) L'étourdit: First Turn. Translated by C. Gallagher. *Scilicet* 4: 5–25 (July 2009). www.lacaninireland.com/web/wp-content/uploads/2010/06/etourdit-First-turn-Final-Version2.pdf

Chapter 8

Interpretation with-out meaning

Christian Fierens

In chapter II of the *Traumdeutung* (*Interpretation of Dreams*) (Freud, 1900), Freud sets out his method for interpretation: we have to recount the dream and then for each bit of the story we have to give free associations. As an example, he interrogates the dream of Irma's injection. When he has finished his own free associations, he suddenly says: "I have now completed the interpretation of the dream" (1900, p. 118). And then, at the end of the chapter, he adds, "*When the work of interpretation has been completed, we perceive that a dream is the fulfilment of a wish* (*Wunsch*)" (1900, p. 121). What do we perceive here? What is the fulfilment of the wish in so far as it is impossible to completely satisfy a wish?

Between these quotations, Freud tells us the story of the leaky kettle. A man had been accused by his neighbour of having brought back a kettle that he had borrowed, damaged and leaky. The man's defence was threefold: firstly, he had returned it in a good condition; secondly, the kettle was already leaky when he borrowed it; and thirdly, he had never borrowed a kettle from his neighbour. With this kind of explanation for the dream, we don't have one meaning, but three, and they are quite inconsistent, or conflicting. Where is the interpretation, or where are the interpretations of the dream? Of course, one could say that Freud feels guilty and that the dream is a wish to be innocent in the same sense as the kettle man's plea. But it is much more complicated than this because perhaps the man feels guilty but also innocent, and maybe Freud could also have wished to be guilty about other things, for example of having killed his father in order to live his own life. These contradictions are the very reason that Freud tells us the story of the kettle. Now what is the interpretation of the dream? Do we have to put together an explanation of the different and contradictory drives and the corresponding guilt, which constitute the dream? Do we have to put these different meanings together in order to complete the interpretation of the dream?

Following the free associations, but not after an explanation of its different meanings, Freud says, "I have now completed the interpretation of the dream". So, the interpretation is not a complicated structure of meanings. On the contrary, it's much simpler. The word "interpretation" is a translation of the German word "*Deutung*", but "German" is "*Deutsch*" in German. *Deutung* is *Deutschung*. When Freud speaks about *Traumdeutung*, he speaks about the *Deutschung* of the

DOI: 10.4324/9781003212720-10

dream, a Germanisation (Germanising) of the dream. Of course, in English we would have to say: "interpretation" is "Englishing" or "Englishisation". Interpretation consists of translating the dream into common language. So, we can better understand the sentence: "I have now completed the interpretation of the dream", as "I have translated it into common language" . . . "completely", or as far as I can.

If an analyst says to the analysand: "here you have the scopic object", "here you are guilty of having wished to kill your father", "behind this woman, you love your mother", or "it's your mother", and so on, no doubt he gives a lot of more or less clever, possibly contradictory, meanings. But they are not interpretations; they are complications. They are not in a common language, they are not *Deutung*; they are not Englishing the process. They are the opposite, the opposite of genuine interpretation.

Second quotation: "When the work of interpretation has been completed, we perceive that a dream is the fulfilment of a wish (*Wunsch*)". What is the fulfilment of a wish? Does it imply that we must first understand the wish (*Wunsch*) in order to enact it? The fulfilment of a wish is absolutely not the meaning of an act that is to be done, and the fulfilment of a wish is not at all the carrying out of a meaning, of a program. It has much more to do with the joke of the kettle, with what remains a riddle: we do not know the truth of the kettle.

Nevertheless, the dream carries a lot of meanings and the analyst can possibly add some more with his fake interpretation, like: "here is an Oedipus complex", and so on. The genuine interpretation is surely not inside this kind of meaning, but outside. The interpretation is with-out meaning.

But where? The interpretation must be in the free associations of the analysand. Interpretation must be *quotation*. This is its first characteristic. It repeats what the analysand has said, not in a working through and in a secondary revision, but primarily without any further elaboration. The interpretation is not to be sought in the meaning of a dream, in the meaning of a slip of the tongue or of a symptom, and so on. It is outside of this meaning and without it. But then it happens, as we have seen in the dream of Irma's injection, that we don't achieve coherence; the interpretation is always equivocal and we can't find the interpretation as a meaning that would give us coherence for our thinking and our doing. In the interpretation, we are well aware that a process of saying is at stake, but we do not find the sentence, the said that would restore everything in perfect coherence.

Every interpretation must have the form of the story of the man's kettle: we borrowed the interpretation from the saids of our analysand in good condition, and we brought it back in bad condition, that is, leaky. In fact, the saids were already leaky without our interpretation and, moreover, we didn't even borrow anything from the analysand. So, after the quotation, every interpretation must be a *riddle*, and that's the second characteristic of the interpretation.

What is a riddle? You know the riddle of Stephen in Joyce's *Ulysses*: "The cock crew, the sky was blue: The bells in heaven were striking eleven. Tis time for this poor soul to go to heaven. – What is that?" And the answer is: "The fox burying his grandmother under a hollybush" (Joyce, 1992, p. 32). It remains a riddle, because the answer is another riddle: the meanings of the cock and the fox do not fit. The saids have a meaning, certainly, but the riddle is in the very process of seeking, without finding, the last meaning. So, the essence of the riddle is the saying that does not end in a said: a saying without saids. As Lacan says in *The Sinthome* (1976, p. 74, lesson of 13/1/1976), a riddle is a saying whose saids cannot be located. The interpretation must remain a riddle; it is not at all its solution or its dissolution.

With these two characteristics – quotation and riddle – the interpretation remains outside meaning.

The meaning must disappear to leave a place for sense. For example, the meaning of "the kettle was in good condition" disappears when it obviously looks leaky, and the first meaning disappears to stimulate another thing, another meaning, for example: "I did not borrow any kettle". But it also has to disappear for the sense – skipping from meaning to meaning – and the sense cannot be stopped. With this living sense, we are always expelled from one place to another, from one meaning to another. And that is the usual sense of free association.

Then what is the end of analysis?

In *L'étourdit* (2001), Lacan deals with this question just before speaking of interpretation. The end of analysis does not consist in giving the true interpretation. First of all, the end is the separation of the analysand from the analyst in so far as the analyst is the representative of the object *a*, the cause of his wish. He no longer needs to lean on the analyst to support his wish. But the place of interpretation remains, and this consists precisely in transforming his manner of wishing. The neurotic – but we are all neurotic – thinks that we have a bunch of demands and that these demands are joined by a central wish that unites them. It is the schema of the torus: the demands repeat themselves, whilst the wish accomplishes a turn around the central gap of the torus. We can easily track the demands, but we can never see the wish as such. When Freud says, "the dream is a fulfilment of the wish", we cannot see the wish itself. We see only the demands, that is, the free associations. But when these are completed or fulfilled, as Freud notes, "the work of interpretation has been completed", and that "we perceive that a dream is the fulfilment of a wish (*Wunsch*)".

The problem of the place of interpretation is to say how the demands and the wish are combined, although they are quite different. How can we find something of the wish (that is not possible to be seen) in the crowd of demands (that are always to be seen)? First of all, we must leave the meaning of the demands as if it were the *matter* of the demands to find a new *form* that would fulfil the structure of these demands. But this form is not a meaning; it is in the process of transforming the demands, and in this process, what is at stake is the phallus.

In chapter IV of his *Interpretation of Dreams* (1900), Freud arrives at the point in which his own method no longer works. The free associations stop. And Freud proposes to clutch onto an auxiliary method, the old "symbolic" method (key of dreams). But be careful! As we can read in his book, there is just one symbol: the phallus, which is not to be understood as the masculine organ. It would be easy to say that everything is phallic. To look for the meaning would always lead to the same answer: the meaning is the phallus. This would be a very odd interpretation: the phallus would mean everything, but to mean everything is to mean nothing. As I proposed, the phallus is not a meaning but a structure of transformation. This implies that we cannot remain with any one meaning; we always have to switch to another thing in an endless process. This is merely a formal process, so the significance (*Bedeutung*) of the phallus – the significance not in the sense of meaning, but the importance – is to be outside of any meaning. The phallus is paramount precisely because it is outside of any meaning. In this way, we are no longer stitched to any demands, and the demands are always mixed up with the wish represented by the phallic process.

In *L'étourdit* (2001), Lacan explains the transforming of the torus that clearly distinguishes the demands and the wish, the transforming of the torus into the Moebius strip where everything is moving in the phallic process of transforming and relaunching the demands inside the form of the wish. With this transformation, the demands, which are always visible and obvious, and the wish, which is always invisible and obscure, are put on the same level; there is a flattening. At the end of analysis, there must remain the flattening of the visible demands with the invisible wish. Lacan writes: "There remains the stability of the flattening of the phallus, in other words of the strip" (Lacan, 2001, p. 487, 2010, p. 17). The editor of *Autres Ecrits* continues: "où l'analyste trouve sa fin" ("where the analyst finds his end"). Of course, it is quite wrong! As analysts, we do not have to search our own end, but rather, the aim of analysis. And the flattening of the phallus is: "où l'analyse trouve sa fin" ("where the analysis finds its aim"), as it was written in the first edition of *L'étourdit* in Scilicet. The first condition for the end of an analysis is that it has more or less reached its aim. It is not to say "bye-bye" to the analyst for having found a central meaning. On the contrary, it is to be in the infinite movement of skipping from one meaning to another, outside of meaning to create his own thinking, his own doing, his own saying. And that is the phallic process, the aforesaid "flattening of the phallus". So, when the analyst is no longer necessary for this flattening of the phallus, the analysis is ended, that is, *with this analyst*. But analysis is not ended for the analysand. He must continue.

Here is the cutting edge of one of the first sentences of *L'étourdit*: "That one might be saying remains forgotten behind what is said in what is heard" (Lacan, 2001, p. 449, 2009, p. 1). We have the *said* of the analysand, we have the *heard* of the analyst, but the *saying* is forgotten. The saying is running around the saids and the heards, but it is forgotten. Perhaps, we take the saids or the heards as interpretations, but they are fake interpretations. Certainly, the saids and the heards are quite concrete; they are beings and we can follow their footsteps. But they are not the saying. The saying is aside, outside, beside or beyond the beings of the saids and heards. Lacan says that the saying must "par-être", that is, "the saying should appear", and so it seems, it almost appears possible. At the same time, "the saying is *beside* the being", and so it is not, it seems, without any consistency. The task of interpretation is to let the saying "appear" as a semblance and to let the saying take a place beside every said and every heard, and outside any being.

The saying is absolutely fundamental for the unconscious. It is not so much a set of meanings, of saids and heards, but rather the movement of saying that appears and is beside the saids and the heards. These are the primary processes. And in this sense, "the unconscious is structured like a language". It is not at all a given language like German or English; it is the changing, the process and the cancelling of any stability of language, in the very process of *Deutschung* or Englishing.

Beginning from this point, that "the unconscious is structured like a language" – in other words, that it is always moving – we can easily understand that the interpretation must keep moving. We can follow this moving in the Lacanian explanations of three equivocations: the homophonic equivocation, the grammatical equivocation and the logical equivocation.

Firstly, the *homophonic equivocation*: A set of sounds has two different meanings. This kind of equivocation occurs in free associations. It helps for the process of condensation. Thus, one word has two different meanings. The dream seems to be quite simple by comparison with the complexity of the unconscious thoughts. So, it must condense the latter ones. From a linguistic point of view, we cannot have a specific word for every being in the world; so, there must be equivocations. We are never outside these equivocations. Lacan says that "no holds are barred there" ("tous les coups sont là permis") (2001, p. 491, 2010, p. 20), since we are not playing with these homophonic equivocations. They are playing with us and we fail to recognise ourselves in them, although we are done with them.

The very reason for these equivocations is not the lack of words to speak of the multitude of unconscious thoughts or the multitude of things in the word. In *L'étourdit*, Lacan quotes three examples of homophonic equivocations. He chooses them, and, for each of them, the meaning refers directly to a logical process, more precisely to a logical equivocation. It means that for each homophonic equivocation in general, it is not so much a matter of looking for its different meanings that would explain the unconscious thoughts, but to try to catch the form that it comes from, the logical equivocation, as we shall see later.

With the homophonic equivocation, it seems that we have to deal with different images. We do not know to what image the equivocal expression refers. It seems like an imaginary problem: we would have to find the right meaning, the right image, but we fail to find it. The problem, however, is not to find the good image, it is far more to use them correctly, "where it suits" ("là où il convient") (Lacan, 2001, p. 491, 2010, p. 20). The space "where it suits" is precisely the space of the flattening of the phallus: we have to use the homophonic equivocation in a symbolic process to transform the demands or the saids in the structure of the wish. Of course, with the flattening of the phallus, it is always possible to promote an imaginary meaning and to inflate the phallus as an imaginary balloon. That would lead us to fake interpretations with many meanings. But the phallus is far more a process of symbolic transformations as can be followed in the letter, in the Greek "gramma". We now pass to the second type of equivocation.

The *grammatical equivocation*: The letter is not aimed at writing down and fixing what would be fleeting in the sense of "spoken words fly away, written words remain". On the contrary, the letter is the meeting point of quite contradictory thoughts, for example, that the mother has the phallus and she does not possess it. Thus, the letter does not remain. It moves from one thought to the other. And we can see that the letter is precisely what is at stake in the phallic function. In so far as the letter is the convergence of contradictory tendencies, it is also at stake in interpretation and its grammatical equivocation.

For example, in his study of President Schreber, Freud provides a grammatical account of the different forms of paranoia. All are related to the narcissistic sentence: "I (a man) love him (a man)". And the different forms of paranoia are grammatical transformations of this sentence. For example, persecutory paranoia would be the product of two grammatical transformations. The first is from love into hate: "I love him" becomes "I hate him", and the second inverts the subject and the object: "I hate him" becomes "He hates me". Of course, we couldn't easily give this grammatical interpretation to the paranoid, first of all because it remains equivocal: we do not know exactly what part is love and what part is hate, and we do not know who loves whom and who hates whom. But we know the stakes of these grammatical equivocations, and, with Freud, we can try to let the analysand "recite his lesson" in grammar. So, it is quite possible that when he says he loves his mother, as a matter of fact, he hates her. Or that she hated him. The analyst does not have to choose between these grammatical forms; he only has to let them unfold in the saying of the analysand. But he knows that "I love you" can mean, "I hate you" or "You love me" or "You hate me", and so on. Thus, the transference consists not in the explanation of this love or hate, but in the grammatical equivocation that skips from one form to another, following the saying of the analysand.

I quote Lacan: "'I'm not making you say it'. Is that not the minimum of interpretative intervention? But it is not its meaning that matters . . ." (ce n'est pas son sens qui importe. . .). However, it is the grammatical equivocation which is also at stake between the analysand and the analyst, "the equivocation between 'You have said it' and 'I take it all the less to be my responsibility in that I did not in any way make you say such a thing'" (Lacan, 2001, p. 491, 2010, p. 21). So, the analyst can transform the said of the analyst in so far as it goes with the saying of the analysand. Easy to say, but we never have the saying of the analysand as such. We must have a support point or a fulcrum for the grammatical equivocation: this is the third equivocation.

The *logical equivocation*: Without logic, "interpretation would be imbecilic", from the Latin *imbecillus*, without baculum, without a walking stick, without any support, without any fulcrum. The support of interpretation is not at all the meaning or the meanings; it is the so-called logic. But what logic is that? Of course, one can emphasise the unconscious that would be without any contradiction. One

Interpretation with-out meaning 67

could then assert that the unconscious is outside of any logic. But this is quite wrong. On the contrary, the unconscious can deal with any contradiction without difficulty, as we have seen in the grammatical equivocation. It doesn't matter if love becomes hate, and so on.

Far from being without logic, the unconscious is based on a logic, but not on the logic of truth that implies the contradiction between true and false.

So, we must try to expose the specific logic on which the unconscious is based, and this is not the general logic of the truth. Lacan said that it can be "formalised, which means proper to the matheme". We can do it; it's always doable. Here Lacan reminds us that "no logical development, this starting from before Socrates and from elsewhere than in our tradition, ever proceeded except from a kernel of paradoxes" (Lacan, 2001, p. 491, 2010, p. 21).

"Paradoxes" – doxa means what appears, the phenomenon – and beside it, there is what disappears: "para-doxes". As we have seen, demands appear, but the wish does not appear. We can track some pregenital drives, but how might we see the so-called genital drive? One could possibly see the birth of a child, or we can posit the genital drive from pregenital manifestations. But we always have to deal with an impossibility of saying the ultimate truth of the most important things.

The first step of this logic for the unconscious is to differentiate what we can see from what is absolutely invisible, between the phenomenon and the noumenon, between the demands and the wish. Regarding the first, we can say: "it is that" . . . but in regard to the second, we must always add: "it is not that". Everybody can observe that it is so . . . and then add: "it is not that"; there is another space which I cannot master. Everybody can undergo this passage from "it is that" to "it is not that". It is doable. That is the principle of the matheme.

In the practice of psychoanalysis, we have the Freudian concepts – the four fundamental concepts – and we can see the repetition, the formations of the unconscious, the different drives and the transference. Each time one could say: "that is it, I can see it". But each of these concepts leads us to its own impossibility: the repetition is always incomplete, the unconscious always has to deal with contradiction, the drives are impossible to demonstrate, and the transference is impossible to decide. It does not suffice to follow these phenomena (repetition, unconscious, drive and transference); we must deal with the logical limits of these phenomena, that is, the genuine impossibility of each of them, and more precisely, the genuine object that elucidates this impossibility. It is impossible to find an object that puts an end to the repetition, and that is the oral object. It is impossible to find an object that puts an end to the conflicts of the unconscious, and that is the anal object that is always contradictory. It is impossible to find an object that would demonstrate the complete framework of the wish, and that is the scopic object. It is impossible to find an object that could decide about the course of the transference, and that is the vocal object.

So, for each of these four concepts and from the four forms of object a, we must add: "that is not it; I have to suppose something that I cannot see". And these suppositions – outside the clinic in the narrow sense of the term – are Lacanian concepts: the subject in question, the phallic function, and the big Other. I have already spoken of the first two.

Let us put forward that the big Other is the symbolic. The interpretation would be then a symbolic event in which . . . in which what? In which a particular meaning or a general one is given? But we know perfectly well that the four forms of object *a* don't fit; they never fit. When we give such a meaning, that is, a fake interpretation, we know that "it is not that". There is nobody to guarantee your so-called interpretation: the big Other does not exist. And the big Other is neither the imaginary nor the symbolic. Lacan would say: it is "ex-sistence"; that is: it is outside sense, outside the imaginary and the symbolic. We can see sense as the movement between different meanings which follow each other. Therefore, the movement is the symbolic and the meaning is the imaginary. When Lacan speaks of "ex-sistence", we must hear this as outside sense, outside the imaginary and the symbolic. It is the Lacanian real.

With the real, we can understand that the big Other is not the symbolic, but the space in which the symbolic can work and where the imaginary can rest. It is the locus of the code (*le lieu du code*), not the code itself. The big Other would be the framework for everything. . . "would be" because we do not have it. It's simply a supposition. No more. But in psychoanalysis we are working only with suppositions: the subject, the phallic function, and the big Other. And we have to deal with all the delusions that escape the reality principle; we have the phenomena and we *should* have the noumena. Lacan adds, "les noumènes nous mènent"; in other words, the noumena are leading us.

Without this support of the noumena, of the question of the subject, of the phallic function and of the big Other, interpretation would be imbecilic, without support, without fulcrum. Therefore, we support the interpretation with something that does not exist; however, that can be done in this process of thinking.

Now the very reason for the homophonic equivocation is not at all the lack of words in a language, but the necessity of dealing with the noumenon, which leads us to deal with the real that escapes us.

We are turning in a roundabout between the three types of equivocation: homophonic, grammatical and logic. And every interpretation must be put into this roundabout. Of course, we cannot be aware of every step of this roundabout in a particular interpretation. But can we still speak about a particular interpretation when it must be put in the general framework of these three equivocations?

We can notice a big shift in the use of the word "interpretation". In Freudian times, one often spoke of interpretations. Nowadays, the word "interpretation" almost seems to disappear in the psychoanalytic field. This can be understood as follows: the interpretation as a meaning must take its leave in order to allow the opening of a space for the movement of interpretation as we have seen in the three equivocations.

To conclude, I would say that the three equivocations are linked in a Borromean knot. The homophonic equivocation concerns meaning and is imaginary; the grammatical equivocation concerns the transformations of the syntax of the said

Interpretation with-out meaning 69

and is symbolic; the logical equivocation is not the logic of truth, but the logic of the real. It would be easy to follow the different meanings (imaginary). However, we have to transform them with grammar following the work of the unconscious (symbolic). With this, we are already led outside of meaning, but this does not suffice. We have to deal with the difference between the so-called clinics of what can be seen and the suppositions of the subject, of the phallic function, of the big Other. And this leads us beyond the phenomena of the imaginary and of the symbolic, to the real. But this real is impossible to approach outside the framework of the imaginary, the symbolic and the real. The interpretation is both inside and outside of meaning, with-out meaning in the Borromean knot.

Of course, we always fail to mastermind this framework, and we mix the three equivocations into one sense, one meaning, one real. Then, we have lost the Borromean knot. We have lost the dimension of equivocation. The interpretation is no longer a riddle, also perhaps no longer a quotation (citation), and we are plunged into a paranoid interpretation. This occurs very often, always I would say. But it must always be possible to find the track of the genuine interpretation once again, not just another meaning supposed to be better, not just a transformation, but the track of the real. Lacan's sinthome reminds us of the structure of the real. The interpretation must take account of the sinthome not because it is the matter that has to be cured, but because it entails the form or the structure of the interpretation in the very life of the analysand.

References

Freud, S. (1900) *The Interpretation of Dreams*. Standard Ed., 4–5. London: Hogarth.
Joyce, J. (1992) *Ulysses*. London: Penguin.
Lacan, J. (1976) *Le Sinthome*. Paris: Editions de l'Association Lacanienne Internationale.
Lacan, J. (2001) *L'étourdit in Autres Ecrits*. Edited by J. A. Miller. Paris: Éditions du Seuil.
Lacan, J. (2009) L'étourdit: First Turn. Translated by C. Gallagher. *Scilicet* 4: 5–25 (July 2009). www.lacaninireland.com/web/wp-content/uploads/2010/06/etourdit-First-turn-Final-Version2.pdf
Lacan, J. (2010) L'étourdit II: Second Turn: The Discourse of the Analyst and Interpretation. Translated by C. Gallagher. *Scilicet* 4: 25–52 (May 2010). www.lacanin ireland.com/web/wpcontent/uploads/2010/06/etourdit-Second-turn-Final-Version4.pdf

Part III

Lacan's inventions – the school, the cartel and the pass

Chapter 9

Psychoanalysis or . . . psychoanalysts?[1]

David Pereira

A necessarily perennial question

The annual conference of the Freudian School of Melbourne, the Homage to Lacan, is an occasion in which the School makes open to the public the working of certain theoretical questions with which its members have substantially engaged in the preceding year: opening them to interrogation by those who are interested to engage with the School in this work.

The title of the Homage in 2016 was *Psychoanalysis . . . or worse*. It well defined the institutional preoccupations of the School not just in that moment, but periodically over the entire history of the School, in recognition of the fact that there is always an "or worse" that nips at the heels of psychoanalysis. At that particular time, in 2016, the "or worse" had concerned the extent to which the relations between analysts – whether cordial or hostile it matters not – gets in the way, or better said, at times fails to get out of the way of the transmission of psychoanalysis and the training of analysts.

Getting out of the way

This, "getting out of the way", has also a somewhat more personal bearing for me insofar as something else of great significance occurred in my life during this time – the death of my father-in-law. He was a man born and raised in the harsh, red-earthed part of the Mallee district near the Victorian, South-Australian border. We find in him a man who was forced by necessity to rely on first principles; something which he tried to impress upon me, and which is also the best that I have learned from psychoanalysis – from my analysis, in my supervision – the imperative to maintain psychoanalysis as a perpetually inaugural experience.

I mention him in this context because his close to dying words reminded me of the fact that they had been something of a signatorial expression of his – perhaps typical of country folk of his era, but one nonetheless that he had made his own. It might have belonged to *many* but he had, in his life, in the way in which he used it, in the manner in which he lived it, made it his *One*. That expression, his way of bidding you farewell, was: "I'll be getting out of your way".

DOI: 10.4324/9781003212720-12

74   David Pereira

This perennial institutional question, one that has not left me unaffected, together with the study in particular of Lacan's Seminar of 1971–1972, *Ou pire* (Or worse. . .) with my colleagues in the School, is what I bring to my interrogation of what Lacan was proposing at the time of this Seminar.[2] In interrogating it, I propose firstly to draw out the implications it has regarding the possible relations between analysts, and secondly between analysts and psychoanalysis itself. Through this, to inquire as to the way in which analysts may be able to get out of the way of psychoanalysis.

The psychoanalyst or psychoanalysts

My point of departure concerns how this "or worse" can be brought to bear specifically upon the relations between analysts. Given that the title of the Homage was *Psychoanalysis . . . or worse*, my title – "Psychoanalysis or psychoanalyst*s*" – places "psychoanalysts" in the plural, in the place of the "worse". The argument anticipated by my title therefore is that the collective, aggregate or weight of analysts, supportive of relations between analysts – a union of analysts – obscures the gravity of the singular or one analyst, and thereby gets in the way (or fails to get out of the way) of the transmission of psychoanalysis and the training of analysts.

The question that follows and that I will endeavour to draw out today, particularly in light of Lacan's Seminar of 1971–1972, concerns what a School of psychoanalysis is, and how it may sustain the transmission of psychoanalysis and the training of analysts given the existence, and perhaps *despite* the existence, of analysts. Lacan formulated this perennial question as a "critique of the psychoanalytic institution as such insofar as it is in strict contradiction with what is required by the very existence of *the* psychoanalyst".[3]

Now, this question forms part of an established critique in Lacan's teaching that had long cautioned against the decline in the discourse of psychoanalysis when it lapses into the collective. In the founding act of the *Ecole Francaise de Psychanalyse*, later to become the *Ecole Freudienne de Paris*, we find Lacan founding the School "alone as I have always been in my relation to the psychoanalytic cause".[4] The *Ecole* was proposed as an "inaugural experience",[5] an inaugural experience with reference to transference.[6] What followed was an attempt to preserve the enthusiasm and vitality of an inaugural experience: a first *One* that does not simply become unionised, collectivised, totalised, and therefore no longer an inaugural experience. In short, how psychoanalytic discourse might not be reduced to what Lacan quipped to be a professional insurance plan against analytic discourse, guaranteed by the weight of numbers of analysts.

As I have kept insisting, there is something of the weight of analysts in the plural that potentially gets in the way, or at least struggles to get out of the way, of psychoanalysis. And yet psychoanalysis cannot be sustained in a position of splendid isolation; it cannot be sustained by one person only. There have to be others in order to sustain an analytic discourse as a "social bond determined by the practice of an analysis".[7]

The question returns therefore to the nature of the relations between these others, on the one hand, and between each one and psychoanalysis on the other. This is something that can be elucidated through a working of Lacan's proposition-cum-provocation, that there is no sexual relation. It would, however, be an error to suggest that this induction could stand as the argument; because there is no sexual relation, that therefore, there can be no relations between analysts, or for that matter no relation between any of us. Clearly, some relationships are possible and even fruitful and enjoyable. The question becomes how this might be produced; what relationships are possible between analysts and between psychoanalysis and the psychoanalyst given the absence of the sexual relation, without lapsing into what's worse? The question suggests that something might be conceived and delivered from the absence of relation.

At the level at which we are speaking of the one and the many of analysts, the importance of the assertion that there is no relationship is to be found in the fact that even in the two or the many, each remains *One*.[8] If not, we end up with a class or union of analysts. So, whilst there might be a School of psychoanalysis, there can be no class of analysts.

The *One*, the singular, has to be separated from its potential incorporation into a collective or a class. The question turns and returns, therefore, around a *One*, a very particular *One*, and the importance of differentiating this *One* from the notion of "oneness" as such; from any suggestion of unification, collectivization or aggregation – *Unien*.

Parmenides *One*

Whilst Lacan does not specifically address himself to the question of the relations between analysts and psychoanalysis in the Seminar *Ou pire*, in the seven talks interspersed with this Seminar at Sainte-Anne, which acquired the title *The knowledge of the psychoanalyst*, he indicates that he refers to "*the*" psychoanalyst as a means of putting into question the relation between psychoanalysis and its knowledge, and the singularity or plurality of "the" analyst as *One*, or analysts as Many. It is at the level of his interrogation of this tension between the *One* and the Many that Lacan addresses himself to Plato's *Parmenides*. The following are two passages that form a certain focus.

> "If you like", said Parmenides,
> take as an example this hypothesis that Zeno entertained: if many are/if there are many, what must the consequences be both for the many themselves in relation to themselves and in relation to the one, and for the many in relation to itself and in relation to the many?[9]

And then the conclusion: "For if none of them is one, they are all nothing".[10] The convolutions apparent in this passage from Plato's *Parmenides* well justify Lacan's assertion that "there is nothing as slippery as this One",[11] which is nonetheless fundamental to the existence of others, of the many.

76   David Pereira

The *One* that Lacan encounters in Plato's *Parmenides* is only the first stage of this *One*, which at this point does not gain the traction necessary to not slide to worse. It is unable to hold its position, always sliding along the axis of being to a totality, a unity, a oneness; in short to that which sustains the idea of a relational totality which is the object of Lacan's critique in this Seminar and beyond. Indeed, in the text of Plato, Lacan discerns a difference between the way in which the *One* appears between the first and second hypotheses of the argument. The distinction is between the "It is One" of the first hypothesis and the "One is" of the second hypothesis. Whilst the first retains the possibility of offering a *One* of "pure difference", an absolute difference, the second – that of "One is" is already, as you can hear in its promissory note, primed and ready to offer an attribute, some quality, to follow. The One, of the second hypothesis, therefore, constitutes a collectivizing oneness, and therefore veers off into attribute and consolidated being.

Whilst Plato kept returning to place the *One* at the level of being, it requires recourse to the theory of sets, in order to effect a separation.[12] The ones, the unifying oneness which the One of Plato's Parmenides tends towards, the unionizing of the class or aggregate of analysts, is something which is to be differentiated from the set, which is only constituted as a set of *Ones*, thereby not forming a class. Whilst what is particular to a class and membership of a class is a shared attribute or attributes, for Lacan the assertion that there is no sexual relation is a statement of the fact that: ". . . there is a *One* distinct from what unifies a class as an attribute".[13] Such is a *One* that Lacan designates as difference itself.

Whilst the One of Oneness – of the unity of a relation – seeks the consolidation of a bond between the analyst and others of his kind, the *One* of the set is, Lacan tells us: "something that has nothing to do with belonging to a register that could be described as universal, namely, something that falls under the influence of an attribute".[14] The point of differentiation between the *One* of absolute difference and the one of attribute is referenced by Lacan in regard to the transference in the following quite brilliant clinical observation. In the analytic experience, Lacan tells us that

> the first step is to introduce into it the One as the analyst that you are. You make him take the step into it, as a result of which the analysand . . . is obviously (going) to reproach you with only being one among others. As a result of which he shows – but naturally without noticing it – (that it) is very precisely that he wants nothing to do with these others.[15]

So, you are an analyst but you are also caught up – even by your analysand's reproach – in being part of a collective, an association, a class. She nonetheless demands that you be singular to her analysis as an inaugural non-collectivisable, non-repeatable experience. Now we are all aware of these occasional reproaches by our analysands: "You Freudians, you Lacanians, you psychoanalysts, you men, you women, people like you, what would you know about suffering". And the list, the list of the ana-lyst in his attributes, goes on. In all these cases, the analyst, the

One analyst, is relegated to a class, a union, a oneness with others. Whilst in this is heard the proposition of a relation, it is through the absence of relation that the singularity of the analyst in his function might be restored.

The *One*, the semblant and getting out of the way

To show you that these considerations are not mere abstractions, I will share something with you from my practice. A couple of years ago, I received a telephone call from a young man who some 20 years previously had been an inpatient in the psychiatric unit at the Royal Children's Hospital, Melbourne, as a 10-year-old. He said: "I was the *One* who was the craziest kid there. I am just ringing to tell you that you were the *One* who helped me to make a difference in my life". He went on to tell me how well he was doing in life and that he had gone on to study and was now working in the field, had a family of his own and so on. This is not what really interests me on this occasion, whilst I will not contest that they were nice things to hear. What was interesting to me and is of importance to what I am trying to draw out about this *One* is what he specifically said. For the *One* that he was, the craziest one, I was the *One*, not that made a difference – that would make a nice couple – but helped him to make a difference in his life. What I heard in this "make a difference" was the very creation or manufacture of a difference.

Whether I did or didn't allow him to make a difference in his life really isn't the issue here. What may be of interest, in light of the argument thus far, is the specification of the *One* which is the agent of this difference. This *One* is not a unifying oneness guaranteed by the relational couple, but the *One* of pure difference, born of the absence of relation stated by Lacan as the absence of sexual relation. This is only possible to the extent that I was able to get out of his way; that he was able to do this despite me.

Now, I use this term – "despite me" – in the very specific sense it is introduced by María-Inés Rotmiler de Zentner in a paper titled *Le psychanalyste malgre lui*, published some 20 years ago, coincidentally around the same time this young man would have been an inpatient. The "analyst-despite-himself" is a way in which that paper gives clear expression to the place the analyst occupies in the transference – the position, Lacan insists, of the semblant of the object.

And what about the analyst? . . . *The psychoanalyst is always despite himself* and it is true that whilst many are capable of sustaining an analysis, only a few are capable *despite themselves*.[16]

It is clear in this that the function of the "analyst-despite-himself" is one through which he separates himself from the *many*. No doubt, as Rotmiler de Zentner contends, this may be a capacity that belongs to the few, but perhaps only insofar as this "few" does not form a list. Rather, in light of my argument, this few "is One", makes *One*. Not, however, the mythical or absolute One, which is gained through identification with the Other of the list, but the *One* of absolute difference which in separating the analyst from the many – you Freudians, you

78 David Pereira

Lacanians, you analysts – affords accession to this status of being in the place of the "despite-himself".

The analyst is *One* – is despite himself – insofar as he is without list; a *One* without attribute. Therefore, "Neither the air nor the song of the semblance is appropriate to the analyst",[17] is to say that to occupy the place of the semblant of the object is to appropriate a place without attribute. This fruitful position of the analyst which is conducive to the making of a difference, a position which the analyst is to occupy in the transference, is only able to be conceived and produced from the absence of relation and the *One* which such an absence is able to generate. It is this *One* of pure difference, this *One* of absolute difference, which therefore paves the way for the desire of the analyst to obtain a maximum difference between the object and the ideal; an ideal underwritten by the "or worse" of the sexual relation.

Implications for a school of psychoanalysis

In order that a School maintain something of the inaugural experience of psychoanalysis and not be overtaken by the collective, and yet at the same time not find itself alone in its own splendid isolation, institutional interventions are from time to time called for. Such interventions might be understood, in light of what arises from Lacan's proposition concerning the absence of relation, as the generation of a *One* of absolute difference affording the re-founding of the desire of the analyst. Historically, several such important moments may be identified, their status as singular acts – *Ones* in themselves – ensuring that none can be repeated in order to create the same desired effects. It is therefore an inaugural experience which is called for.

I will conclude by identifying two of these. The first Lacan's dissolution of his School. In conceding that there was a problem with the School, he proposed the solution to be one of dissolution. It being enough, he contended, for one to go away – referring to the One that he had become, the mythical One – for all to be free. In regard to the dissolution of the School therefore he "resolve(d) himself to it since it would function, were I not to put myself in its way, contrary to that for which I founded it".[18] Lacan was trying to find a way of "getting out of the way".

The second example comes from the history of the Freudian School of Melbourne itself, specifically that moment in 1992, announced in a letter of February 22, 1992, when the founders of the School resigned from the School.[19] It is a work to be read and studied, but I will cite only two passages as they bear upon what I have been arguing today. Firstly: "Our resolution to resign from the School is intrinsically linked to the transmission of psychoanalysis. This nevertheless engages us and those who want to pursue the task, to further work this different answer". Secondly:

> It is a time when in order to complete the act we should allow for the present, as well as for our presence, to become past and for the future to become

present; otherwise, at this stage our presence would be more of an impediment than a contribution, a kind of blockage, a resistance.

As I noted earlier, these acts – ways of getting out of the way – are such insofar as they are singular and therefore unrepeatable. They invite us, however, to consider the implications of the absence of relation, and the *One* it generates, for this School of psychoanalysis; the Freudian School of Melbourne: School of Lacanian Psychoanalysis, now. The specific implication that I am drawing is that whilst there might be a School of psychoanalysis, there can be no School of psychoanalysts. There can therefore be a member of the School, perhaps even an analyst-member of the School, but can there be such a thing as an analyst of the School? The author note attached to this paper introduces me as being an "Analyst of the School". My argument strips me of this attribute to the extent that it is not possible to say – without convoking the "or worse" of the sexual relation, that ONE IS an "Analyst of the School". This is the question I propose ought to be worked in constructing a necessary intervention at this point in the life of the School in order to do what is necessary, and perhaps possible, to bear the impossible discourse of psychoanalysis in the face of a relentless slide to what's worse.

Notes

1 I am grateful to the Editor, Linda Clifton, for reminding me that published in the *Papers of the Freudian School of Melbourne*, in 1981, is an article by Gustavo Etkin titled "Psychoanalysis or psychoanalyst". There, Etkin also addresses this perennial question concerning the problems that arise when analysts aggregate, problematizing the relationship of the analyst to the School. The present paper raises this question specifically in light of Lacan's arguments in his Seminar *Ou pire*.
2 Lacan Jacques, *The Seminar of Jacques Lacan, Book XIX, 1971–1972. . . . Ou pire/ . . . Or Worse*, translated by Cormac Gallagher from unedited French manuscripts. For private use only.
3 J. Lacan, Impromptu at Vincennes, in *Television. A Challenge to the Psychoanalytic Establishment*, edited by Joan Copjec, W.W Norton & Co, New York, 1990, p. 119. (My emphasis)
4 J. Lacan, *The Founding Act*. Translated by C. Gallagher, 2010, p. 97, www.lacanin ireland.com/web/wp-content/uploads/2010/06/The-Founding-Act1.pdf.
5 Ibid., pp. 102–103.
6 Ibid., p. 103. "The teaching of psychoanalysis can be transmitted from one subject to another only by way of a transference. . . . The 'seminars', including our course at the *Hautes Etudes*, will found nothing if they don't refer back to the transference".
7 J. Lacan, *Television*. Op. cit., p. 14.
8 J. Lacan, *The Knowledge of the Psychoanalyst. Seminar 1971–1972*, translated by Michael Gerard Plastow. Éditions de l'Association lacanienne international (For Private Use Only). Seminar of 4th May 1972.
9 Plato, Parmenides, in *Plato. Complete Works*, edited by John M. Cooper, Hackett, Indiana, 1977. p. 370, Line 136a.
10 Ibid., p. 396, Line 165e.
11 J. Lacan, *The Knowledge of the Psychoanalyst. Seminar 1971*–1972. Op. cit., Seminar of March 8, 1972.

12 Ibid., Seminar of June 1, 1972. "as regards the yad'l'un there are 2 stages. Parmenides and then subsequently we have to get to set theory".

13 J. Lacan, *The Knowledge of the Psychoanalyst. Seminar 1971–1972*. Op. cit., Seminar of 17th May 1972.

14 Ibid.

15 Ibid., Seminar of March 15, 1972.

16 María-Inés Rotmiler de Zentner, Le psychanalyste malgre lui, in *Papers of the Freudian School of Melbourne*, FSM, Melbourne, 1996, Vol. 17, p. 159.

17 J. Lacan, *The Knowledge of the Psychoanalyst. Seminar 1971–1972*. Op. cit., Seminar of 10th May 1972.

18 J. Lacan, Letter of Dissolution, in *Television. A Challenge to the Psychoanalytic Establishment*, edited by J. Copjec, translated by J. Mehlman, W. W. Norton & Company, New York and London, 1990 [1980a], p. 129.

19 Oscar Zentner and Rotmiler de Zentner María-Inés, Letter of Resignation, in *Papers of the Freudian School of Melbourne*, FSM, Melbourne, 1992.

Chapter 10

On the necessity of becoming dissolute

Megan Williams

Dis-solution

In 1980, Lacan proposed a solution to what he saw as the ills of his school. The solution he proposed was a dis-solution (Lacan, 1990 [1980a], p. 129). Dissolution. What if we take this up as a solution proper to the discourse of psychoanalysis?

Dis-solve. Re-solve. There's a curious slippage in the term dissolution. It means to dissolve, which in turn means to make a solution. Yet dissolution could also mean its opposite: the undoing of solution. Lacan's dis-solution was intended to undo the solution (in a chemical sense) that was being made in his school, a solution, I suggest, of love and identification. Lacan resolves to put himself in the way of this solution that makes the school function contrary to the purpose for which he founded it – the purpose for which he founded it being, one would think, to sustain the discourse of psychoanalysis (Ibid.). His formulation here echoes an earlier one, made in 1967, of an atmosphere of narcissism and prestige in psychoanalytic societies which "re-establishes, with the reinforcements of the backslider, what the training analysis aims to dissolve" (Lacan, 1995 [1967], p. 2). The phrase ". . . aims to dissolve" speaks again of dissolution as a solution – here, one proper to the analysis. A solution to what? A dissolution of what? If we continue with Lacan's words from the later time, the time of the dissolution of his school, we would say that it aims to dissolve "the malaise" particular to each *parlêtre*; a malaise which is responded to, he says, only by the truth particular to each one (Lacan, 1990 [1980b], p. 133). Thus, there is a link between the particular truth and dissolution. The truth dis-solves something.

In the same 1980 text that references the particular truth, Lacan writes: "the Other is missing" (Ibid., p. 134). There is a link, then, between dis-solution and the revelation of the absence of the Other. If the Other is missing as guarantor of truth, then there is no truth that can be stated as universally true; only singular sayings that half-say this truth that is particular to the *parlêtre*: for each one, a particular truth. There is no common impasse and therefore no common solution.

Recently, in the Freudian School of Melbourne I spoke of how my own analysis came to an end with an interpretation that brought a particular truth to respond to a malaise that I called melancholy. I spoke of how the symptom formed after

DOI: 10.4324/9781003212720-13

the death of my mother in my childhood, the symptom that I called *the insistent presence of an absence*, was transformed into the *absence of a presence*. The insistent presence of an absence had been made symptomatically present in my life through identification: it had been that which could not be missing; that which I always found and, ultimately, found myself to be. To use Lacan's language from *The Four Fundamental Concepts of Psychoanalysis*, these representations formed an automaton which, in turn, made my encounters with any absence or loss into a *tuché*, a real and traumatic encounter (Lacan, 1979, pp. 53–54).

The penultimate interpretation that my analysis produced, the words "a fault without remedy", made me grasp that the fault in the Other, the wrong of missing, was not mine alone. I heard in those words that the fault is universal, the Other is missing, and this is not the same thing as the missing of a loved one. The object that had resonated like a hungry ghost in all the times of my life was extracted from its solution with identification. It was no longer necessary for me to embody it and enact the fault. It became possible to encounter others as real presences rather than as re-presentations of the absent object.

The object *a* has no representation. To make a representation of it is to make a solution (in both the chemical and metaphoric senses). It is to dissolve it into an idealising identification, as Lacan proposes in *The Four Fundamental Concepts of Psychoanalysis*, and he marks that identification with the letter *I* (Lacan, Ibid., pp. 267–274). A solution of *a* and I. A solution of love and knowledge. The fall of that object was a separation of *a* from I, a dissolution of the fantasm that bound them. The transformation of a present absence into an absent presence meant also that my analyst could no longer support the ghostly presence. The object fell from the analyst; a dis-solution of it from the ideal of a masterful knowledge.

Knowledge of the psychoanalyst functions as particular truth

This separation concerns the truth that the psychoanalyst knows: the truth that the Other is missing or, otherwise said, that there is no sexual rapport. Is this not a common impasse, a universal truth, a generalised knowledge? No, because the psychoanalyst doesn't know it as a *general* knowledge, and because it's not that the *person* who is a psychoanalyst knows it, but that the *psychoanalyst* knows it, in the way that knowledge of the psychoanalyst operates, which the discourse schema tells us is from "under the bar", from the other place (Lacan, 2007, p. 79, 93). "[W]hat psychoanalysis reveals is that it is a knowledge that is unknown to itself" (Lacan, 1971–1972b, lesson of November 4, 1971, p. 16). This knowledge can only be made to *function* – and according to the Discourse of the Analyst, the knowledge of the psychoanalyst functions *as truth* – and only in singular moments, in particular sayings that respond to a particular malaise (Lacan, 2007, pp. 69, 93). It can't fund a common technique. It comes or it doesn't come; it's not at the disposal of the *person* but in the saying of the *analyst*. The final interpretation that my analysis produced concerned the function of this knowledge as truth.

On the necessity of becoming dissolute   83

The interpretation was: "It's not that you know, or that I know, but that your tears know". It dissolved the propriety of knowledge, the "I" or the "you" which might make of analysis a tutelage of reasoning.

In *The Knowledge of the Psychoanalyst*, Lacan makes a neologism combining the words for "reason" and "resonate": *réson* (Lacan, 1971–1972b, lesson of January 6, 1972, p. 10). *Réson* is the purring of jouissance in speech, where it is parasitic on signifiers. The particular truth concerns this dissolute jouissance and therefore leaves knowledge beneath the bar, in the other scene, improper and outside convention. Thus, dissolution establishes a not-all, a one by one, not a society.

Dissolute is given by Dictionary.com as the past participle of *dissolvere*, to dissolve. This suggests that it is that which has been dissolved – the jouissance that purrs in speech. Yet its meaning suggests the *un*-dissolvable: "being indifferent to moral restraints; given to immoral or improper conduct; licentious; dissipated; promiscuous; undisciplined; disregarding of accepted conventions".

Dissolution of transference

That psychoanalysis become a conventional discipline is what Lacan puts himself in the way of by his solution of dis-solution: namely, that the School become a society, a place of accepted conventions, idealised leaders and hierarchy, a discipline of the generalised knowledge proper to the Discourse of the Master. A master discourse establishes a common theoretical solution for the overcoming of a common impasse. The common establishes the norm, replacing psychoanalysis with a psychology in which normalisation leaves no place for the psychoanalytic act of encounter with a singular truth. Lacan indicates that a training analysis should dissolve something, and typically the dissolution in question has been thought of as the dissolving of transference at the end of analysis. For Lacan, in the passage I cited earlier from *The Four Fundamental Concepts of Psychoanalysis*, the desire of the analyst ought to operate such that it maintains the greatest possible distance between I and *a*, or between idealising identification – "the point at which the subject sees himself as loveable" (Lacan, 1979, pp. 270, 272) – and the object *a* (Ibid., pp. 272–273). He doesn't say that the dissolving of transference entails a dissolution of the bond between them, but I hear this in what he calls the fall or separation of the object *a* (Ibid., p. 273).

In 1976, François Roustang published a book titled *Un Destin funerare*, translated as *A Dire Destiny* (Grotjahn, 1982). It considered the question of the destiny of psychoanalytic institutions in light of the end of analysis and what happens to transference afterwards. Roustang, somewhat like Lacan, held that analytic theory must be continually reinvented within each analysis, in a process that involves "learning that which has never been heard before" (Ibid., p. 808). If we replace "learning" with "hearing" – *hearing that which has never been heard before* – the phrase evokes *réson*. Roustang goes on to write that this makes psychoanalysis incompatible with a "hierarchical organisation based on master-disciple relations"

(Ibid., p. 809). And yet, for Roustang, the Other cannot be missing, since he nevertheless writes that we do become disciples, and this in order "to forestall madness" (Ibid.). That psychoanalytic theory is invented anew in each analysis makes analysts susceptible to madness, since "delusion is the theory of one" (Ibid., p. 809). An impasse thus emerges for Roustang on the path between invention and theory: there where Lacan locates a particular truth, he locates theory, which must have reference to that which is held in common. In the institution, therefore, his argument goes, we need leaders, designated by transference, who will function as "theoretical referents" for all, and thus as the guardian and guarantee of our sanity (Ibid.). This makes impossible the complete resolution of transference or dissolution of infantile dependency. Only a madman is free of transference. That is, singularity is madness.

Another author who considers the dissolution of transference, Jessica Benjamin, draws in 1994 a conclusion which also concerns identification with an Other of authorised knowledge (Benjamin, 1994). Whilst she critiques the notion (attributed to Freud) of analysis as a form of tutelage that passes on authority, she nevertheless retains it with the modification of countertransference. Her formulation is that the identification which the analysand makes with the analyst in transference love must be reciprocated by the analyst's attitude of "I remember being like you", which will dissolve the analysand's idealisation of authority, resulting in self-respect and freedom rather than submission (Benjamin, 1994, pp. 542–543). Thus, while transference love involves identification, yet its dissolution also comes about by identification – as long as the identification is mutual. The erotic idealisation of transference love will be dissolved by the analyst's "counter transference communication" of respect, empathy and attunement, as much as by his "modeling" (*sic*) of self-knowledge and self-mastery (Ibid.). What she proposes is thus an internalised master-disciple relation and another solution (in the chemical sense) of love and identification: a sexual rapport, based on a seeming incest or merging of generations. The erotic is dissolved by making one – that is, by Eros.

This is akin to the hope which seems to underlie many of Freud's writings: that the surplus which the symptom testifies to could be bound by Eros. It is a hope that, in writing "Analysis Terminable and Interminable", he acknowledged had been disappointed (Freud, 1937, pp. 223–230). What is of interest, though, in all three theories, is the idea that resolution should come from solution or binding rather than from dissolution. The account that they give of the efficacy of analysis is that the singular jouissance particular to each *parlêtre* – that excess which Lacan's term "parasitic Real" characterises as unbindable – comes to be bound (Lacan, 1975–1976, lesson of January 13, 1976, p. 15). And what it is bound to is an idealised identification. For Lacan, on the contrary, the particular truth which responds to that singular jouissance un-binds it from identification.

Morality, propriety, discipline, convention: does analysis aim to dissolve the civilising bonds with a truth particular to the speaking being, to extract the object *a* from its solution, only to re-solve the resulting dissolute? Freud asked the same question: is it the analyst's role to entice a spirit from the underworld only to

On the necessity of becoming dissolute   85

order it back again in fright (Freud, (1915[1914], p. 164)? In the end, however, he didn't unequivocally say no. And that, I think, is why Lacan argued that, where Freud had ground to a halt at the castration complex, his own approach could pass beyond it. He specified in 1963 that the way beyond it is by the analyst taking the seat of the object *a*: in the later language of the Discourse of the Analyst, by becoming its semblant (Lacan, 1971–1972a, lesson of June 21, 1972, p. 8). He defined the transference this way – which I would characterise as the analyst as a solution (in the chemical sense) of knowledge and the erotic bond to the object or, put otherwise, of the I of identification and the *a* of the object. I have said that Lacan then proposes that the analysis function such as to make a dis-solution or separation of what has been in solution, producing as residue the dissolute, the falling out of the object. His position is thus contrary to those of Roustang, Benjamin and, although it's arguable, at least certain writings of Freud.

Also in. . . *ou Pire*, while still defining transference as a location of a the object *a* as semblance in the place of the analyst, Lacan identifies this object with *the being forgotten in saying* (Lacan, 1971–1972b, session of June 21, 1972). The "particular truth" of the parlêtre referred to above could be thought of in this way: as the being of jouissance forgotten in speaking, which it is the function of the analysis to extract from the solution it has made with identification, by hearing its *résonnance* echoing in the spoken reasoning. This might include, for instance, the notion I have drawn from Roustang of hearing that which has never been heard before, or the author Gerald Murnane's notion of writing in order to write "*that which only [he] can say*" (Murnane, 2012, pp. 117, 119).

The analyst, the dissolute

Thus, I am linking this *hearing* and *saying* to Lacan's notion of a particular truth which dis-solves, to arrive at a characterisation of *the psychoanalyst as dissolute*. Dissolute in being the place of that object which falls out of reason and identification. Dissolute in functioning with the jouissance that purrs in speech. Dissolute in being attuned not to convention nor propriety but to *this* hearing and *this* saying: which belongs to the "I" of neither the analyst nor the analysand. It *résonne*, resonates: hosted by the signifier yet consisting not in its meaning but in its singing, its purring. That singing or purring, I think, doesn't necessarily refer to its physical sound. It might refer to the way it resonates in the halls of history, in the vaults of suffering, in the echoes of that which repeats.

Recently, I listened to an analysand who had over the course of some years repeated certain family stories as an unvarying set. On this singular occasion, words came from my mouth without pre-meditation, surprising me. I said: "You are saying your love". I had heard what had never been heard before, even though we had both heard the same words many times. The analysand, unusually, was silent, and then began to cry. The interpretation brought a turn in the analysis. It was, I would say, a moment of separating the *a* from the I; separating a real presence in the body and affect from the history and consolidation of identifications;

something of the real of sexuality from the Eros which binds it into the family. It would have been more accurate to say, not, "you are saying *your* love", but "you are saying love" or even better, "love is saying you", in that there is an object cause there which had been dissolved in an ideal identification to a giant of a grandfather. Naming it love in that moment was not, I think, to bind it in the sense of Eros, but rather to mark something real as separate from the identification and as belonging to the *parlêtre* alone, not explicable by the spoken representations. There was a momentary and contingent real presence or trans-substantiation of the dis-solute and ultimately un-dissolvable object.

Against Roustang, then, I would hold that the singular produced in an analysis is not mad, but dissolute. It is not mad because it has an effect, not of theory, but of truth.

What is striking in the theories of Roustang and Benjamin in contrast to Lacan's is that there is no place for singularity; for an encounter which might not become theoretical knowledge. It's striking to me in that it highlights Lacan's taking up of that singularity, his having become dissolute in act, continuing to make heard that which had never been heard before. It was demanded of him that he become dis-solved in the *herd*, identified to a common "theoretical referent", and he refused, choosing instead the *heard*. It makes sense to me in a new way of what might have been at stake in his assertion that he spoke in his seminars as an analysand, since it is from the saying of an analysand that one might hear that which has never been heard before.

The school

So, what of the destiny of the dissolute in a school? The theories of Roustang and Benjamin propose to deal with that which is dis-solved by re-solving it in a "better" solution but of the same kind. They propose that the erotic excess, the singular truth, be bound again in identification: to a leader, to a father-become-alter-ego or to an agreed convention: in all of which the big Other returns and is not missing. They send the spirit back to the underworld; do what I suppose Lacan wanted to put himself in the way of when he dissolved his own school. Their implicit argument that the identification to the leader of the society or to the analyst is a *better* identification than the one that was brought to the analysis is irrelevant, since the fundamental structure is opposed to the movement of an analysis as dis-solution. It's the difference between saying that analysis makes the same knot but with better, more conventional elements, and saying that it makes a different knot, in which the real surmounts the symbolic such that there is no solution, no dissolving (Lacan, 1974–1975, session of January 14, 1975).

A singular saying cannot be made into theory, as Roustang observes: that would be delusion. Its singularity itself, however, gives rise to knowledge: the knowledge of the psychoanalyst that the Other is missing. During the analysis this knowledge is dissolved in transference but the passage out extracts it such that it can function as truth, in a form particular to this analysis. Therefore, it also

On the necessity of becoming dissolute   87

dissolves the subject supposed to know and con-vention, the con of transference, which can only leave the field to in-vention; singularity. It will therefore influence the practice of the new analyst in singular and unpredictable ways which make each analysis a matter of invention. Thus, it's not *theory* that is made anew with each analysis, but *psychoanalysis*.

In 1964, Lacan said that he had always stood alone in relation to psychoanalysis (Lacan, 1990[1964], p. 97). It's quite an extreme position, but I have come to realise that it's not the position of *Lacan the person*, but of *an analyst, any* analyst who doesn't "backslide" into identification. In presenting something of my pass in the Freudian School of Melbourne, I spoke of what I called several moments of backsliding. Each one involved a solution of love and identification; that is, an identification with an ideal position adumbrated by an Other whose love might therefore be captured by occupying that position. For example, in my first approach to the pass, I spoke from a position given by my father's childhood name for me, a name which designated the place in which I was loved. In that the solution was presented to the Other of the jury of the pass, where I hoped to find a solution of love and knowledge, it indicated a continuation of transference. Moreover, this name given by my father not only carried his love, but designated what he thought I was for my mother, the missing one, the one standing in the place of the lost object. Thus, it indicated a familiar knot made of Eros: a knot of love, knowledge and the object *a*. Only in making a second turn around where I was tied into that knot did I retie it, and pass to a position of saying that which only I could say, and by that I'm not referring to the content alone, but to a saying which allows for the forgotten being to not be identified.

Conclusion

Clearly, it's not for nothing that the authors I have cited terminate analysis with new, or rather, substitute identifications. The pull to identify is strong. Roustang, indeed, observes that the members of Lacan's school had an un-analysed transference to Lacan as the subject supposed to know how to interpret Freud (Grotjahn, 1982, p. 808). Identification promises belonging, love, knowledge and mastery of the promiscuous, un-principled forces the speaking being is subject to. The pull of the Discourse of the Master is strong. This is what drew from me the word "necessary" of my title and of the paper that I presented in the Freudian School of Melbourne. If the only solution is dis-solution and the dissolute ex-sists alone and appears contingently, then is it not necessary to continue to speak in order that one produce opportunities for this contingent emergence? – to speak in order to say that which only I can say and which has never been heard before.

What else does one do with the dissolute? The question about the destiny of that which one stands alone with makes it clearer, perhaps, why there are analysts. The *analyst* – not the *parlêtre* nor the *person*, who have other destinies – is given to *functioning* with the dissolute: to finding something to do with it, in the Discourse of the Analyst. And since the analyst cannot function as such by making solutions,

88   Megan Williams

by displacing the particular truth into conventional theory, the school cannot be a society. It is a place where each psychoanalyst operates with a particular dissolute, and not of psychoanalysis taken as a common endeavour.

Afterword

It may seem that in this paper I have conflated two separations – that of the object *a* from I/idealising identification; and that of love from knowledge – thereby suggesting that the object *a* of the first formula is equivalent to the love of the second. It would be a Freudian move, to speak of desire and love in the same breath, and I am not equating them. But I think there is a point to be made. Love has something of a bad press in psychoanalysis, as narcissism or as the passion for being that one brings to transference, along with hate and ignorance: *hainamorignorance*. However, if the movement of an analysis is to extract the object *a* from sameness in order to obtain absolute difference, then isn't love also separated from identification, to become what I called in the case of my analysand *a real presence*? Jean Allouch wrote a book examining what it might be to not only do without the father but to remove all traces of him: to go beyond God, exit the temple. He concludes that what it involves is a different kind of love: love that goes towards difference, "love in the time of the object *a*" (Allouch, 2012, p. 174). Ab-solute difference. Dis-solute. No solution. The love which emerged in my analysand in that singular moment was not a love *for*. It will no doubt find channels of signifiers to run through, but at that moment it was *ab*, as in ab-solute: without the limits of the signifier.

References

Allouch, J. (2012) *Prisonniers Du Grand Autre: L'Ingérence Divine I*. Paris: Epel.
Benjamin, J. (1994) What Angel Would Hear Me? The Erotics of Transference. *Psychoanalytic Inquiry*, 14(4): 535–557.
Freud, S. (1915[1914]) *Observations on Transference-Love (Further Recommendations on the Technique of Psycho-Analysis)*, Papers on Technique (1911–1915[1914]). Standard Ed., XII. London: The Hogarth Press and the Institute of Psycho-Analysis.
Freud, S. (1937) *Analysis Terminable and Interminable*. Standard Ed., XXIII. London: The Hogarth Press and the Institute of Psycho-Analysis.
Grotjahn, M. (1982) Un Destin Si Funeste. By François Roustang. Paris: Editions de Minuit, 1976, 203 pp. *Journal of the American Psychoanalytic Association*, 30: 791–814.
Lacan, J. (1971–1972a) *The Seminar of Jacques Lacan Book XIX: . . . Ou Pire*. Translated by C. Gallagher. London: Karnac Books.
Lacan, J. (1971–1972b) *The Seminar of Jacques Lacan: The Knowledge of the Psychoanalyst*. Translated by C. Gallagher. London: Karnac Books.
Lacan, J. (1974–1975) *The Seminar of Jacques Lacan Book XXII. R. S. I*. Translated by J. Stone. Unpublished.
Lacan, J. (1975–1976) *The Seminar of Jacques Lacan Book XXIII: Joyce and the Sinthome*. Translated by C. Gallagher. London: Karnac Books.

Lacan, J. (1979) *The Four Fundamental Concepts of Psycho-Analysis*. Edited by J. A. Miller. Translated by A. Sheridan. Harmondsworth, Middlesex, England: Penguin.

Lacan, J. (1990 [1964]) Founding Act. In: *Television. A Challenge to the Psychoanalytic Establishment*. Edited by J. Copjec. Translated by J. Mehlman. New York and London: W. W. Norton & Company.

Lacan, J. (1990 [1980a]) Letter of Dissolution. In: *Television. A Challenge to the Psychoanalytic Establishment*. Edited by J. Copjec. Translated by J. Mehlman. New York and London: W. W. Norton & Company.

Lacan, J. (1990 [1980b]) The Other is Missing. In: *Television. A Challenge to the Psychoanalytic Establishment*. Edited by J. Copjec. Translated by J. Mehlman. New York and London: W. W. Norton & Company.

Lacan, J. (1995 [1967]) Proposition of 9 October 1967 on the Psychoanalyst of the School. Translated by R. Grigg. *Analysis*, 6: 1–13.

Lacan, J. (2007) *The Seminar of Jacques Lacan Book XVII. The Other Side of Psychoanalysis*. Translated by R. Grigg. New York and London: W. W. Norton & Co.

Murnane, G. (2012) *A History of Books*. Sydney: Giramondo. Vol. 117, 119.

Chapter 11

Writing out of school[¶]

Peter Gunn

I last visited this place in 2005. The occasion was the Joyce-Lacan Symposium. It was with this gathering that the full weight of Dublin pressed itself upon me. If the first of these names, Joyce, can be identified as the chief artificer of this impression, there is no doubt that the effect was sheeted home by its tie to the second, Lacan.

One articulation of this concatenation of names took the form of a paper, titled "The Joyce Effect". Delivered by a psychoanalyst, this paper, or, more accurately, this performance, was structured by writing. That is, it was presented as an encounter, in the form of an exchange of letters, between these two, Joyce and Lacan.

The effect of this delivery was in no way lessened by the dawning realisation that this encounter was entirely fictional. This is despite the fact that, in opening what must, in retrospect, be called the first Joyce-Lacan Symposium, Lacan himself gives chapter and verse of an actual meeting with Joyce.[1]

Not only that. With the subsequent publication of "The Joyce Effect", it became clear that what was being performed, both in 2005 and in 1975, was something quite fundamental. It was an enactment of Lacan's own formula, "there is no sexual relation" [*il n'y a pas de rapport sexuel*].[2]

In their reaction to this performance, some in the audience, many of whom also laid claim to being psychoanalysts, demonstrated a compulsion to make One of "them-two" [*la relation d'eux*]. For psychoanalysis, however, this is of the order of the impossible.[3]

For Lacan, with Joyce, there could be no correspondence other than by way of the *one* of the symptom. This is Lacan's own symptom, but a symptom now re-named, as a result of his entanglement with Joyce, by this concatenation of names.[4]

But for me, in addition, there was a re-doubling of this Joyce effect. This was due to the fact that the psychoanalyst in question, Oscar Zenter, to name him, is one of the founders of the *Freudian School of Melbourne*, that being the school of psychoanalysis of which I am a member.

This brings me to my paper. Here I want to pose the question, "What is the relation of the group to the school?" Or, in order to not close off the question, "What

DOI: 10.4324/9781003212720-14

is the relation of the group to the school when the group in question is already, as it were, out of school?"

And need it be said that the school in question is already something of a misfit? This school cannot be made to fit into the classrooms of any known teaching institution. This is a school which, through the transmission of psychoanalysis, *institutes*. And what it institutes is naming in its essential, and irredeemably singular, function.

Now, it was probably no coincidence that in the course of trying to write this paper something quite weighty arrived from Dublin. It was *The Letter*, that is, the Irish journal of Lacanian psychoanalysis by that name.

As it turns outs, the first article of this issue of *The Letter* is written by the man whose work we are here to honour, Cormac Gallagher.[5] As many of you know, Dr. Gallagher is also a founder; he co-founded the School of Psychotherapy at St. Vincent's University Hospital. Along with University College Dublin, this, of course, is the institution whose insignia are stamped into the very material of this conference.

But something almost equally pressing also arrived with the same package. Pressed onto the outside of the envelope was a €6 Éire stamp. And those of you who are native to this place will know that what this stamp carries: an image of the Springmount wax tablets.

These tablets are one of the earliest surviving examples, in Ireland, of writing which uses the Latin alphabet. It is because they were easily able to be transported that items such as these were such an important aid to bringing Christianity to the Irish heathens. And, indeed, the text which is pressed into the wax comes from the Psalms.

The tablets are now housed in The Treasury of the National Museum of Ireland. I went there yesterday to have look at them. The impact of seeing them in the flesh, as it were, took me to Lacan's own visit to a similar museum in 1961, a visit which he recounts, with great verve, in the seminar on identification.[6]

In that museum, the National Archaeology Museum of France, what Lacan saw, also behind glass, was a fragment of bone carrying a series of markings. They were probably made by a deer hunter of the late Palaeolithic.

What these repetitive incisions transmitted to Lacan was much more momentous than any message, whether mundane or spiritual. What endured for Lacan in that moment, even through glass, and at such an immense distance in time, was the signifier.

It is in fact in enduring that the signifier remains quite new, even for us today. It is new in two senses. It is new in the sense that it is only since Lacan that we can even say that the signifier exists. But we can also, again following Lacan, speak of a more fundamental sense in which the signifier is new. It is only inasmuch as the signifier is taken as always already existing that we can be said to be saying something new.

This newness of saying is made possible because the signifier introduces difference into the otherwise indifferent real. In its persistence as *the letter*, that is, as the primordial inscription of pure difference, the signifier introduces that gap or hole which Lacan names as *the subject*. This is the subject of the unconscious, or, to put it another way, it is the subject of the enunciation; in a word, it is the speaking-being, the *parlêtre*.

As a response to his encounter with this primeval writing, what Lacan performs in the seminar on identification is the *parlêtre* itself, in the very act of naming-in-speaking. This becomes clear from what he says in a subsequent lesson:

> In the act of enunciating, there is this latent nomination which can be conceived of as the primary kernel as signifier of what is subsequently going to be organised as a turning chain, such as I have always represented it for you from this centre, this speaking heart of the subject which we call "the unconscious".[7]

For Lacan, it was in encountering the hunter's incisions on the fragment of bone as the very inscription of the *parlêtre* that he himself was caused to exclaim:

> There, I said to myself addressing myself by my secret or my public name, this is why in short Jacques Lacan your daughter is not mute, this is why your daughter is your daughter, because if we were mute she would not be your daughter.[8]

In his article in the latest issue of *The Letter*, Dr. Gallagher is responding to a question about founding: "Why was psychoanalysis founded by an emigrant?" He asks in turn, "what is specific about founding psychoanalysis as opposed to a whole lot of other things like the Christian Brothers. . . ?"[9]

He points out that in establishing their teaching institutions throughout the English-speaking world, the Brothers were also emigrants. In their case, "they started here [Ireland] and . . . headed off . . .".[10] The point remains, however, that in their founding activities, they came from elsewhere.

Now, for psychoanalysis founding is an act, an act underscored by writing. In the case of the *Freudian School of Melbourne*, it is also an act that must, albeit only *aprés coup*, be interpreted as a failure, that is, as a parapraxis.[11] A prior question therefore presents itself: Who, or what, is acting? And this is a question that takes us to the heart of the unconscious, no less. This, in turn, is very much the question at hand for me in the writing of this paper.

I had thought, at the outset, that the paper would be something like a report on the work of the small group with which, for some years, I have been involved. But a report would situate this group within a universe, a universe supposedly already founded, even enshrined, by the *Freudian School of Melbourne*, the school of psychoanalysis with which, nevertheless, it does have some relation. Such universalising would have amounted to suffocation; it leads not to the unconscious but to unconsciousness.

By contrast, in 1975, during the *Journées des cartels de l'École freudienne de Paris*, Nicole Guilet spoke of the upsetting effect of the madman in the little groups at La Borde.[12] Like those groups, the group that I am talking about does not seek to make peace with this same upsetting effect, but rather make space for it. It does so by exposing the territory of psychoanalysis to an infiltration from elsewhere. The infiltration comes from practices, whether in literature or in art more generally, which might themselves be considered mad.

This intrusion of madness is prefigured in the group's name which, in its most recent incarnation, is *My Barbaric Yawp*. The phrase comes from a poem, *Song of Myself*, by Walt Whitman. At its core, the "myself" of this poem cannot be said to be the "real" Whitman of 1855. It is, rather, the other, poetic self. That is, it is the self as structured in and by language.

But in fact, in both writing and presenting this paper, I am already taken elsewhere. I am taken to the clinic, my own, what is more.

Quite recently, one of my analysands said: "It proves my living". In saying this, he understood himself to be referring to his incessant busyness over the many years which have followed the death of his beloved sister. This was a death, need it be said, that was both sudden and violent.

In responding, I found myself playing up. I played up this break, not the one that is constituted by the event of his sister's death, however tragic, but the breaks and stutterings in his own speech as he attempted to speak of this point of impasse. That is, I played up what opens up, between, on the one hand "prove", and, on the other, "improve"; in that equivocal opening, "improves my living" slips to "proves my living".

What does this imply about what I am trying to say to you now concerning this group, *My Barbaric Yawp*? It implies, I think, that I too must make play with the word "report". If something of the work of the group is to be conveyed to you by what I am saying, it will only be as an *effect* of what I am saying. In other words, whatever is conveyed must approach the effect, in this very room, of a report, a sudden, violent report.

I have to confess, however, that I come to this task already disturbed. And it is the work of the group which has had this effect. This can be confirmed, after the fact, by a bungled action. Let me try to account for myself.

I was trying to send an email to a member of *The Yawp*, that diminutive having now become, in practice, the group's name. Not sure that I had actually sent it, and blaming technology, I sent it twice, in different versions. My correspondent responded as follows: "I got one response from you, plus one from the writer".

This is more than brilliant. And, again, it is this *more* which had the effect, so much so that even now I struggle to keep pace with it. More than that, I am beside myself.

As I understand it now, the writer, that is, *The Writer*, capitalised and italicised in order to underline its status now as alien, *The Writer* as such caught out in pure differentiation from any rapport between one correspondent and the other, functions, at that moment, as "plus one". *The Writer* is itself more, but a more borne on the work of the group. In addition, at that moment, in referring to this "plus one", my correspondent is also not herself; she too becomes *The Writer*.

And perhaps it is worth noting that, although my correspondent would not be categorised as mad, this act, the act of taking up the position of *The Writer*, was unconstrained by any affiliation, whether to the *Freudian School of Melbourne* or even the group itself.

Lacan (2010e) first writes of the *plus-one* in *The Founding Act* of 1964. In that *Act*, Lacan specifies that the work of the School is to be structured by "a principle of elaboration". Under this principle, the work is distributed amongst small groups each of which "will be composed of three people at least, of five at most, four is the right measure . . . plus one . . .".[13]

Lacan furthers specifies that this distribution does not accord with what any one individual might champion. It gives weight instead to what each one carries from one group to another. In this circulation or transmission of work, the fixation of individual knowledge is bypassed in favour of the dynamism of not-known knowledge. In this way also, the "permutation" of groups through the movement of their "elements" bears on a constancy given not by the mastery of any single individual but by what insists by way of structure.

In using the terms "element" and "permutation", here Lacan is adopting the nomenclature of mathematics. In the *Journées*, Lacan makes frequent references to mathematics.[14] One such remark occurs in the context of an exchange with Daniel Sibony. Sibony was a practising mathematician who had recently completed his formation as an analyst with Lacan's school.

In reflecting on the cartel in the light of the discussion of the previous day, Sibony asks what it is which makes a set of *parlêtres* hold together. As I read Sibony, if, in the case of a meeting of individuals, each takes himself to be *only* an individual, nothing intrudes beyond the specular. The group is taken to be encompassed by the imaginary dimension, in its "manifest finitude", to use Sibony's term.

But if such an aggregation makes place for the extra which is carried by speech, it becomes what Sibony calls a "human set". The effect of this extra is that of an imposition; it "crushes" the individuals who would seek to account for the group only in its finitude.

Given what Lacan writes in the *Founding Act*, we can say that it is the effect of this extra which reduces the individuals of the group to *elements*. Now, *aprés coup*, it is as elements that they populate Sibony's "human set".

Sibony calls this imposition the "latent infinitude" of the human set. It is the radical externality of this point of infinitude which holds the elements of the set together. And it is not coincidental that it is precisely here that Lacan intervenes, naming this point, in turn, as the *plus-one*: "latent infinitude", he says, "that is precisely what the *plus-one* is".[15]

Now, on the previous day of the *Journées*, Lacan had already singled out an aggregation of mathematicians as just such a set. They constitute a set, he says, neither on the basis of identification, nor on the basis of knowledge, that is, of knowing *what* they are talking about. They do, however, form a set on the basis of knowing *who* they are talking about.

The oddness of this assertion can be credited to the peculiarity of the position to which this "who" is assigned. In coming to personify the *plus-one* of the group, this "who" is itself extra. To quote Lacan again:

> When mathematicians get together, there is incontestably this "plus-one". Namely, that it is quite striking that the mathematicians, I could say, they don't know what they're talking about, but they know who they are talking about; they are talking about mathematics as if it were a person.[16]

Lacan then goes on to comment, perhaps rather wistfully, that he wishes that the functioning of groups, and, more particularly I think, the groups which make up his School, would function in the same way as "any group of mathematicians".

Taking these assertions of Lacan together, I take him to be saying that when mathematicians get together around a project of work, what is woven, what is knotted, and by that very aggregation of *parlêtres*, is this "who" of mathematics. Precisely because this *Who* (which again, in order to underline its external status, I now capitalise and italicise) cannot be thought of as an actual person, *It speaks*; *It* speaks, in a word, mathematics. So substantive is this effect of speaking that mathematics, mathematics as such, becomes, we could say, personified.

In being made in this way, this *Who* of mathematics cannot be identified with any member of the group. A little like Mary Shelley's Frankenstein, in being brought to life it remains always already outside, including outside the human group. But, to make use of another of Lacan's terms of art, it is only in being *made* to speak that this *Who* comes to *ex-sist*, already outside.

Let us look more closely at this *ex-sistence*. In *RSI*, the Seminar which Lacan was conducting contemporaneously with the *Journées*, he credits it to Søren Kierkegaard.[17]

It was, Lacan says, by giving testimony to his symptomatic repetition of the excess of his father's sin that Kierkegaard wove this relation into something tangible. He did so by putting it into writing, that is, by inscribing it in letters. This led to the publication of a book by that same name, *Repetition*. It was in making the repetition tangible that this testimony made an impression.

In the same way as my *Yawp* co-respondent, in writing, Kierkegaard differentiates *The Writer*, here named as Constantin Constantius, from himself. The insistence of both the morpheme "con", from Latin "with" or "together", and the word, "constant", from Latin "standing firm", only serves to redouble the name's hypostatic effect.

Beyond the stifling repetition of his dead father's sin, *Repetition* stamped Kierkegaard's symptom as having the force of life, his life. Taken to that point, the knotting which this writing enacts becomes a subjective, but necessary, point of structuring. As such, it must, now, be designated as *ek*. In ancient Greek, this "ek" is a preposition; it has the sense of a point of origin, but one which is, at the same time, *ek-stra*, that is, outside.

But, as I read what Lacan says in *RSI*, if Kierkegaard was able to put the effect of this outside point into practice, within the domain of psychoanalysis it is given *existence* because he, Lacan, names it. And, having regard to the fact that the effect of this extra, being the extra of the symptom, is very much in play even in his own speech, in his very saying of it there is already a latent nomination. It is for this reason that Lacan can be said, *aprés coup*, to have named it *jouissance*.

Thus, whatever existence Lacan's naming gives to *jouissance*, it can only be said to exist in a space defined by the negation of existence. It does not exist but yet it is from Lacan's very *saying*, in *RSI*, that it is situated or placed.

In saying this, however, Lacan does go back, once again, to mathematics, in this case, to begin with, to the projective geometry of Girard Desargues in the 17th century. To put this very summarily, *jouissance* is further situated in being constituted in a knotting, a knotting which Lacan also names, for psychoanalysis, as Borromean. This is a knotting taken to the impossible point at which the apparent finitude of the circle is revealed, when considered topologically, to be equivalent to the infinitude of the straight line.

It is at this point of infinitude, a point which is also a point of con-junction or buckling of the three registers, R S I, that jouissance is produced as a hole, but a hole which ek-sists "It is [says Lacan] to the Real as making a hole that *jouissance ek-sists*".[18]

With the constitution of this hole, *jouissance* is isolated in its peculiar consistency. This consistency is given only by the name; it is naming as singularity. This, says Lacan, again in *RSI*, is what the psychoanalytic experiment has contributed: this *ek-sistence*, which is "what is touchable, tangible in something that is defined by the knot".[19]

In using the term "buckling" just now, rather than "knotting", to refer to this hole, I have in mind something which Lacan had already said in 1966, in *The Object of Psychoanalysis*, that is, almost 9 years before *RSI*. On this occasion, however, he was speaking not so much about the end of the analysis as the transmission of psychoanalysis, that is, of psychoanalysis as such.

He formulates this as a response to a challenge, which he reports as follows: "'How', it was said to me, 'can you believe that there is the slightest interest in stating what you are stating here in front of people who are so little prepared to understand it? Do you think that this exists in a sort of third or fourth space?'"[20]

Here is Lacan's response:

> [T]hat a certain buckle [*boucle*] had been effectively looped and that something of it, however little it may be, remains indicated somewhere, this is something which is perfectly sufficient to justify one giving oneself the trouble to state it.
>
> It is here that the notion of intersubjectivity becomes quite secondary; the plan of the structure can wait; once it is there, it is sustained by itself and in

the fashion, I would say, – the metaphor only comes to me here extemporaneously – in the fashion of a trap, of a hole, of a ditch. It is waiting for some future subject to be caught in it.[21]

Making the approach to this un-imaginable point of buckling is not easy, however. Impressed, as he himself is, by what Kierkegaard's writing was able to put into effect, Lacan compares it to the pilgrimage of the sinner. He says the following in *RSI*:

> I approach so penitentially [*péniblement*], my God! that everything that concerns Borromean-knot-thinking will give you pain. Because I told you, it is not easy to imagine it, which gives a proper measure of what all thinking [*pensation*] is, as I might say.[22]

Despite, or perhaps because of, the pain, let us persist.

Thinking of this pilgrimage in terms of how, by its work, the group writes its relation to the school, what falls out? I can only respond in the particular.

The place of *My Barbaric Yawp* is outside, including outside the ambit of the *Freudian School of Melbourne*. But it is in being situated, situated, that is, as *The Writer*, that this group puts something into effect.

To further locate this, we need to go back once again to 1960, in this case to Lacan's seminar on transference: *Transference in its Subjective Disparity, Its Putative Situation, Its Technical Excursions*, to give the full title. What *My Barbaric Yawp* puts into effect is the symptomatic excess of the *plus-one*, pure and simple. That is, it is the *plus-one* as *subjective disparity*.

In the first instance, this is not, therefore, the *plus-one* of the group, let alone the *plus-one* of the School. It is the *plus-one* of the subject, as such, of psychoanalysis. To misquote *The Writer*, the one who, in *The Founding Act of 1964*, named Lacan's (2010e) school *École freudienne de Paris*, it therefore "stands alone as [it] has always been in [its] relation to the psychoanalytic cause".[23]

At the same time, however, this *plus-one* does bear the name. It does so in three senses: bearing the name as insignia, being borne on it, and bearing its weight. That is, it does so in terms of the Imaginary, the Symbolic and the Real.

Now, Lacan tells us, in *RSI*, that these three are linked in a purgatorial Trinity;[24] that is, they are linked by suffering or, to be more precise, by *jouissance*. So long as this Trinity is kept in mind, *My Barbaric Yawp* can be said to function as *plus-one* of the *Freudian School of Melbourne*.

If it might be said to be an adornment of the *Freudian School of Melbourne*, in being borne on it, borne on the work of the School by that name, *My Barbaric Yawp* must also bear the pain of being outside it. What falls out then from *My Barbaric Yawp*, and from that very act of naming, is *The Yawp*.

As I say that, however, I am forced to recognise that, in the case of the *Freudian School* as well, *The Writer* has got there before me. There also a supplement is already being written.

98 Peter Gunn

The name of the School, to give it in its fullness, is the *Freudian School of Melbourne* plus. . . *School of Lacanian Psychoanalysis*. What falls out there, between these two names, Freud and Lacan, is, once again, a redoubling. For us, analysts, the effect of this redoubling is to bring us back, again and again, to the point of struggling to keep pace with the impossible.

It is to this same impossible task that Lacan was returned by his encounter with Joyce. It was also this task that imposed itself on Nietzsche at Sils Maria in his encounter with the demon: "Do you want this again and innumerable times again?"[25]

Coming to him as it did from outside, this voice crushed Nietzsche as an individual. In his madness, it was not Nietzsche, the individual so-named, who took up the burden of this impossible but chronic infinitude, but the subject. It was *this* Nietzsche who made it, in that moment, his own, "ultimate eternal confirmation and seal".[26]

If *The School* can be said to be already giving vent to this same impossibility, *The Yawp* trumpets it yet again, differently.

Notes

¶ This is an expanded version of a paper originally presented at *The Symptom of the Psychoanalytic Group and the Transmission of Psychoanalysis, A Tribute to the Work of Cormac Gallagher*, a conference held at University College Dublin on 30 November and 1 December 2018. This version of the paper has also published as part of the proceedings of this conference in *The Letter, Irish Journal for Lacanian Psychoanalysis* (Gunn, P, 2019). It is published here with the kind permission of the editor of The Letter, Monica Errity. Out of respect for this dispensation, and in order to try to retain something of the immediacy of that occasion, I have kept the local references.

1 Jacques Lacan, Joyce le symptôme I, in *Joyce avec Lacan*, edited by Jacques Aubert, Navarin, Paris, 1987, p. 23. This text seems to approximate what Lacan said in inaugurating the Symposium. It is based on notes made by Eric Laurent at the time. Following the Symposium, Lacan reportedly gave a quite different text to Jacques Aubert. This is now known as "Joyce le symptôme II". Both texts make the claim that Lacan met Joyce at Adrienne Monnier's bookshop in Paris, but they differ as to his age. In "Joyce le symptôme I", Lacan is 17, making the year of the meeting either 1918 or 1919; "Joyce le symptôme II" has him aged 20, making the year either 1920 or 1921. The second version corresponds to what we know of Joyce's movements. According to his biographer, Richard Ellmann, Joyce did not arrive in Paris until June 1920, that is, 2 months after Lacan's 19th birthday. But if what Lacan said in opening the Joyce Symposium appears not to correspond with the historical record, this lack of correspondence only goes to the subjective disparity which the encounter with Joyce seems to have induced in him. As he puts it later in the same year, such was the exigency of this Symposium for Lacan that it was itself inaugurating: "at the time . . . I let myself be hauled up to . . . by a pressing solicitation . . . I let myself be hauled up to inaugurate, to inaugurate under the banner of a Joyce symposium" (Jacques Lacan, *Seminar XXIII – Joyce and the Sinthome*, translated by Cormac Gallagher, www.lacaninireland.com/web/wp-content/uploads/2010/06/Book-23-Joyce-and-the-Sinthome-Part-1.pdf, lesson of November 18, 1975, consulted March 2019, translation modified). For more on the fictional status of the encounter between Joyce and Lacan, see, e.g., Luke Thurston, *James Joyce and the Problem of Psychoanalysis*, Cambridge University Press, Cambridge, 2004, esp. Chapter 1, "An Encounter", pp. 17–30.

Writing out of school 99

2 Oscar Zentner, 'From the Lacan ⟷ Joyce Correspondence', in Linda Clifton (ed.), Writing the Symptom, *Papers of The Freudian School of Melbourne, The Freudian School of Melbourne*, Hawthorn, Vol. 23, 2007, 275–292.

3 Jacques Lacan, *Seminar XX – Encore*, tr. Cormac Gallagher, lesson of 12 December 1972, consulted January 2019, translation modified.

4 In *The Sinthome* seminar, Lacan admits, "I am embarrassed by Joyce like a fish with an apple". (Jacques Lacan, *Seminar XXII – Joyce and the Symptom*. Op. cit., lesson of January 20, 1976, consulted February 2019).

5 Cormac Gallagher, 'Opening Remarks', *The Letter*, Issue 66/67, Autumn 2017/Spring 2018, pp. 1–2.

6 Jacques Lacan, *Seminar IX – Identification*. Op. cit., lesson of December 6, 1961, consulted November 2018.

7 Jacques Lacan, *Seminar XXII – Joyce and the Symptom*. Op. cit., lesson of January 10, 1962, consulted November 2018.

8 Ibid., lesson of December 6, 1961.

9 Cormac Gallagher, Opening Remarks. Op. cit., p. 2.

10 Ibid., p. 1.

11 Toro de Psicanálise, "The Situation of Psychoanalysis – Interview with Oscar Zentner", in *Ecritique, Newsletter of The Freudian School of Melbourne, School of Lacanian Psychoanalysis*, Vol. 7, 2010, consulted February 2019.

12 'Journées of the Ecole Freudienne de Paris' (Cartel Study Days), 12/13 April 1975', tr. Cormac Gallagher, consulted November 2018.

13 Jacques Lacan, "The Founding Act", tr. Cormac Gallagher, consulted November 2018.

14 "Journées of the Ecole Freudienne de Paris" (Cartel Study Days), April 12/13, 1975. Op. cit.

15 Ibid.

16 Ibid.

17 Jacques Lacan, *Seminar XXII – RSI*, tr. Cormac Gallagher, lesson of 18 February 1975, consulted November 2018.

18 Ibid., lesson of December 17, 1974, translation modified.

19 Ibid., lesson of February 18, 1975.

20 Jacques Lacan, *Seminar XIII – The Object of Psychoanalysis*, translated by Cormac Gallagher, www.lacaninireland.com/web/wp-content/uploads/2010/06/13-The-Object-of-Psychoanalysis1.pdf, lesson of June 1, 1966, consulted November 2018.

21 Jacques Lacan, *The Object of Psychoanalysis*. Op. cit.

22 Jacques Lacan, *RSI*. Op. cit., lesson of April 8, 1975. I am here departing from Cormac Gallagher's translation, and also taking liberties with Lacan's French. Gallagher's translation of *péniblement* as "painfully" is more usual.

23 Jacques Lacan, *The Founding Act*. Op. cit.

24 Friedrich Nietzsche, *The Gay Science*, ed. Bernard Williams, tr. Josefine Nauckhoff, Cambridge bUniversity Press, Cambridge, 2001, p. 194.

25 Friedrich Nietzsche, *The Gay Science*. Op. cit., p. 194.

26 In his Mallarméan reading of Nietzsche, Deleuze draws our attention to an order of repetition which, because of its temporal structure, is inherent to the act. It is in appropriating as fatality what falls out from the repetitive act of the dicethrow that chance becomes the affirmation of necessity (see Gilles Deleuze, *Nietzsche and Philosophy*, tr. Hugh Tomlinson, Continuum, London, 1986, pp. 23–31.

References

Deleuze, G. (1986) *Nietzsche and Philosophy*. Translated by H. Tomlinson. London: Continuum.

Gallagher, C. (2018) Opening Remarks. *The Letter*, 66(67) (Autumn 2017/Spring).

Gunn, P. (2019) Writing Out of School. The Letter. *Irish Journal for Lacanian Psychoanalysis*, (68): 47–61.

Journées of the Ecole Freudienne de Paris 2014, (Cartel Study Days) 12/13 April 1975. Translated by C. Gallagher. www.lacaninireland.com/web/wp-content/uploads/2014/03/Cartel-Study-Days-1975.pdf.

Lacan, J. (2010a) *Seminar XIII – The Object of Psychoanalysis*. Translated by C. Gallagher. www.lacaninireland.com/web/wp-content/uploads/2010/06/13-The-Object-of-Psycho analysis1.pdf.

Lacan, J. (2010b) *Seminar XX – Encore*. Translated by C. Gallagher. www.lacaninireland.com/web/wp-content/uploads/2010/06/Book-20-Encore.pdf.

Lacan, J. (2010c) *Seminar XXII – RSI*. Translated by C. Gallagher. www.lacaninireland.com/web/wp-content/uploads/2010/06/RSI-Complete-With-Diagrams.pdf.

Lacan, J. (2010d) *Seminar XXIII – Joyce and the Symptom*. Translated by C. Gallagher. www.lacaninireland.com/web/wp-content/uploads/2010/06/Book-23-Joyce-and-the-Sinthome-Part-1.pdf.

Lacan, J. (2010e) *The Founding Act*. Translated by C. Gallagher. www.lacaninireland.com/web/wp-content/uploads/2010/06/The-Founding-Act1.pdf.

Lacan, J. (2011) *Seminar IX – Identification*. Translated by C. Gallagher. www.lacanin ireland.com/web/wp-content/uploads/2010/06/Seminar-IX-Amended-Iby-MCL-7.NOV_.20111.pdf.

Nietzsche, F. (2001) *The Gay Science*. Edited by B. Williams. Translated by J. Nauckhoff. Cambridge: Cambridge University Press.

Toro de Psicanálise (2010) The Situation of Psychoanalysis – Interview with Oscar Zentner. In: *Ecritique, Newsletter of The Freudian School of Melbourne, School of Lacanian Psychoanalysis*. Vol. 7. www.fsom.org.au/assets/7_e_critique-7.-2010.-o.zentner.th-e-situation-of-psychoanalysis.2.pdf.

Zentner, O. (2007) From the Lacan ◇ Joyce Correspondence. In: *Writing the Symptom, Papers of The Freudian School of Melbourne*. Edited by L. Clifton. Hawthorn: The Freudian School of Melbourne. Vol. 23, 275–292.

Part IV

Psychoanalysis and the child

Chapter 12

Antigonal

Michael Currie

Introduction

Not long ago, in a public mental clinic, I was faced with the treatment of some children whose mother had suicided. After the suicide, a 5-year-old daughter who barely remembered her mother was beset by a dog phobia, walked in her sleep, turned on the lights at night and told her family to wake up. She suffered from night terrors and bedwetting. After some months of this, her father and stepmother brought her for treatment, understandably wanting to know what to say to the daughter about her mother's death. What utterance could address the symptoms the child was showing?

The brother and meaning

I didn't directly treat this little girl. I did treat her older brother who was 11 years old. The children's father was a practical man. His son had started, after the suicide, to withdraw at school, began to refuse to eat his dinner, commenced an endless series of angry outbursts at home and often retreated to his room. The father told me, "I know he is upset about his mother. But this can only go on for so long. There have to be consequences for what he does". The father was remarkably consistent in the application of consequences. After a series of meetings with the older brother, he came to me with a solution, which he recited to me with a dull look in his eye. "I've got to get over the fact that she killed herself and get on with my life". In this statement, the boy had received his father's opinion that his son's discontent was explained by the death of his mother.

As an explanation, as a cause, it has a strange status. In the "She killed herself", the mother takes both the subject and the predicate and all the whys and wherefores to the grave. The impenetrability of such a self-contained act leaves an unexplained absence foreclosed by the good work of the father. The sayings that the brother might have put forth remain forgotten behind the saids of the withdrawal, anorexia and anger. By this, I mean that there is an unspoken and unshaped discontent behind the brother's symptoms that remains untapped. Such is life.

DOI: 10.4324/9781003212720-16

The brother made the comments about getting over his mother to me after a break of some weeks. He had returned changed from a child to a boy-man on the cusp of puberty. His statement of adaptation came alongside the sudden appearance of the badges of adolescent haircuts and dressage. His words seemed his ticket of entrance into the revolving ritornellos of adolescence. A series of fads, fashions, new knowledges, girls, in the end, new masters had suddenly come in place of his father's consistent parenting. Such are the outcomes of good fathering. The son was embracing the world.

No doubt this is a fate, all going well, which awaits the daughter of this story, particularly if her father does parent the daughter in a similar way to the son. This would be to make of her dead mother's self-contained suicidal act an exception to the idea of the mother. For mothers don't suicide. Following the failed, suicided mother comes the stepmother. The enigma of the suicided mother is foreclosed, by inserting the dead mother into a series of mothers.

This method of dealing with the dead mother was shown to me in a performance of a version of the Greek tragedy Antigone that I saw in Melbourne. In the version I saw there is a different ending to Sophocles' play (Sophocles–Montgomery Griffiths, 2015). There is not the disaster that unfolds at the end of the Sophocles' play after the deaths of Antigone and Hemon. Rather, Creon steadies himself to give an identical political speech to the one he gave after the death of Eteocles at the opening of the play. Creon praises his son Hemon as a patriot and a hero, despite his suicide; just as he had praised Eteocles for dying defending Thebes against his brother Polynices. Creon explains the deaths of the two men completely, as if without contradiction, in exactly the same terms.

So, the effect of the consistency of Creon's unchanged story – speech about Hemon is to quash Antigone's act within the play. Antigone's death as a result of burying Polynices against Creon's edict has no effect. She is indeed obliterated. The world remains unchanged. Antigone is merely an exception, a speck in the back and forth of political discourse of meaning, which remains unchanged by her death. This is the method of the son of the vignette, encouraged by the father: "Forget about her and move on". The enigma of the mother's suicide has been filled with saids. That one might be saying remains forgotten. The problem with such forgetting is that it leaves no room for the son to make whatever he makes in regard to his dead mother.

The ritornello

What made me wonder about the fate of the daughter in the clinical vignette was a presentation of one of her play-therapy sessions by a colleague to a clinical review meeting of a multi-disciplinary team where I was present.

The colleague was discussing the daughter's play with a doll's house. The house had three levels and three rooms open to the child on each level. The daughter had placed a female doll on a chair in the central room of the centre floor of the house. She then played with the remaining figures, a father, grandfather and other siblings in all the rooms avoiding the central room. Where the figures had to enter the room with the silent female figure, they passed through without noticing or interacting with the female figure. The female figure remained untouched until she was packed away at the end of the session.

This session, as described by my colleague who was treating the girl, was the focus of much discussion in the clinical review meeting. The question was really one of what to make of this carefully placed yet untouched and unvoiced doll in the play session.

In the clinical review meeting, my colleagues advanced many hypotheses. The doll is the dead mother and the child's attempt to grieve for her; it is the child's attempt to keep the mother alive so she has a maternal object; it is the symbolization of the phobia; it is the child's refusal to accept the reality of the death; it is the love/hate of the mother; it is the child's attachment. . . . All the formulations focused on the imaginary link between the dead mother and the child and led to a suggestion, based on the loss of the primary maternal object, about what technique to use, or theme to encourage in the child's play. One suggestion was that the child should be told a story about her mother, so she could understand what had happened.

What was curious was the absence of reference to any playing that the child was enacting around the figure that apparently represented the dead mother or to the symptoms the child had produced.

In the meeting, as the explanations and techniques based on these explanations mounted, I was filled with the urge to say to my colleagues: "It is not that". What stopped me from saying "it is not that" was the supposition of a glare from my colleagues and the response, "Well if it is not that, what is it?"

There I was, caught in what Lacan describes in L'etourdit as the ritornello between the master and the academic discourses. Within the ritornello, there is an insistence on hearing the child's symptoms as demands for maternal care; an insistence on a meaning relationship between S1 and S2 (in the master's discourse, for example, the doll is the mother); and the production of certain signifiers as a support of a knowledge about the meaning relationship (in the academic's discourse, for example, to "make up" for the maternal loss). This ritornello has come to drive the knowledge industry that now exists between universities and mental health. The term "ritornello" is well chosen, to my ear, by the Lacan of L'etourdit.

A ritornello is a musical term denoting a short, striking section of music that is returned to. Nowadays, we refer to the ritornello as a refrain, chorus or the hook of the pop song. Or the slogan of a theory. It is obvious, tired and expected. One goes away from it only to return.

Beyond the ritornello, there is a riddle this little girl presents with her mysterious doll. There is a position implied by "it's not that". This position attempts to find a method of not being stuck within the universal or the good, what I might call the Antigonal path, where "It does not go without saying". What are the ethics implied by this path?

The ethics of antigonality

First thread – antigonal to the good

There is another way of hearing the child's play. The silence of the doll creates a separateness from the play of everyday dealings within the doll's house. The silent presence of the doll in the play of the child is unique; all the words and the interaction go on in the house, but the mother doll remains silent and un-moving. The silent presence of the doll marks a place beyond and separate from the world of goods. The child wordlessly insists on this separateness. This separateness suggests to me that the child is not demanding a mother that is good enough. Rather, the child's play implies that goods are not enough for a mother. To put this another way, the child's symptoms are not demands to be answered within the goods of mental health discourse, but markers of her singular, synchronic place in regard to the death of her mother. As Lacan says of Antigone: "The pure and simple relationship of the human being to that of which she happens to be the bearer" (Lacan, 1992, p. 282). The doll is an exhumation from underneath the slagheap of the good that has been piled on top of whatever the doll-mother represents. For this daughter, the doll is of course a signifier, and it is her synchronic relation with this signifier that puts her doll between the two deaths of absolute obliteration and physical death, a la Antigone.

In rendering Antigone in the way he does in his Seminar on Ethics, Lacan (1992) passes through a moment in his theorizing that allows him to point out the place of the analyst. This place is Antigonal to the good. Antigonality does not take the basis of the child's future neurosis as a repetition stemming from the failure to reach developmental goals. Rather, the child's neurosis is the method she can find to move the fathers of her city-state. Neurosis becomes a creative nexus that has a part in founding a law. Psychoanalysis attempts to harness this creative force.

This involves a shift from taking this mother doll as the said of the clinician's theory, to proposing the fixed unmovingness of the doll as a locus for saying that of which the child just happens to be the bearer.

Second thread – death, melancholia and the master

There is more than a tinge of melancholia in this doll. Having recognized the synchronic structure the child bears, the clinician is drawn to the work of mourning: a repetition of the saids of the loss of "the mother". Such a project risks trapping the child in her own master discourse of maternal loss and suffering. If we think of the structure of melancholia outlined by Freud, such a project supporting the saids of loss and mourning would be to maintain a fantasy that the second death does not exist. But the second death of absolute obliteration does exist, despite Lacan's mysterious rendering of the concept of the second death in his reading of Antigone in seminar VII. Melancholic effacement of the second death has real consequences in the clinic. One can imagine in this case the consequence of a forgetting of the sayings of mourning behind the returning saids of melancholia. For Freud showed us 100 years ago that there is always a forgotten saying lurking in the static saids of melancholia.

Lacan (1992) rendered Antigone as "between two deaths". Moustafa Safouan (1980), in his paper "In Praise of Hysteria", calls the first death *"narcissistic birth, the model of all corpses"*. The second death Safouan puts forward as the realization that fantasy is only fantasy. The example he gives is Hegel's fantasy (that Hegel took as reality) that the death of parents is the beginning of life for the child.

In Safouan's formulation, for us fortuitously rendered from the child's point of view, to give life to the child subject, the parent object must die. The second death is to know this is a fantasy. One can hear how important such a notion is with the prospect of a master discourse of melancholic suffering that I mentioned earlier. After reading L'etourdit, and Fierens' reading of L'etourdit, I might not able to look at the matheme of fantasy again without thinking of the divided subject and the object *a* being dragged, one after the other, through the roundabout of discourses.[1] For the child, a better metaphor for the second death, for the realization that fantasy is always one's own, we can take up Lacan's fantasy as that window through which one desires. Perhaps, that would be a start of an analysis for this little girl – to know that the window through which she chooses to view her mother is her own window where the view always changes.

Third thread – the non-universality of the doll

We are all born of a mother and all mothers die. There is no getting around this universal. But, rather than the universality of the mother, the object that might be represented by the doll is a mother. A mother who has exempted herself from motherhood. Theoretically, each exception – such as the exception/mother of the brother I discussed at the start – bears within her the seeds of the jump to the other side of the formulae of sexuation, to the third formula of sexuation. Contrary to the clinicians of the vignette, Fierens says in the "The Psychoanalytic Discourse", of the third formula, "Let us dare the exception by making a radical absence fundamental". The masculine and feminine sides of sexuation are not Antigonal to each other, but some Antigonality is necessary to make the jump to the other side of sexuation. This is a jump that could not be made in the work with the brother of this vignette. He was "the one that got away". But, as resistance is with the analyst, I turn to think on how to help the analysand submit to the delirious fecundity of psychoanalysis. How can a saying be provoked?

Fourth thread – the impossible

It should be clear by now that the jump of which I write cannot be made via filling the absence with the meanings of master theory. Not filling the absence is why theory should not intrude into the clinic. Being able to not stand in the way of it is why one theorizes outside of the clinic, indeed the reason for the existence of this paper. This is the beginnings of an answer to a question that has bothered me at some level in nearly every treatment session I have conducted with a child: Why am I allowing this play, posing as a treatment, to continue?

According to the Lacan of l'etourdit, "It is not that" as a refusal of meaning is still "the wail of an appeal to the real". A wail, perhaps, to the same gods that Antigone appeals to in Sophocles in following her Ate. A wail to the gods of theory that I suppose in my colleagues' response: What is it then?

One sense of the Antigonal orientation of the analyst (non-universal and not informed by the good) is to facilitate the blunderings of the child. Children blunder back and forth (across) and up and down (along) the bar of signification. A definition of play is that whilst it takes up many little objects, play itself has no object. A child's play, with its tendency towards intransitivity, promotes inconsistency. A child's play exists in the realm of "not without". In the clinical work with the daughter of the vignette I've described, "It does not go without playing". A play that amounts to a laughing in the face of death.

In the face of the child's demand about the mother/not mother, the cause (in this case, the mother's suicide) has to be effaced in favour of a playing saying.

The conditions under which to work with a child who has suffered such a loss was given to me earlier this year by another child, my daughter. We had been to see a performance of the opera Madame Butterfly. My daughter, who was watching as the singer who played the protagonist stepped forward to take her bows, told me of her relief to see Madame Butterfly "come alive again". My reply was that during the opera I couldn't wait for Madame Butterfly to kill herself and get it over with. I realized the killing I couldn't wait for was the killing of meaning. There bows the singer who played Madame Butterfly. The one who has bourne meaning but is now not so attached to it. It is a moment quivering with equivocation. Such is the intermediary status of this doll that allows the effacement of cause. Such effacement supports a saying – playing.

There is no grandmother who can give us a saying about this mother who has suicided. The playing – saying about and around the mother has no guarantee apart from its own playing – saying. There are no means of deciding about it apart from the saying. The mother is how the child plays her. That is perhaps true of all mothers, except that most often the child has a mother who provides an illusion that the sayings about her belong to her. But, in psychoanalysis, in the end, there is no such guarantee of decidability. We are stuck with a problematic equivocating mother, an effect, Fierens says, of having dared the exception and taken the radical absence of the third formula. We can't decide about her, yet on the child plays.

Note

1 I am thinking here of the master discourse, which hides fantasy, the academic discourse which appropriates the absence of the object a to knowledge, the psychoanalytic discourse, which takes the absence of the a-object and questions what this saying is for the subject, and the hysteric's discourse where the master is questioned without knowing why.

References

Lacan, J. (1992) *The Ethics of Psychoanalysis. The Seminar of Jacques Lacan, book VII.* Edited by J. A. Miller. Translated by Dennis Porter. London: Routledge.

Safouan, M. (1980) In Praise of Hysteria. In: *Returning to Freud: Clinical psychoanalysis in the school of Lacan.* Edited by S. Schneiderman. New Haven, CT: Yale University Press, 55–60.

Sophocles – Montgomery Griffiths, J. (2015) *Antigone by Sophocles.* Edited by Jane Montgomery Griffiths. Sydney: Currency Press (e-book).

Chapter 13

Falling into silence

Michael Gerard Plastow

It is very common to hear – whether in clinical practice or outside of it – a mother or father say of their child, "He, or she, doesn't listen". Parents who make this complaint often go so far as to have the child's hearing tested. We might think that this is displaced, that effectively their complaint is that the child does not respond to their demands, or does not obey their commands. That is no doubt true. But we must give credence to the parents' saying that the child does not listen. The child – or the subject in the child – strives to not hear. He doesn't listen to the voice of the Other that attributes meaning to what the child says, that demands satisfaction, the voice of the Other that commands the child to obey. The child endeavours to find a "deaf spot"[1] in order to not be drowned in this voice of the Other, to endeavour to find a place, a foothold from which to speak in his own voice. In the face of the overwhelming din of the Other's voice, the child – or any speaking being – in order to establish a place as subject, responds with the other side of the voice: the subject answers with silence.

Claude Lévi-Strauss, who had always taken an interest in aesthetics even in the most anthropological of his works, in 1993 published a book primarily regarding aesthetics titled *Look, Listen, Read.*[2] The *listening* part of this book focuses on a particular section of Rameau's opera *Castor and Pollux*, a section that might be of interest in our investigation of the function of the voice and its counterpart: silence. In the first act of this opera, everything is ready for the celebration of the nuptials of Pollux, king of Sparta, with Télaïre. But Télaïre is in love with Pollux's brother Castor. At the beginning of Act II, following Castor's violent death, there is a lament by a chorus of the Spartan people which begins and ends with:

Let the whole earth groan with *one voice*![3]

Lévi-Strauss cites an article from the 19th century by an author by the name of Masson, which already notes that after the last chord of the chorus, there is "a long silence",[4] following which we hear three notes that immediately precede Télaïre's aria. This aria expresses Télaïre's singular grief for the loss of her love. This silence was in fact written into the score, as Lévi-Strauss demonstrates by reproducing a section of the partition written in Rameau's own hand as *Petit Silence*[5]

DOI: 10.4324/9781003212720-17

or "A Little Silence". The interest of Lévi-Strauss, as well as that of others, is primarily upon the three notes, considered a mark of Rameau's genius, notes that so simply and elegantly effect the transposition between one key and the next.

The silence, in one sense, replaces a whole scene which was part of the original 1737 opera, but omitted in the 1754 reworking, a remake that became an artistic triumph in the face of the aesthetics of Italian opera of the time. Lévi-Strauss does not make anything further of this silence, but again cites Masson who notes that "in Télaïre's monologue, the slow and heavy accompaniment, with long chords and numerous silences, produces an effect of doleful sadness and of despondency".[6]

There are many different silences: there might be the silence of an inhibition of playing a musical instrument or singing in public, or of beginning to speak in a session. There are the silences or pauses between arias, or the silences that punctuate a session, or produce a scansion in a piece of music or speech. But there is something quite particular to a mode of silence that is written into the score, a silence that has a density and a weight by virtue of the fact of its refusal to be part of the "one voice", a silence that irrupts into the fabric or text of an opera, an analysis or a family. It is a silence that is not just an absence of sound, it is one that is a presence that can be inscribed by letters.

It was at this point in my looking at – and listening to – a recording of this opera, that my younger daughter joined me and asked me to tell her what had happened in the story up to that point. I told her that Castor and Pollux were said to be twins, the Gemini, but were actually half-brothers, conceived on the same night by the same mother. The fundamental disparity between them, however, is that Castor is mortal, whereas Pollux, who was conceived by Zeus, is immortal. And after Castor's death, Pollux tries to bring him back from the dead. My daughter asked, "So, it's about families?" I hadn't quite thought about it like that, but maybe she is right. Perhaps, today it might be called a blended family. She asked me if Pollux went to the Underworld to find Castor. My other daughter, overhearing this conversation, asked, "Why is opera always about love?" "It's not just about love", I replied, "It's also about death". And of course, if it's a *grand* opera, it's also about incest.

Freud wrote of an oceanic feeling in which one sacrifices oneself to the enjoyment of the Other. He wrote that Romain Rolland supposes that this feeling, "is present in millions of people. It is a feeling which he would like to call a sensation of "eternity", a feeling as something limitless, unbounded – as it were, 'oceanic'".[7] Freud endeavours to problematise this experience. But, in Greek, a πρόβλημα, or problema, is anything thrown forward or projecting, a tongue of land, or an escarpment. Pascal Quignard tells us that *problema* was the escarpment, projecting over the first waves, from which the town would throw a victim who then plunged into the sea below.[8] And that the victim – sacrificed by the High Priest, thrown into the ocean, he writes, "in other words into affect" (the "oceanic *feeling*") – is an emissary of Sound, of the Sonorous, according to Quignard: "The-man-who-is-the-victim-of-language. The-man-who-is-obedient", he writes.[9] Obey, though, is derived from *ob-audire, audire* to hear. To hear is to obey. Quignard writes that "Men resurface from the underworld and err on the sonorous sea. All living beings", he writes, "risk being engulfed in the sonorous sea",[10] *la mer sonore*, which could also be the sonorous mother (*mère*).

Jean-Michel Vivès proposes that opera maintains a tension between desire and jouissance, desire and enjoyment. Perhaps, we could say that the function of the family is to *decrease* this tension, it regulates the affects, as is commonly said today. The family protects the child from the unremitting noise of the world, as well as the continuity of its silence, through regulating sound, by making the sound musical. Much has been written of the musicality of the mother's voice by which the child is bathed in her warm waters, her amniotic fluid, her milk. This musicality continues in the nursery rhymes that every child learns, the rhymes, the rhythms that convey the cadence of language. Through these rhymes, the rhythms of the body are submitted to language. They punctuate sound and make it pleasant. The ancient poet Archilochus wrote, "take pleasure in what is pleasant, yield not overmuch to troubles, and understand the rhythm [$\dot{\rho}\upsilon\sigma\mu\grave{o}\varsigma$] that holds mankind in its bonds".[11] These are the family ties that bind, the bonds that promote the harmony of family life. The word *harmonia* in Greek describes the means of attaching ropes so that they can be tightened.[12] The family that prays together, stays together.

Josef Hayden wrote in his diary that he composed music in order to appease a long-standing sonorous suffering. His father was a wheelwright in Rohrau in eastern Austria, and Quignard tells us that "the whole pathos of his childhood bonds was hurled into the rhythms" of the hammer, the mallet and the saw. He defended himself against this by composing.[13] This noise persecuted him his whole life long, and, in the months preceding his death these rhythms hammered away at him with such a fierce acceleration that he was no longer able to transform them into melodies.

The musicality strives to reduce what is beyond the pleasure principle, endeavouring to resolve it into pleasure or unpleasure. In this sense, the family is normativising, and it is for this reason that Lacan says that the Oedipus complex is normativising. The normativisation provides a screen across jouissance, across the incest and death carried by Oedipus. There is a reduction of *enjoyment*, into joys that are meant: meant to give some pleasure. Baby bundles of joy, become petty parcels of pleasure. There are, for instance, little birthday presents of meaning that ritualise the means by which the child was conceived and borne. These presents, this pre-sense, a preconceived sense, avert the pure presence of silence. Enjoyment or jouissance is resolved, then, into little pleasures.

Freud, as we know, had an aversion to music – strange, in such a musical city as Vienna – but something perhaps that ran the risk for him of oceanic feelings. In his paper on the Moses of Michelangelo, he wrote that he was "almost incapable of obtaining any pleasure"[14] with music, as this is conveyed in the Standard

Edition. Except that he didn't write "pleasure", or *lust*, he wrote *Genuß*: enjoyment or jouissance. Notwithstanding, on December 12, 1897, Freud had written to Wilhelm Fliess: "Recently the *Meistersinger* afforded me a strange pleasure".[15] So, Masson, Jeffery Masson this time, translates as *pleasure* what Freud writes as *Genuß*.[16] Something keeps slipping in the translation, it lets slipping dogs lie, no doubt with the best of intentions, in order to not leave things in tension. Nobody wants any tension in the family. But Freud was, after all, susceptible not just to familiar pleasures, but to a strange enjoyment.

Such a strange enjoyment derived from song is potentially lethal, as we know from Odysseus' encounter with the Sirens. But even before Odysseus sailed past them, there were other encounters with the Sirens, such as the one recounted in Apollonius' *Argonautica*. On that occasion, Jason, in search of the Golden Fleece, set out with a number of heroes including our old friends Castor and Pollux, Odysseus' father Laertes, as well as Orpheus. On this occasion, the ears of the sailors were filled, not with beeswax, but with the melody from Orpheus' lyre, in order to overcome the song of the Sirens. Nonetheless, "the Sirens kept uttering their ceaseless song", writes Apollonius, the voice as object is continuous, it is as ceaseless as it is relentless. Two of the heroes, despite the precaution taken, threw themselves overboard, their souls "melted by the clear ringing voice of the Sirens".[17]

Odysseus did not have Orpheus on board, but he did have the enchantress Circe who gave him fair warning about the Sirens and how to withstand their cry and their song: it was both of these.[18] Following her instructions, Odysseus stopped the ears of his fellow sailors with wax and had himself bound hand and foot to the mast. Family harmony comes at a price: that of attachment.

The arrival at the Sirens' Island was presaged by a "dead calm". Odysseus alone left his ears unstopped in order to hear the Sirens' cry and song. Their song was a-semantic, at once conveying nothing, but knowing all:

> *We know all the pains that the Greeks and Trojans once endured on the spreading plain of Troy when the gods willed it so – all that comes to pass on the fertile earth, we know it all!*[19]

How can one find a place when the Other knows it all, when there is no lack in the Other's knowledge? This is a force, a seduction, that is difficult to resist.

Vivès draws our attention to a short text by Franz Kafka titled "The Silence of the Sirens".[20] Kafka prefaces this text with the following conclusion: "Proof that even inadequate, indeed childish measures can suffice for one's preservation". Childish measures like *not listening*, for instance. Kafka gives various versions of Odysseus' encounter with the Sirens, but what insists is Odysseus' *not listening* to the Maidens. For instance, he begins by saying, "To protect himself from the Sirens, Odysseus stopped his ears with wax and had himself chained to the mast". In this version, Odysseus listened, not to their song, but to their silence.

114 Michael Gerard Plastow

Furthermore, Kafka goes on to say that "the Sirens have a still more terrible weapon than their song, namely their silence". Or again, he writes that

> when Odysseus came, these mighty singers did *not* sing, whether they believed that against this opponent only silence could achieve anything, or whether because the look of bliss on the face of Odysseus . . . made them forget all about their singing.[21]

What matters here is that in this encounter, like in our beginning, the "childish measures" are able to produce a silence in the Other, an encounter with a silence, a silence that risks being even more unbearable than the voice that threatens to drown one out. There is an encounter here with this point at which the Other no longer responds, and the Other is no longer listened to. This is a silence that, of course, cannot be spoken, but, like Rameau, we might endeavour to write it.

When Odysseus had left the Sirens in his wake, his steadfast crew loosened the bonds holding him to the mast. This "loosened" was given in Greek, in the version of the Odyssey that has come down to us, as ἀνέλυσαν.[22] Quignard tells us that this is the first time that the word "analysis" is recorded in a Greek text.[23] Analysis, then, is an unloosening from that to which we are attached, a loosening from the mast of the good ship Oedipus, so that we can be set adrift. We might be able to move a little more freely, but more importantly, the wax may fall from our ears so that for the first time we can hear, even if it is to hear a silence. Here lies the possibility of a loosening of one's bonds, through an encounter with the voice as a-semantic, and the other side of the voice: a deafening silence.

Notes

1 J. M. Vivès, *La Voix sur le Divan*, Aubier, Paris, 2012, p. 36.
2 C. Lévi-Strauss, Regarder Écouter Lire, in *Œuvres*, edited by C. Lévi-Strauss, Gallimard, la Pléiade, Paris, 1993.
3 Accessible at: www.opera-comique.com/sites/TNOC/files/uploads/documents/152-rameaucastoretpollux1754-francaismodernise-philidor-cmbv.pdf My italics.
4 C. Lévi-Strauss, Regarder Écouter Lire. Op. cit., p. 1517.
5 Ibid., p. 1527.
6 Ibid., p. 1530.
7 S. Freud, *Civilization and its Discontents*. S.E., 21, Hogarth, London, 1930, p. 64.
8 P. Quignard, *La Haine de la Musique*, Calmann-Lévy, Paris, 1996, p. 35.
9 Ibid., p. 61.
10 Ibid., p. 200.
11 Cited in: W. Jaeger, *Paideia: The Ideals of Greek Culture. Vol. 1 Archaic Greece: The Minds of Athens*, translated by G. Highet, Oxford University Press, London and Oxford, 1965, p. 125.
12 P. Quignard, *La Haine de la Musique*. Op. cit., p. 193.
13 Ibid., p. 18.
14 S. Freud, *The Moses of Michelangelo*. S.E., 13, Hogarth, London, 1914, p. 211.
15 J. M. Masson, (Ed. & Trans.), *The Complete Letters of Sigmund Freud to Wilhelm Fliess: 1887–1904*, Belknap, Cambridge, MA, 1985, p. 286.

Falling into silence   115

16 M. Schröter, *Sigmund Freud: Briefe an Wilhelm Fließ 1887–1904*, Fischer, Frankfurt am Main, 1986, p. 312.
17 Accessible at: http://classics.mit.edu/Apollonius/argon.4.iv.html
18 *Phthoggos* and *aoidè*. P. Quignard, *La Haine de la Musique*. Op. cit., p. 183.
19 Homer, *The Odyssey*, translated by Robert Fagles, Penguin, Harmondsworth, 1996, p. 277 (XII, 206–208)
20 F. Kafka, The Silence of the Sirens, in *The Great Wall of China and Other Short Works*, edited by F. Kaka, Penguin, London, 1991.
21 Ibid., p. 101.
22 Accessible at: http://cdn.textkit.net/ram_odyssey_bookXII.pdf.
23 P. Quignard, *La Haine de la Musique*. Op. cit., p. 183.

Chapter 14

The words "Papa" and "Mama"

From the cave of language

Debbie Plastow

Introduction

Sabina Spielrein was one of the first analysts to work with children and to write theoretical psychoanalytic papers on the child. However, her work remains largely forgotten, or even repressed and rejected by many analysts, with a number of her papers not yet published or translated into English. Yet the writings that we do have access to give us insight into Spielrein's original theoretical ideas regarding language. One publication of particular interest from a psychoanalytic perspective is her paper titled: "The origin of the child's words Papa and Mama: Some observations on the different stages in language development" (1922b). Through interrogation of this paper, we will consider the following questions. Firstly, what can Spielrein's theorisations contribute to our understanding of language in psychoanalysis? And how might a child take up his own position as subject within language?

Spielrein's paper was preceded by a presentation that she delivered at the International Psychoanalytic Congress in The Hague in 1920. There is no written account of the presentation made by Spielrein at the Congress; however, we do have access to her abstract titled "On the question of the emergence and development of spoken language" (1920). The earlier abstract and her published paper seem to be different, and her theorisations in the latter may have been influenced somewhat by her association at that time with Piaget. By 1920, Spielrein already had a long association with Freud, who published *Beyond the Pleasure Principle* (1920) in the same year that she presented her paper at The Hague. In 1921, Spielrein moved to Geneva and met Piaget, who was at the beginning of his career. In a footnote, Spielrein writes that she attended Piaget's course on "Autistic Thinking" in the winter of 1921–1922 (1922b, p. 299), and Piaget was analysed by Spielrein for a number of months. In 1922, Spielrein's paper was published in *Imago* (1922a), but it was not until 80 years later that it was translated from German to English by Jungian analyst Barbara Wharton (1922b). We will cite the original German paper at times for a translation *à la lettre*, to allow a closer examination of the words and signifiers that insist in Spielrein's writings.

DOI: 10.4324/9781003212720-18

Spielrein's notions in this paper are underpinned by her theorisation of three different fields of language, which we will consider in relation to Lacan's later formulation of the three registers: the real, the symbolic and the imaginary. Spielrein's conceptualisation of the *Wunschwort* – the word of wish/desire – is fundamental to the question of how a child might begin to speak; the task of the infant is to separate the word or name from the referent. However, we contend that the words central to Spielrein's thesis – "papa" and "mama" – are alternating signifiers, and that a pair of opposing signifiers is integral in allowing the possibility for the child to take up his place as subject within language.

The fields of language

Spielrein's central question in this paper is how the child can accede to spoken language. Of interest to note is that from the very beginning of her paper, she introduces a theorisation of three contrasting fields of language. Spielrein clearly considers language in a broader sense than the aspect of verbal language alone, recognising that spoken language is just one part of language. She contends that musicality, rhythm and melody constitute the most primitive form of language, and commences her paper thus:

> When we adults speak of languages we think of verbal content and overlook the role played, even in written texts, by contributions from the field of rhythmic/melodic language, such as exclamation marks, question marks, and so on. These melodic means of expression become even more important in spoken language.
>
> (1922b, p. 289)

Spielrein distinguishes verbal or spoken language from the language of melody or rhythm. Her theorisation of language and its different forms therefore takes in other experiences that we would not necessarily consider as language. Nonetheless, we contend that Spielrein's notion of a melodic language pertains to respiration, the heartbeat and the rhythm of the body's sphincters as they open and close. Such rhythmic language of the body, heard also in the wail of the infant, is, perhaps, an aspect of language, or perhaps an aspect of some other realm of experience, in its most primitive or primal form. The primal experience, including the primal scene, is necessarily outside of our experience, outside our grasp. The melodic points of punctuation described by Spielrein – the exclamation marks, question marks and so on – are also a form of discontinuity in this rhythm in which something happens to the body: a puncture, interruption or cut. Likewise, the written – including punctuation marks in a text – can be read as anticipating Lacan's notion of the real.

Spielrein continues:

> here a third factor is added, imitation and gesture, means of expression which we could call visual language. . . . Accordingly we must differentiate from verbal language other types of language such as that of melody, visual (picture –) language, the language of touch, and so on.
>
> (1922b, p. 289)

In imitation and gesture, the picture, the image or in what is seen, there is an illusion of meaning. Spielrein's notion of visual language gives an illusory harmony or fullness. Her theory of visual or picture language can be considered as corresponding to the imaginary. Spielrein's remarkable theorisation of the different forms of language – spoken, musical and visual – resonate with Lacan's later conceptualisation of the symbolic, the real and the imaginary. Further, Spielrein's formulations of the three fields of language can be read as an attempt to tease apart three different aspects or dimensions of the one experience of the subject.

The emergence of spoken language

Spielrein centres her theorisation of the emergence of spoken language on two words – "papa" and "mama" – words that she proposes are popularly accepted in culture as the child's first words, and which, she posits, emerge largely from the mouth movements involved in suckling. Spielrein proposes that the child's verbal language emerges in three different modalities: "autistic", "magical" and "social". Although in her paper she refers to these modalities as "stages", they are not conveyed as distinct developmental phases. The first term, "autistic", was adopted from Bleuler's description of psychotic patients: "This detachment from reality with the relative and absolute predominance of the inner life, we call autism" (Bleuler, 1911, p. 131). This modality of language put forward by Spielrein is not associated with the diagnosis of autism, but rather comes from the features associated with schizophrenia.

In *Three Essays on the Theory of Sexuality*, Freud takes up the concept of auto-erotism, its defining feature a sexual drive that "is not directed towards other people, but obtains satisfaction from the subject's own body" (1905, p. 181). In her paper, Spielrein takes up this concept to theorise specifically about language, introducing "autistic language" as "a language which exists only for its own sake" (1922b, p. 290). The notion of autistic language also features at the beginning of Spielrein's earlier abstract:

> The presenter differentiates autistic languages, which do not foresee the transmission of a message or understanding on the part of other people, and "social languages". It is proposed that autistic languages are the primary languages.
>
> (1920)

The words "Papa" and "Mama" 119

Drawing upon the work of Bleuler and Freud, Spielrein elaborates a theory of her own centring on language, contrasting autistic languages – as primary languages, which exist purely for one's own enjoyment or self-satisfaction – to social or spoken languages. In creating this distinction between autistic languages and social languages, Spielrein's formulation provides a remarkable perspective. Taking auto-erotism as a starting point, she puts forward a theory of language founded on the enjoyment of one's own body. We are aware that Freud, in his "On Narcissism" paper (1914), makes an artificial distinction between auto-erotism and object-based libido. Lacan, in his revision of Freud's notions (1953–1954, lesson June 2, 1954), makes it clear that the phenomenon of auto-erotism does not exist without an object. We can also read Spielrein's theorisation of the libido as not unrelated to the object. Spielrein's conceptualisation of an autistic form of language, moreover, provides an early formulation of the place of jouissance in language.

Spielrein's notion of "magical" language is influenced by the ideas of Freud, as well as her own experiences in working with psychotic patients. In her paper, "The origin of the child's words Papa and Mama", Spielrein quotes Freud's *Totem and Taboo*, proposing that: "The person who believes in magic is like a child for whom 'objects as such are over-shadowed by the ideas representing them. . .'. We often meet this kind of magical belief in mental illness, in so-called 'schizophrenia'" (1922b, p. 296).

In making this proposition, Spielrein concurs with Freud's theory that: "Primitive men . . . are *uninhibited*: thought passes directly into action" (Freud, 1912–13, p. 161). We can consider Spielrein's allusion to primitive man also as a reference to the mythical, a primal experience. In the original German paper, she notes:

> The separating of the word (name) and the event is a secondary occurrence; originally it was a oneness. In magic it becomes once again a oneness in which the name takes the place of a person, of an occurrence, and the word for an action.
>
> (1922a, p. 358)

Spielrein's notion of "event" or "action" refers to attributes of the primal experience of suckling, an imagined oneness experienced in relation to the mother.

Spielrein, again in her German paper, goes on to write:

> In the first stage of development, when the child does not yet know a world separate from himself, and a world to be conquered, the word is singularly and alone determined by self-enjoyment. It calls up certain clusters of sensations that it ends up "signifying" [*bedeutet*].
>
> (1922a, pp. 358–359)

Again, in Spielrein's adoption of developmental terms, we perceive the influence of Piaget. Despite this, we consider Spielrein's theorisation to be structural rather

120   Debbie Plastow

than developmental, as her formulations of language describe an experience that occurs throughout life. The child's experience of suckling necessarily occurs in a world separate from himself, outside of itself. Spielrein elaborates this idea of the child making sounds related to the experience of suckling to support her thesis on the emergence of the word "mama". She contends that the sound "mö-mö", a sound closely associated with the act of suckling, originally *was* the action itself. Moreover, she proposes that: "By uttering a certain group of sounds the child could finally call up this specific cluster of sensations as often as it wished" (1922b, p. 301).

In Spielrein's formulation, there is initially a oneness in the "mö-mö" sounds uttered by the child and the actual experience of suckling. The sounds and event are not separated out by the infant, although the sounds uttered and the act of suckling are clearly not the same. We propose that it is the task of the child to separate out the signifier from the event. Separating of the word from the event is also a means of separation for the child from his primal oneness with the mother or the other.

The *Wunschwort* or wish word

Spielrein proposes that the child's "mö-mö", a sound associated with the pleasurable sensations experienced in suckling, arises as an expression of a wish. This wish of the child is central to Spielrein's earlier abstract, in which she specifically refers to the words "papa" and "mama":

> It is proposed that these words are the bearers of pleasure/enjoyment [*Lust*] that the child experiences whilst suckling and which would have the tremendous signification of satisfaction of desire in the fantasy, since desire here, turned upon an external object, cannot be satisfied at will.
>
> (1920)

According to Spielrein's theorisation, it is through the uttering of this certain group of sounds, the repetitive syllable "mö-mö", that something is signified. Thus, the child's words "mama" and "papa" (or the more rudimentary forms "mö-mö" and "pö-pö") are the bearers of enjoyment for the child. However, we contend that it is the child's experience of non-satisfaction that is vital here. It is precisely because something cannot be satisfied at will, that something is lacking or absent, the thing that cannot be obtained, that the child comes to experience such longing or a wish. Spielrein continues:

> As a consequence of the initial experiencing of pleasure whilst suckling through another living being, it is proposed that the child comes to perceive an external pleasure-giving object for which one longs and which can be obtained by calling out the word of desire [*Wunschwort*] derived from suckling.
>
> (1920)

The German word *Wunschwort* does not have a precise translation in English, but is closest in meaning to "word of desire/wish". Spielrein proposes that this word is called at moments when the child experiences non-satisfaction. In her description of the child calling out the word of desire, we discern an eroticisation experienced by the child in the act of uttering these sounds. However, we contend that the *Wunschwort* is not a form of naming or communication. What is important is not the idea that one word can name or represent a thing, but that there is another, contrasting cluster of sounds that signifies difference. In other words, the *Wunschwort* is essentially a signifying pair.

Papa and Mama

Much of Spielrein's discussion in the "Papa and Mama" paper centres on the word "mama", and it appears that she gives only lip service to the word "papa". Yet, from the beginning, including in the title of this paper, "papa" is in prime position. Why is this so? Spielrein proposes that the word "papa", which she notes, means "bread" in Russian nursery language, also has at its origins the question of nourishment and suckling. But, beyond this, she contends that the sound "pö-pö" contrasts with the sound "mö-mö", as each arises in a different phase of suckling. Spielrein writes: "The word 'mö-mö' reproduces suckling in its truest sense. 'Pö-pö', 'Bö-bö' etc correspond more with the time when the satisfied infant is playing with the breast, now letting go of it, now latching on to it again" (1922b, p. 303).

Spielrein's contention here is not simply that the child produces one sound, "mö-mö". Another, contrasting sound – "pö-pö" or "bö-bö" – is produced, the sound linked with the mouth movements of the satisfied infant when no longer suckling but playing with the breast. Spielrein proposes that these alternating sounds are produced at different moments, that the child says "mama" when sad or when longing for something, and "papa" when playing or content. She points out that the labial nasal sound "m", and the unvoiced labial occlusive "p", although articulated somewhat differently, are the easiest for the infant to produce, as "these particular sounds were produced in . . . the act of suckling" (1922b, p. 294).

We note that the "m" sound in "mama" is produced with uninterrupted airflow, which contrasts with the "p" sound in "papa", produced when the airflow is impeded or interrupted at the level of the lips. We contend that what is essential is that there are two fundamentally opposing signifiers – "mama" and "papa" – two different signifiers that function to mediate between the I, the child as subject, and the outside world. In this formulation, the contrasting signifiers mark difference; through this difference, a paternal function is instilled. The signifier "papa" functions to produce a cut, intervening in the eroticism experienced by the infant in relation to the imaginary object of desire.

In *Seminar X*, Lacan considers the opposing articulations of signifiers "papa" and "mama", stating:

> [I]t is clear that the lip, itself the incarnation, as one might say of a cut, that the lip in a singular way evokes what exists at a quite different level, at the

level of signifying articulation, at the level of the most fundamental phonemes, those most linked to the cut, the consonantal elements of the phoneme, the suspension of a cut.

(1962–1963, lesson May 15, 1963, p. 3)

In Lacan's formulation, the different signifiers, "mama" and "papa", are articulated by the lips, the lips which suckle from the mother's breast, imaginary object of desire. Here, the lip functions as an edge, the opposing signifiers "mama" and "papa" effecting the cut, the cut of weaning, or of birth, of the "no" of being excluded from the primal event, the primal scene, or of what is to become of the subject when "thrown into the outside world" (1962–1963, lesson May 15, 1963, p. 4).

Spielrein's theorisation of contrasting words "mama" and "papa", associated with either longing or satisfaction, strike a familiar chord in psychoanalysis. We recall the case of Freud's grandson, whose alternating words "fort" ("away" or "gone") and "da" ("there") accompanied the disappearance and reappearance of the cotton reel (1920). Spielrein also writes of her young daughter's use of the repetitive, opposing words "where" and "there", which were uttered "without worrying whether this corresponds to reality or not" (1922b, p. 300). We propose that these opposing signifiers, "mama"/"papa", "fort"/"da", or "where"/ "there", function to mark difference. Between one signifier and another, there is difference: each signifier is different to the next.

Spielrein's theorisations of primal words and their meanings are influenced by Freud's paper, "The antithetical meaning of primal words" (1910). In her paper, "Destruction as cause of becoming", she notes: "Freud showed that every dream image means its opposite at the same time, and Freud also shows that linguistics recognizes an 'opposite meaning of the primary words'" (1912, p. 116).

In this paper, Freud uses the German word "Gegensinn", which is literally "antisense" or "against sense", although in the Standard Edition, this has been translated as "antithetical meaning". Freud uses the work of philologist, Karl Abel, to explore ancient languages and to consider the structure of language in relation to the unconscious. Freud defines "antithetical meaning" as, historically, "words that denoted at once a thing and its opposite" (1910, p. 156). He commences the paper with the question of the dream, adds a footnote relating to "slips of the tongue that result in the opposite being said [of what was consciously intended]" (p. 161), and concludes with the comment that more research is needed! He notes: "[W]e psychiatrists cannot escape the suspicion that we should be better at understanding and translating the language of dreams if we knew more about the development of language" (p. 161).

Spielrein takes up this challenge of Freud's in theorising about the emergence of language in the child. In her congress abstract, she writes: "The presenter will especially consider the question of whether the child himself invents a language to which infantile 'word transformations' can be attributed" (1920). Lacan's later theorisations of speech and language are relevant here. Lacan contrasts the notion of language – something the subject is born into and subject to – and speech. In his seminar of February 24, 1954, he refers to Melanie Klein's patient, Little Dick, stating: "Language and speech are not the same thing – this child is, up to a certain point, a master of language, but he doesn't speak" (1953–1954, p. 84).

Thus, we can take up Spielrein's questioning of whether the child can invent a language, in a different way. The child, following Lacan's theorisations, cannot invent a language, as he is subject to language. He therefore has to invent a way to articulate something, in order to accede to speech.

Spielrein, in her paper, "The origin of the child's words Papa and Mama", notes:

> Only when reality is recognised alongside phantasy, when fellow human beings are perceived alongside oneself, and when words contain not an enforcing meaning but an optional one, does that emerge which we adults generally understand as language.
>
> (1922b, p. 301)

Spielrein's notion of language, "when words contain not an enforcing meaning but an optional one", makes reference to words and their multiple meanings, or, we might propose, the signifier which does not have a specified signified. Thus, Spielrein is delving into the question of something akin to the signifier, whose multiple signifieds are inherently "against sense".

In her abstract, Spielrein writes: "the first formations of social oral-language, it is proposed, are at the same time signs of mediation between I and the outside world" (1920). Thus, to take up his own position as subject in language, the child's task is to produce another, different signifier, an opposing signifier that might function to mark a lack, an absence, longing, or even something "against sense".

The cave of language

Lacan takes up the notion of contrasting signifiers, each different to the other, in *Seminar XVII*. In his lesson of January 6, 1972, Lacan speaks of, and to, the walls. He adapts Plato's cave and what can be seen inside it, the shadows cast upon its walls, to consider what can be heard emanating from the different parts of the cave. Thus, Lacan takes up his conceptualisation of the imaginary, of the shadows in the cave, and creates a theory of language based on the resonance of contrasting articulations of the mouth, lips, teeth and tongue. He states:

> [F]or a long time now man has been wailing like any small animal; well, he whines, to get the maternal milk. But in order to become aware that he is capable of doing something – that, of course, he has been able to hear for a long time, because in the babbling, the spluttering, all is produced – but in order to choose, he had to become aware that the $/k/$ resonates better from the depth of the cave, the last wall, and the $/b/$ and the $/p/$, well, it sprang forth better at the entrance, that's where he heard the resonance.
>
> (1971–1972, lesson January 1, 1972, pp. 95–97)

Lacan proposes that it was within the walls of the cave, in this void, that language was born. Plato's cavern becomes a mouth that articulates speech, with its associated sounds, sounds which, we can hear, resonate with Spielrein's theory of the child's use of opposing sounds and words as bearers of enjoyment. Such theorisation of the origins of language – whether originating in a cave, a primal event, or the primal scene of suckling – is based on a mythological proposition.

In Plato's "Republic" (1999), Socrates is convincing Glaucon about the qualities one must have to rule the state, including knowledge of science, geometry, philosophy and, above all, reason. He introduces the idea of a cave in which men are educated for this purpose. The men's legs and heads are restrained from childhood, preventing them turning their heads to look behind them, reflecting the human condition, with the real behind us impossible to grasp. In the cave, there are shadows reflected on the walls, and sounds from outside the cave that resonate within it. For the man in the cave, much less is learned from what is seen, from the illusion, the shadows on the walls, than from what is heard, from the voice, the words and their musicality.

In the cave, Plato's emphasis is on the perception of the world outside, through the play of shadow images on the wall of the cave. With Lacan, the cavern has now become a mouth, an organ for producing language, a form of the symbolic that mediates the apprehension of the real. The object that cannot immediately be grasped can at best be approached through the voice and its alternating articulations and signifiers.

Conclusion

One of the aspects of greatest interest to us in Spielrein's paper is her original and elaborate theory of language, underpinned by the subject's separating out of the name from the referent. Spielrein not only proposes a theory for the emergence of verbal language, her conceptualisation of language and interrogation of its elusive origins, with particular emphasis on the child's first words, but also elucidates the structure of language through the opposition of signifiers. Moreover, her notion of three different fields of language can be read as anticipating Lacan's later formulations of the three registers – the real, the symbolic and the imaginary. Through such theorisations, Spielrein is able to contribute to our discussion on how, through an absence or longing, and the *Wunschwort* or pair of contrasting signifiers, a child might take up his own position within language.

References

Bleuler, E. (1911) Dementia Praecox oder Gruppe der Schizophrenien. In: *Handbuch der Psychiatrie*. Edited by G. Aschaffenburg. Leipzig: Deuticke. Quoted in: Parnas, J., Bovet, P., & Zahavi, D. (2002). Schizophrenic Autism: Clinical Phenomenology and Pathogenic Implications. *World Psychiatry, Oct. 2002*, 1(3): 131–136, p. 131. www.ncbi.nlm.nih.gov/pmc/articles/PMC1489853/. Last accessed on 16/5/17.

Freud, S. (1905) *Three Essays on the Theory of Sexuality*. Standard Ed., 7. London: Hogarth.

Freud, S. (1910) *The Antithetical Meaning of Primal Words*. Standard Ed., XI. London: Hogarth.

Freud, S. (1912–1913) *Totem and Taboo*. Standard Ed., 13. London: Hogarth.

Freud, S. (1914) *On narcissism: An Introduction*. Standard Ed., 14. London: Hogarth.

Freud, S. (1920) *Beyond the Pleasure Principle*. Standard Ed., 18. London: Hogarth.

Lacan, J. (1962–1963) *The Seminar of Jacques Lacan: Anxiety. 1962–1963. Book X*. Translated by C. Gallagher. (Non-commercial edition).

Lacan, J. (1971–1972) *Seminar 1971–1972: Le Savoir du Psychanalyste/The Knowledge of the Psychoanalyst: Séminaire 1971–1972* (bilingual edition). Translated by M. Plastow. Paris: l'Association Lacanienne Internationale, 2013. (Non-commercial edition).

Lacan, J. (1953–1954) *The seminar of Jacques Lacan: Book I: Freuds Papers on Technique 1953–1954*. Edited by J.A. Miller. Translated by J. Forrester. New York: W.W. Norton & Company, 1988.

Plato. (1999) Republic. Book VII. In: *Plato: The Collected Dialogues including the Letters*. Bollingen Series LXXI. Edited by H. Cairns & E. Hamilton. Translated by P. Shorey. Seventeenth Printing. Princeton, NJ: Princeton University Press.

Spielrein, S. (1912) Destruction as cause of becoming. Translated by S. Witt. *Psychoanalysis and Contemporary Thought*, 18: 85–118.

Spielrein, S. (1920) *On the Question of the Emergence and Development of Spoken Language*. www.psyalpha.net/chronik/ipv-internationale-psychoanalytische-vereinigung/internationale-psychoanalytische-kongresse-seit-1908/1920-haag-vi-internationaler-psychoanalytischer-kongress. Last accessed on 27/2/18.

Spielrein, S. (1922a) Die Entstehung der kindlichen Worte Papa und Mama: Einige Betrachtunger über verschiedene Stadien in der Sprachentwicklung. *Imago*, 8(3): 345–367.

Spielrein, S. (1922b) Part II: The Origins of the Child's Words Papa and Mama: Some Observations on the Different Stages in Language Development. In: *Sabina Spielrein: Forgotten Pioneer of Psychoanalysis*. Edited by C. Covington & B. Wharton. Translated by B. Wharton. Hove: Routledge, 2003.

Part V

Intersections
Painting, writing and psychoanalysis

Chapter 15

Between destruction and becoming

Sabina Spielrein[1]

Michael Gerard Plastow

> *Wo Es war, soll Ich werden. Es ist Kulturarbeit etwa wie die Trockenlegung der Zuydersee.*
>
> Freud[2]

> *τῷ οὖν τόξῳ ὄνομα βίος, ἔργον δὲ θάνατος*
> *The bow's name is life (βίος), but its job is death.*
>
> Heraclitus[3]

I want to speak of Sabina, I want to write of Spielrein.
But not for the titillation of imagining a sexual relation.
And not to join the fashion of the fascination for her analyst.
No! I'm not Jung at heart. But I want to write
in my own hand, of my interest today
that lies in how she concludes her analysis.
There was analysis. Thanks to Jung, and Bleuler.
It was luck that took her to the Burgölzli,
rather than to any other Zürich asylum of the time.
But how does she conclude? How does she finish,
despite Jung, with this impossible transference-love?
How do any of us leave our analysis? How do we conclude
what is otherwise interminable?
How can we transform our pain into something we can use?
I'm interested in how she leaves and the part that writing plays.

It's precisely because she wrote that we know anything at all.
When Sabina left Geneva to return to Russia in May 1923
she left a heavy brown suitcase
in the hands of Claparède, founder of the Rousseau Institute.
In it were her diaries, personal and official papers,
letters to her parents and brothers, friends and colleagues,
and notably her correspondence with Freud and Jung.

DOI: 10.4324/9781003212720-20

130   Michael Gerard Plastow

It was found in 1977 in the basement of the Wilson Palace,
Sabina continued to write and publish papers, from 1911
until it was no longer possible to write psychoanalysis in Russia.
So many writings, precious few translated into English.

She writes to Freud in May 1909 requesting an "audience".
She asks to speak with him, for him to listen to her.
She has not met him but writes, "You . . . have made me feel awkward".[4]
Freud replies honestly, "You have put me in a predicament",[5]
but it's not the predicament he says.
He has heard of the case in bits and pieces,
from Jung's unflattering account.
But not of the love affair that followed in its wake,
and not all the details. And not clarified
that it's all the one analysand, the one Jung wrote,
"was obsessed by a poem by Lermontov",[6]
or the case he presented in Amsterdam,
"The Freudian Theory of Hysteria".[7]
The one who recognized that "her greatest wish,
he said, was to have a child by me".
The Siegfried of whom they had spoken.
Except it was not just Sabina's desire, and the poem was by Pushkin.
"Naturally" Jung wrote to Freud, I will have to let the bird fly free.[8]

And Jung was still the crown prince of psychoanalysis,
the future leader, the Christian who would take it,
beyond its Jewish ghetto. "The Swiss will save us",
said Freud, "Me and all of you".[9]
Freud forwards her letter to Jung,
asking for an explanation, a telegram for clarification.
He buys himself some time; asks her,
"to let me know in *writing* what it is all about".[10] And write she does.
But when Freud discerns the love affair in question,
He elaborates upon his "predicament", and urges her
to examine herself, to overcome the feelings
that have outlived the relationship, and whether it would be best,
if they were not better suppressed,
"an eradication without external intervention:
the involvement of third persons".[11]
But it is not so easy for the bird to fly free,
while she is still in the cage.

She continues to write.
In one of these early letters she replies to Freud
that she is not seeking, regarding Jung, any intervention,

Between destruction and becoming   131

but rather to be heard, to make something understood.
"Suppressing an emotion will not work for me,
for if I do it with Dr. Jung,
I will never be able to love anyone else. . .
I would like to part from Dr Jung completely, and go my own way".[12]
She wants to fly. It's for this reason she writes to Freud,

"Four and a half years ago Dr Jung was my doctor,
then he became my friend, and finally my 'poet',
i.e., my beloved. Eventually he came to me and things went
as they usually go with 'poetry'. He preached polygamy;
his wife was supposed to have no objections, etc., etc".[13]
"My love for him transcended our affinity,
until he could stand it no longer and wanted 'poetry'"[14]
So much poetry, but only metaphorically speaking.

Sabina to Freud:
"At that time Prof. Freud appeared to me
as an angel of deliverance. I wrote a poem to you".[15]
With Jung she enacts "poetry", with Freud she writes it.
What that poem is we'll never know.
But as an analyst and a poet she plays with the signifier:
"I go to bed with *Rauber's* Anatomy
and first quickly write a letter to Dr Jung;
I do not want anything that might *rob* me of him
as my deeply respected friend, doctor, beloved;
I want to be his absolutely unselfish friend, etc.
I place the letter in *Rauber's* book and tell myself indignantly,
'I don't want to be the *robber*!'
'No', my other component replies,
'You won't be the *robber*, he will!'"[16]

Wagner's initial name for the first part of his ring cycle
Was *Der Raub des Rheingoldes*,
the robbery of the thing, of the pure [*rein*] gold
In another of Sabina's letters to Freud we read these lines:
"Oh, once there was a dream so wondrous strange
One fine, cool night the Rhine sang long ago. . .
It sang of a poet, black eyes, golden hair".[17]
Black eyes, the part of the Jewess – the Egyptian
as Jung called her – for her poet Siegfried.

Sabina continues to write to Freud:
"I liked *Das Rheingold* best . . . Dr Jung's eyes fill with tears. . .
He, too, always liked *Rheingold* best".[18]

132   Michael Gerard Plastow

The Rhine gold that from Wagner's libretto,
"the *robber* . . . stole [*raubte*] in revenge
[and] deems it now the holiest good, greater than woman's grace".[19]
Perhaps she read in Hölderlin's hymn to the Rhine,
whose "voice . . . was of the noblest of rivers",
that "An enigma is of pure origin (*Reinentsprungenes*) . . .
Even song may hardly unveil it"[20]

Spielrein to Freud:
"After all, didn't Dr Jung sigh,
'I love you for the magnificence of your passion?'
Yes, yes, I'll tell you why! After all,
my friend has told you a number of things in a distorted light!
It was Wagner who planted the demon in my soul
with such terrifying clarity. I shall omit the metaphors,
since you might laugh at the extravagance of my emotion.
The whole world became a melody for me:
the earth sang, the lake sang, the trees sang,
and every twig on every tree. I feel as if . . ."[21]
She omits the metaphors, it becomes realized
when it is written, when it becomes poetry:
between *Destruction* and *Becoming*.

Regarding Jung:
"He told me he was going to the theatre and once more
something made me ask what play was being performed.
He laughed: 'A silly story: *The Rape of the Sabine Women*'
(My name is Sabina). Naturally I was taken aback, and he continued,
'The director did not realize there was a people by that name,
and in order to make the play sound more appealing,
he called it *The Rape of the Sabinettes.*'" [*Der Raub der Sabincherinen*][22]
Jung didn't realize there was a woman by that name.

Spielrein lets herself be played by her name:
"Today I had to have my card checked by Dr Lutz.
I was one the last one of a small group.
He reads off my name, which is written clearly enough as Spielrein,
and he asks me twice, 'Are you called Spielerein [play clean], or Spielerei
[play around]'.
With the straightest face in the world I replied, 'Spielerein' . . .
my attention was blurred by the colossal effort I had to make
to keep from bursting out laughing".[23]

What is the place of this writing, of her *Autopsychography*,
As Fernando Pessoa called the product of the poet,

in a little poem by that name.
A writing of one's psyche, of one's soul?
Let us read the first two stanzas:

The poet is a feigner.	O poeta é um fingidor.
So completely does he feign	Finge tão completamente
that the pain he truly feels	Que chega a fingir que é dor
he even feigns as pain.	A dor que deveras sente.
And those who read what he writes	E os que lêem o que escreve
Feel in the pain they've read	Na dor lida sentem bem,
Not the two pains that were his	Não as duas que ele teve,
But one that's not theirs instead.	Mas só a que éles não têm.

If it's not theirs, the reader is also a feigner then,
necessarily, so that something is passed on,
some *thing* that belongs neither to the poet nor to him.
Translating poetry is of course impossible.
How can one translate when the signifiers are not the same?
Even this word 'feigner', in Portuguese *fingidor*,
Already contains the *dor*, the suffering or pain.
But the many translations,[24] whether we consider them
bad or good, each one creates something new,
they literally make the poet, not just a feigner,
but a dissembler, a pretender, and a concealer,
a fancier, an imaginer, and a faker,
a liar, a forger and also an inventor:
someone who makes a semblance.

Sabina writes, she feigns her pain.
Her first paper, her psychiatry thesis,
is published in the *Jahrbuch* of 1911,
"About the psychological content of a case of schizophrenia",[25]
alongside Freud's Schreber[26] and Jung's "Metamorphoses of
the libido"[27]
Spielrein's paper is an account of a psychotic woman,
one who is captivated by her love for Dr Jung.
"She authorizes herself to hear in the analysis
a love story that has turned out badly".[28]
We are struck, when her patient says:
"Sistine art can give rise to sexual art:
Through a beautiful painting one can become poetry [*Poesie werden*],
perhaps forget one's duty".[29] For Spielrein,
"The phrase, 'to forget one's duty',
from the mouth of a married woman

allows to be seen undisguised, the erotic element in 'poetry'",
and she proposes "that 'poetry' = 'in love'".[30]

Whilst Sabina is working the delusions of her patient,
She is also writing the fiction of her transference.
In 1912 she publishes another paper,
"Contributions to the knowledge of the child's soul",
whose first part is literally an account of her own analysis,
the story of a young girl who is fascinated
to see olives, and other plants and animals grow.
And by the metamorphosis of a stick of zinc
dipped in a solution of lead salts
that "became a 'real' tree:
So one can really create artificial 'life' . . .", she writes,
"There must be supernatural forces in order to realize
this marvellous metamorphosis that I witnessed".[31]

In 1911 she goes to Vienna where she is admitted
to the Vienna Psychoanalytic Society on the strength of her thesis,
only the second woman to be recognized as analyst there.
She does a presentation: "On Transformation",[32]
that is used to criticize Jung, including by Freud himself.
It is based on the third part of her new paper:
"Destruction as cause of becoming"[33] in which she posits,
that "death is necessary for the advent of life".[34]
In it she proposes a death drive,
separate to the self-preservation drive,
a notion that Freud opposes, at least until 1920.
Wagner's *Flying Dutchman*, she writes
"yearns in vain, for an object".[35] He longs for love,
a love that will lead to his long-sought death.
A death, a separation: a love that robs him of his life,
a rapture that is replaced by a rupture.

So how then, can we conclude?
When Sabina married, Freud congratulated her
but wrote there still remained,
the other half of her cure:
"Analysis terminable and interminable".
Her situation always remained precarious,
she never got back the *Geld*, the *Spielreingold*,
that her father had possessed, that Jung,
who married well, had got hold of
and of which she was robbed.

This, her other half, the other component,
of her cure: a remainder that is incurable.

On Fernando Pessoa's tomb we can read the words
of his semi-heteronym, Álvaro de Campos:

No, I want nothing.	*Não: não quero nada.*
I already said I want nothing.	*Já disse que não quero nada.*
Don't come to me with conclusions!	*Não me venham com conclusões!*
The only conclusion is to die.	*A única conclusão é morrer.*

But the nothing, the enigma of pure origin,
that even poetry may hardly unveil,
takes a different form for each one.
Sabina never came back to Switzerland,
the origin of the Rhine,
to get her heavy brown suitcase,
the Nazis made sure of that.
She had a chance to escape,
but remained behind with her daughters,
in Rostov on the Don.

To become an analyst, to conclude her analysis,
she wrote a thesis and papers, letters and poetry,
so moved away from Jung, directing her work elsewhere.
It's quite something to realize your analyst is a feigner.
Nothing personal! But maybe something *Pessoal*,
since if you're lucky, he or she is also a forger,
an inventor, even a poet or poetry.
But for this realization there's a work to be done,
a work of writing, writing a type of poetry,
attaining, through the writing, a *poiesis*.
We continue to write, we continue to re-cite,
between destruction and becoming.

Notes

1 First published as "Entre destruction et *werden*: Sabina Spielrein", in: *Essaim*, n° 37, Toulouse, Erès, 2016.
2 S. Freud, Vorlesung die Zerlegung der psychischen Persönlichkeit, *Gesammelte Werke*, XV, 1933, 85.
3 M. T. Robinson, *Heraclitus: Fragments. A Text and Translation with a Commentary by T. M. Robinson*, University of Toronto Press, Toronto, 1987, p. 35.
4 A. Carotenuto (ed.), *A Secret Symmetry. Sabina Spielrein between Jung and Freud*, Pantheon, New York, 1982, p. 91.

5 Ibid., p. 113.
6 W. McGuire (ed.), *The Freud/Jung Letters*, translated by R. Manheim & R. F. C. Hull, Princeton University, Princeton, 1974 (Fourth printing, with corrections and additions (in the notes)), 1994, p. 72.
7 C. Jung, The Freudian Theory of Hysteria, in *Freud and Psychoanalysis: Volume 4 of the Collected Works of C.G. Jung*, Bollingen, New York, 1913, 1961, pp. 3–24.
8 M. Guibal & J. Nobécourt (eds.), *Sabina Spielrein: Entre Freud et Jung*, Aubier Montaigne, Paris, 2004, p. 104.
9 Cited in: S. Richebächer, *Sabina Spielrein: de Jung a Freud*, translated by Daniel Martineschen, Civilização Brasileira, Rio de Janeiro, 2002, p. 179.
10 A. Carotenuto, *A Secret Symmetry*. Op. cit., p. 113. (My italics).
11 Ibid., p. 114.
12 Ibid., p. 92.
13 Ibid., p. 93.
14 Ibid., p. 96.
15 Ibid., p. 97.
16 Ibid., pp. 108–109. (My italics and substitution of "rob" [*rauben* in the original] for "deprive").
17 Ibid., 108.
18 Ibid., 100.
19 R. Wagner, *Das Rheingold*, translated by Frederick Jameson, www.murashev.com/opera/Das_Rheingold_libretto_English Last accessed on 30/04/17.
20 F. Hölderlin, The Rhine, in *Selected Poems and Fragments*, translated by Michael Hamburger, Penguin, London, 1998, pp. 188–189.
21 A. Carotenuto, *A Secret Symmetry*. Op. cit., pp. 106–107.
22 Ibid., p. 109.
23 A. Carotenuto (ed.), *Tagebuch Einer Heimlichen Symmetrie: Sabina Spielrein, zwischen Jung und Freud*, Kore, Freiburg, 1986, p. 112. & A. Carotenuto, *A Secret Symmetry*. Op. cit., pp. 111–112.
24 www.disquiet.com/thirteen.html
25 S. Spielrein, Über den psychologischen Inhalt eines Falles von Schizophrenie (Dementia praecox), *Jahrbuch für psychoanalytische und psychopathologische Forschungen*, III(1) (1911), Hälfte: 329–400.
26 S. Freud, Psychoanalytische Bemerkungen über einen autobiographisch beschriebenen Fall von Paranoia (Dementia paranoides), *Jahrbuch für psychoanalytische und psychopathologische Forschungen*, III(1) (1911), Hälfte: 9–68.
27 C. Jung, Wandlungen und Symbole der Libido, *Jahrbuch für psychoanalytische und psychopathologische Forschungen*, III(1) (1911), Hälfte: 120–227.
28 M. Guibal & J. Nobécourt (eds.), *Sabina Spielrein*. Op. cit., p. 185.
29 S. Spielrein, Über den psychologischen Inhalt eines Falles von Schizophrenie (Dementia praecox), in *Sämtliche Schriften*, Psychosozial-Verlag, Gießen, 2002, p. 15.
30 Ibid., p. 16.
31 S. Spielrein, Beiträge zur Kenntnis der kindlichen Seele, in *Sämtliche Schriften*, Psychosozial-Verlag, Gießen, 2002, p. 150.
32 H. Nunberg & E. Federn (eds.), *Minutes of the Vienna Psychoanalytic Society (Volume III): 1910–1911*, International Universities Press, New York, 1974, pp. 329–335.
33 S. Spielrein, Destruction as Cause of Becoming, *Psychoanalysis and Contemporary Thought,* 18 (1995): 85–118.
34 S. Spielrein, Destruction as the Cause of Coming into Being, *Journal of Analytical Psychology,* 39 (1994): 155–186, 166.
35 Ibid., p. 183.

Chapter 16

To put one's name to what is not a thought . . .

Megan Williams

How to put one's name to what is not a thought?

Where am I in the utterance?

Can that which is thinking itself be thought?

That one say remains hidden behind what is said.

What can be transferred from zero to one?

I ask you to refuse what I offer you (what I offer you in order that you will return it to me) because that's not it.

These are questions, propositions and demands which circulate in or around Lacan's 1971–1972 seminar, . . . *ou Pire*. One can hear in them a plea for being; being identified: who am I?; what is thinking in me?; am I thought?; where do my thoughts come from?; who is speaking? The history of psychoanalysis refers these to a fraught and fragmented couple, albeit fraught only in that it is supposed, by psychoanalysis since Freud, to *be* a couple: Ego and Id, narcissism and object-love, subject and object, signifier and jouissance. Freud (at least in some of his writings) had the idea that the couple is fraught in neurosis but that an analysis can bring its partners to live in harmony. Lacan indicated with his formula of the fantasm, and more explicitly in. . . *ou Pire*, that they do not unite except by thought or fantasy.[1]

Psychoanalysis, in other words, has been haunted by the notion of a duality ever since Freud observed that neurosis is a matter of unresolved conflict which psychoanalysis aims to resolve.

Once upon a time, in one of my repeated panics at one of those repeated moments when the possibility of giving a paper somewhere was faced with becoming a necessity through my furnishing a title and an abstract and inscribing my name on the program, I recall saying in my analysis "I can't. I don't have a thought". The interpretation that emerged was "how to put one's name to what is not yet a thought".

To my mind, this interpretation highlights a distinction drawn by Deleuze, in his book, *Difference and Repetition*.[2] Lacan comments in. . . *ou Pire*, that "if what thinks is not thinkable, and then there is no psychoanalysis", and also that interpretation requires that something have been "thought *qua* real thought".[3] In these and other comments, I think there are traces of his seminar's influence by

DOI: 10.4324/9781003212720-21

Deleuze's book, which had been published three or four years previously, particularly in relation to repetition and what an analysis produces. I will endeavour below to discuss this.

Deleuze distinguishes passive, sensual, unconscious contemplation from the active, representational, conceptual thinking that might be involved in writing, or giving a paper. He considers the unconscious as consisting of three different syntheses of time. The first two comprise a split or caesura in subjectivity and the third in some sense transcends that split but without resolving it dialectically.

The **first synthesis** is made by passive contemplation, which contracts experiences into habits. The narcissistic self is no more than the effect of this synthetic pleasure; not an identified being but an affected one; the instance that Freud called the Id; jouissance rather than the signifying order. The passive synthesis of habit founds time as such, by fusing repeating instants into the living present, to which then belong the past (of preceding instants) and the future (of anticipated instants).[4] It does not remember so much as retain the past. One effect of this is a transcendental synthesis that contracts the past as a whole into an *a priori*, already-there that was – the pure past, which grounds time and co-exists with each new present, yet itself neither passes nor comes forth.

I would equate this passive synthesis with the time of Lacan's lalangue, that erotic tide of speech washing through the living being and leaving the detritus of habit that Freud called the drives – the time of the S1 as that gathering or contracting of an affected self around the excitation produced by a sound-image, as if around an object – one which is thus already missing.

To this synthesis belongs the involuntary form of memory called reminiscence, and Eros as the relation to an object which is forever virtual – hallucinated, in Freud's terms. "Eros tears virtual objects out of the pure past and gives them to us so that they can be lived".[5] As a shred of the pure past, the object of reminiscence is partial, missing and lacking identity; not an actual, former love but an object which always and never was. This is thus the time of transference, not as an undoing of forgetting, but as presence-through-reminiscence; an intensification or penetration of time such that the analyst is the presence of that "was"; such that the Thing which never comes forth in representation, nevertheless speaks. What can be transferred from the zero of inexistence to the one of presence?[6]

The caesura or split in subjectivity concerns this passage from passive and involuntary contemplation of presence to the active and voluntary re-presentation of former presents, which comprises Deleuze's **second synthesis of time** – from involuntary retention to active remembering; from sensuality to reflection and understanding. It is the time of the Ego, which tries to conceptually master the passively experienced, fatal affection of the contemplative self.[7] If we take Lacan's S1 as symbol of this affection, we can relate this active synthesis to the Discourse of the Master linking the S1 with S2's to produce a signifying chain. Lacan in. . . *ou Pire* refers to this keeping-on-representing as a *queue de pensées*, which can be translated as "train (*queue*) of thought", "nothing but (*que de*) thought" or even as a cock or phallus of thought, as distinct from his other term, *really* thought, which I take as referring to the first synthesis.[8]

David Pereira made the point in his seminar of 2015 that the first synthesis is the time of Lacan's "there is no sexual relation", in that the fusing of contrasting experiences makes no place for an Other. The second synthesis, where I locate Lacan's *queue de pensées*, proposes an Other, but it is an Other of fantasy: the *queue de pensées* is, he says, that by which "you only enjoy the Other mentally", by fantasy, so that the jouissance produced is not sexual. The phallus of thought represents a sexual Other where it is lacking. In Deleuze's terms, fantasy incorporates the virtual object into real objects, thus erotising them with a fragment of the pure past (the past such that it was never lived in reality). In this process, memory and recognition function in the field not of presence but of representation. They differentiate the derived copy from a supposedly original model, thus mistaking the pure past for a past present; the virtual for a true first love of which all other loves are copies. We can recognise in this account the Oedipal view of transference as the re-presenting of a former present object, rather than as the *making present* of that which has no representation and is therefore always masked and displaced. In taking the latter view of transference, Lacan characterises the analysand as saying "I ask you to refuse what I offer you because that's not it",[9] while Deleuze has the active subject asking, "Please, give me . . . another mask", and adds, "The pseudos becomes the pathos of the true".[10] We could therefore say that in the passage from passive contemplation to active reflection, in which something exceeds the signifier's capacity to represent, the virtual or mythical first object is constituted as always already lost: the object *a* falls out.

"Thinking" goes on all the time – both the passive and the active. "*A* thought" is something cut from that stream, usually by a saying or a writing. Saying is key for Lacan because, as opposed to the utterance (the said) that one carefully prepares or edits after writing, in saying one says more or other than one means to say – which is what makes speaking in analysis so daunting: that which has fallen out of representation may present itself without warning. Where a stream of thoughts can go on producing the illusion of identity between Ego and thought, saying gapes open, being more than one can grasp, more than one knows that one *really* thinks. Saying produces the caesura or division of the subject, whereas the utterance produces the subject as what I will call "a-thought", in the sense of *a-studié* or *a-sujetti* (a-studied, a-subjected), to evoke Lacan's neologisms similarly attaching the object *a* to a past participle.[11]

If "I think" and "I am" – thinking and saying, thinking and a thought – are not marriageable, it's because of time: they are split apart by time and only God – another name for the Other who is barred – could put them together again, and then only by expelling time. This is how (put very briefly) Deleuze paraphrases the Kantian critique of Descartes' cogito.[12] The subject of the signifier cannot escape being a-thought, partial, by being coupled. Its other half is neither a representation nor a sexual Other, but something which exceeds thought much closer to home, to paraphrase Lacan's words from another seminar: it is the unwanted, *unheimlich* guest already inside the house, though without a designated room.[13] It belongs to a different synthesis of time. Furthermore, while I have loosely called it the subject's other half, it is so only in that it is a residue of the subject's, and not in the sense that it can be returned to complete him. It is the forever virtual which has nevertheless a logical consistency: it must be posed. Lacan phrases the fundamental question of the analysand as: "where am I in the utterance?", and he observes in response that the object *a* is to be found at the place of "speaking as forgotten" – that is, at the same place as the being which escapes the subject and which the analyst occupies in transference.[14]

Would the aim of an analysis then be, not to derive an identifiable, representable being from the jouissance that exceeds thought, nor to eliminate it, but, as Deleuze suggests, to penetrate it in some other mode than that of thought – not to represent it but to allow its presence to in-habit one without mediation? This would then define transference in terms of Deleuze's definition of reminiscence: as a passive, involuntary and sensual in-habiting by the presence of that erotic shred of the pure past in which we locate the lost being, lost object.

The go-between

"The past is a foreign country: they do things differently there". This is the sentence which begins L. P. Hartley's 1954 novel, *The Go-Between*.[15] The story takes the form of a reminiscence, something like an analysis, by a man late in life, and concerns an episode of his early teens which until now, when he unearths from his attic a forgotten and locked diary, has been refused, repressed, ejected from active remembering. I say it is akin to an analysis because it is a passive and involuntary reminiscence, a making-present, of which the protagonist, Leo, says:

> [T]he past kept pricking at me and I knew that all the events of those nineteen days in July were astir within me . . . the more complete, the more unforgotten, for being carefully embalmed.[16]
>
> The cerements, the coffins, the vaults, all that had confined them was bursting open, and I should have to face it, I *was* facing it. . . . Excitement, like hysteria, bubbled up in me from a hundred unsealed springs.[17]

I say analysis also because the reminiscence meets Sloterdijk's definition of transference – in the text commented on by David Pereira in his 2016 seminar – as "the formal source of the creative processes that inspire the exodus of humans into the open".[18] I will argue that Leo's exodus into the open at the end is synonymous with his assumption of the S1, *Go Between*, not as an identity but as a living act which opens to the future of a time no longer circling back to the past. I will also argue that this corresponds to the production of what Lacan calls *unien*, which could be translated as "unian" or "oneian".[19]

The reminiscence which revisits Leo emerges from the pages of a special diary whose year is 1900 – "the first year of the century, winged with hope" – and is decorated with the signs of the Zodiac: each one, to the particular habit of this contemplative mind, suggesting "a plenitude of life and power"; glorious, invested with magic and a "tingling sense of coming fruition".[20] They are translated into Egoic representations in the following fashion:

> The Ram, the Bull and the Lion epitomised imperious manhood [while] the Virgin, the one distinctively female figure in the galaxy, . . . was, to me, the key to the whole pattern, the climax, the coping-stone, the goddess. . . .

For a man:

> There were only two candidates, the Archer and the Water-Carrier.

Yet Leo identifies with neither, choosing to remain:

> A Zodiacal sign without portfolio, [thus having] the Virgin to myself.[21]

It is precisely this refusal to take up a named position of his own that makes Leo susceptible to becoming a go-between.

The previously forgotten events took place during his visit over several weeks that summer to a schoolmate's wealthy family, the Maudsleys, at Brandham Hall. The Hall is the seat of the Viscount Hugh Trimingham, who is present during Leo's visit, and is betrothed to the schoolmate's sister, Marian Maudsley. For Leo, that shred of pure past which is present in the Virgin of his Zodiac re-presents in Marian, with whom he is fascinated. Only a Viscount – even scarred as Hugh is from the Boer war – could possibly be a fit companion to her in Leo's eyes, yet there is also Ted, a farmer and thus from a lower social class, but whose strong and masculine presence imposes itself as an Ego ideal. Ted represents the Water-Carrier, while in the wings waits the Archer, the Father, the God figure to whom the Woman belongs, the Viscount Hugh.

Leo is quickly drawn into the role denoted by the title of the book, but which is never named as such until he himself does so in the epilogue. He carries benign messages from Hugh to his Lady love, which Marian receives with resignation or irritation, and intensely secret and urgent messages between Marian and Ted. Whilst at first he enjoys his importance in bearing them, imagining that he is crucial to the mystical business of higher beings, he is shattered with disappointment when one day he catches sight of the first line of a message from Marian and realises that the whole affair is so base as to be about nothing but . . . spooning!

Spooning becomes the name of that which defies translation, remaining mystically beyond comprehension. Yet its simultaneous, dangerous presence is signalled by Leo's fascination with a deadly nightshade plant on the grounds, growing uncannily *inside* an abandoned outhouse:

> It looked the picture of evil . . . so glossy and strong and juicy-looking . . . I knew that every part of it was poisonous, I knew too that it was beautiful . . . I stood on the threshold [with it] reaching out towards me . . . I felt that . . . if I didn't eat it, it would eat me.[22]

Leo's wish to re-appoint his Gods from his disappointment with them leads him to demand of Ted that, in return for being "Postman", as Ted calls him, Ted tell him exactly what spooning involves. Ted promises to but later reneges, saying that it's a job for Leo's father (who is dead) and that he "doesn't feel like it"; a phrase repeated later in an apologetic letter that he writes to Leo. Leo, fallen from the heights of his Zodiacal fantasy but still wanting to believe that he is central to the outcome of these three lives, takes on himself the responsibility of ending the relation between Marian and Ted, in order that the former marry the Viscount, by slightly displacing the time of the next meeting when he relays Ted's ultimate message to Marian.

There follows the primal scene to which all of the reminiscence has been leading, the repressed heart not only of the recounting but of Leo's entire adult life, the realisation of the caesura between a habit and its missing representation, the traumatic encounter with an object whose virtuality is never diminished. Marian, having gone to keep her appointment with Ted at the incorrect time given by Leo, is thus missing from Leo's birthday tea, even though she was to have been the star attraction by riding in the new bicycle she was to give him as a present (which Leo knows secretly from his schoolmate). Mrs Maudsley, determined that Marian will marry Hugh and suspecting something afoot and Leo's involvement in it, grips him and insists that he take her to Marian. She drags him to the site of the luxuriant and deadly nightshade, where he encounters the sight whose image masks the real which the complex of social arrangements has been circling:

> [I]t was then that we saw them, the Virgin and the Water-Carrier, two bodies moving like one. I think I was more mystified than horrified; it was Mrs Maudsley's repeated screams that frightened me, and a shadow on the wall that opened and closed like an umbrella.[23]

And a postscript to the scene, from the time afterwards when Leo is in a state of mental breakdown:

> I remember very little more, but somehow it got through to me, while I was still at Brandham Hall, that Ted Burgess had gone home and shot himself.

For Deleuze, the **third synthesis** of time is "determined in the image of a unique event" which throws time out of joint by constituting its totality, both constituting

To put one's name to what is not a thought . . . 143

and drawing together *before*, *now* and *after* such that the event repeats itself as contemporaneous with every present; as always past and yet also still to come.[24] The image of the event assumes the status of a symbol to which three moments correspond: a "before" in which the event is apprehended by the subject as "too big for me"; a metamorphosis in which the subject becomes adequate to the event; and an "after" in which the subject is overtaken and put aside by the product of his act.

In this way, the key scene of the novel, the presence of spooning, is already there at the start, as the event which is too big for Leo to face and thus repressed. Even though it is already past, it is yet to come and every moment of the reminiscent recounting takes its significance from this event which is always returning, from either the past or the future, repeating itself. Leo spends most of his reminiscence, as he has spent most of his life, in the "before" of the event which took place in his 13th year and yet is still in his future, too big for him. It is an event of mythic rather than historical time, the time of Freud's primal horde father to whom thinking and being are one; or of God the Father who can expel time. It is to his Ego ideal, the Water Carrier, that Leo accords the mystical power to face it, and his grief for Ted is consequently mixed with both guilt and wistfulness, as for a challenge not taken up, a missed encounter.

When Ted fails the promise made by the Ego ideal; when the mystical link between Marian and Ted is revealed as the repellant spooning; when Ted "doesn't feel like" explaining spooning; when Leo envisions Marian's gift of a bicycle as nothing more than a bribe to the Postman; and finally when he is confronted with the shocking distance there is between postcard representations of spooning and the intensity that invades his passive being in the primal scene – when these things happen, there is the crisis which, for Deleuze, opens the third synthesis of time. The crisis comprises a reflux of libido onto the Ego; a return to the narcissism of thinking; a defusion of Eros and Thanatos; a de-erotisation. Leo has a breakdown, and when, after some weeks, he returns to school, he refuses to hear or remember anything about the event. His older, reminiscing self writes a lifetime later of what followed:

> Gradually my active dread of hearing anything about Brandham Hall passed into indifference, a progressive atrophy of curiosity about people that extended in many directions, in fact nearly all. But another world came to my aid – the world of facts. . . . Indeed, the life of facts proved to be no bad substitute for the facts of life. . . . So I missed [many experiences], spooning among them. Ted hadn't told me what it was, but he had shown me, he had paid with his life for showing me, and after that I never felt like it.[25]

Thus, Leo occupies the place of his object in one of its masks – he remains Virgin, untouched by life, in the "before" of the event, refusing the encounter with it, until his involuntary entry into transference. Lacan in previous years had characterised the object *a* as the one which the subject looks for out in front of desire, thus mistaking its true place which is behind, as cause, in the forgotten place from which speaking emerges.[26] Forgetting his saying in being occupied by the said, Leo speaks from the Virgin place which he had taken to be the one to which his desire tended, but which is rather his seat, a shred of the pure past which has no existence:

> [B]eyond the lover and beyond the mother, coexistent with the one and contemporary with the other, lies the never-lived reality of the Virgin.[27]

Deleuze's third synthesis realises the fracture between the passive, contemplative self and the active master of representation; between "I am" and "I think". It thus equates to a killing of God the Father who had unified them. It is the moment of the event, of becoming adequate to the event, bringing about a metamorphosis. There is a dissolution of the previous self, and of the temporal structure in which the event had remained mythical. This moment corresponds to Le Gaufey's notion of "the instant of the murder" of the primal horde father.[28] Freud had approached the problem raised by his discovery of "psychic reality" – the problem of what is real, outside memory and fantasy – by designating a beyond of it in terms of *time*: a pre-historic or primal time, illustrated by the myth of the primal father of the to-be-human herd.[29] Evidently, there is a caesura between mythic/pre-historic time and historical time, expressed in the "timelessness" of the unconscious according to Freud, or by Deleuze's definition of the unconscious as three different syntheses of time. For Le Gaufey, the mythical time of "before" is transformed into the historical time of "after" by an instant (recall Lacan's evocation in. . . *ou Pire* of the term "the sudden"[30]): in this case, the instant of the killing of the primal horde father, understood as corresponding in lived experience to the momentous event of encountering the failure of a given father to attain the status of Fatherness or true cause.[31] Lacan, too, references the father as the one who is supposed to unify (*unie*). The instant of his fall establishes a place of exception; "the father" as a real outside the series of representations, which has presence but no identity. Thus, the caesura is not so much resolved as realised in an encounter with what Lacan called the lack in, and of, the Other, and which is approached theoretically in various moments of his work as castration or as the impossibility of sexual relation.

The encounter thus realises that by which the "I" is fractured: namely the pure and empty form of time, the third synthesis which has remained hidden until now and is what brings it about that being is determined not by thought but by time. The Kantian cogito is revealed as an illusion that relies on the Father (in the shape of God), wherein "I think" is not the activity of a substantial being but the affection of a passive subject who experiences its own thought being exercised upon it rather than by it.[32] Thus Lacan renders the Cartesian cogito as *I think: "therefore I am"*: as a phallus of thought masking castration.[33]

The trauma of the event is thus defined not in the Freudian terms of an unassimilable excitation, but as the realisation of the split that time makes in the subject. It is not that the living being cannot tolerate jouissance but that the subject cannot assimilate it to the *queue de pensées:* cannot make the present "am" of this being abide in the same place – that is, the same time – as its habitual "I" coupled with or drawn from its virtualised-past object. Here, then, is the caesura between the psychoanalytic couple "I think" and "I am", Ego and Id, narcissism and object-relation. The point highlighted by all three authors cited previously is that the Cartesian cogito, or the promulgating of a Father by religion, or the repetitions of reminiscent memory and fantasised object, mask the fracture which may never-theless be encountered under certain conditions, among them that of transference.

For Deleuze, time in its third synthesis loses the cardinal order given by the cir-cle of Eros and memory (first repetition, second, third, . . .) and becomes ordinal: a straight line leading to the future and, ultimately, to the impersonal death to which Ted succumbs. Emptied of the virtual – virtual object, virtual self – with which memory had erotised it, *it* unfolds rather than things unfolding within it (88). In the third synthesis of time, all is repetition, not in the ordinal register, but in the temporal series (before, after) established by the symbol of the unique event (*go-between*). Deleuze writes:

> Repetition is a condition of action before it is a concept of reflection. We produce something new only on condition that we repeat. . . .
>
> Moreover, what is produced, the absolutely new itself, is in turn nothing but repetition: the third repetition, this time by excess, the repetition of the future as eternal return.[34]

The "after" of Leo's event concerns such a repetition in excess, unfolded in an epi-logue to the reminiscent body of the novel. Having re-activated the living present of his life, Leo is curious for the first time in 50 years, and visits Brandham Hall. Meeting by chance in the street the 11th Viscount Trimingham (Hugh had been the 9th), he is informed that Marian still lives in the village, and he visits her. He is confronted with a Marian fallen far from her Zodiacal heights, an old woman living in reduced circumstances, who tells him the rest of the, now impersonal, story: Ted did kill himself, she did marry Hugh, now dead, their children died in the second war, and now she is retired into this small place in life, waiting in vain for her grandson the 11th Viscount to visit. But he, having discovered that he is the descendent of Ted and not of Hugh, cannot forgive her betrayal. Marian begs Leo to take a message to this new Ted and attempt a rapprochement. Leo thinks this is ridiculous – what can he do? – and considers jumping into his car and leaving:

> But I didn't, and hardly had I turned in at the lodge gates, wondering how I should say what I had come to say, when the south-west prospect of the Hall, long hidden from my memory, sprang into view.[35]

These are the last words of the novel, which thus ends, I would argue, with Leo assuming his S1 as a name, *Go-Between*. Deleuze writes that the trauma persists in the symbol of the event, and opens to "a belief of the future, a belief in the future".[36] Could we not regard this symbol as an S1 – in the novel, *Go-between* – produced only in the event which returns from both past and future, co-existing every present, and conceding to the logic of an act possessing its own secret coherence beyond the fractured self?

The event and the third synthesis of time which opens doesn't cure the caesura of the subject or synthesise one from two. Neither does an analysis. Lacan indicates that when the analyst makes himself the support of the object *a*, the forgotten place of speaking, "what is born of an analysis . . . at the level of the subject" is "this split thing".[37]

What, then, can an analysis produce aside from this "gaping slit"? Can Deleuze's notion of becoming adequate to the event, or Le Gaufey's instant of the father's killing, lend something to this question? As I read . . . *Ou Pire*, Lacan implicitly differentiates the split subject or fractured "I" from the *one* which is produced by the analytic act. The one is alone, the Other having fallen away from where, as numinous pure past, it had formed the erotic ground of the cycling of memory lent to fantasy. The term unian is thus apt for this one which is produced. The term is drawn from the verb *unier*, to unify, yet this unifying occurs beyond the threshold of the fall of the father. It is not a unifying by the Other, but by the coherence of that act which, for one instant, unifies that which had gaped open. Such an act is Leo's turning in the gates. He is not unified with his intention or his knowledge, his *queue de pensees*, but in the moment of acting he turns away from trying to heal the split and allows himself to be moved by that which moves beyond his knowledge in his affected being. Roberto Harari regards unian as a being which is undivided, unlike the subject of the signifier.[38] Lacan's conglomerated phrase *Yad'lun* also suggests a form which is indivisible and non-substitutable. *Yad'lun* could be translated with regard to sense as *some (of) one*, but this misses its form in French, which is holophrastic, indivisible. Univocal being could not be the consistent identity necessary to narcissism: it is a one which could only *be* in an instant of time, "the sudden". What is that instant other than the instant of an act, including an act of speech? If so, neither the act nor the being is repeatable except, each time, as absolutely new.

Unian implicitly references Deleuze's notion of difference-in-itself, which he defines as univocal, without co-respondent. Difference-in-itself requires affirmation as that which produces what was previously inexistent. It leads to a different form of repetition, as the eternal return of difference-in-itself. To affirm this being and take it up is thus to repeat the un-repeatable in the mode of living presence. Leo's final taking up of *go-between* is such an act. Saying can be such an act. In saying, Lacan indicates, the Freudian Thing, which is impossible to speak about (i.e. to represent), speaks, and this speech is both the Thing showing its face (*face*) and a making (*fasse*):

> Either the *therefore I am* is only a thought, to prove that it is the unthinkable that thinks, or it is the fact of saying it that acts on the Thing, sufficiently for it to behave otherwise.[39]

Leo both shows his secret name and, in doing so, *makes* the go-between. Rather than being represented, the Thing makes itself present, each time in a singular way. We could say that this Thing is what is transferred from zero to one and is also the place of speaking as forgotten and thus of the inexistent object.

The symptom's repetition, Lacan says, is necessitated by the inexistence, at its source, of truth and of jouissance. Leo's act affirms that which until then had been inexistent to representation and thus had repeated as a symptom. It brings the repeating one (unary trait) to a halt and produces instead the one based on zero; zero indicating the lack of co-respondent, the lack of any element corresponding to a concept, the one irreducible to the series.[40] The south-west prospect of the Hall is such an element. It is a one based on zero in the sense that there is no object that it represents; it is a one without meaning yet irreducibly present. That Leo had previously been unable to recall it indicates that it was not one of the series created by Eros and Memory cycling around the place of a virtual object, the scene of the fantasm. This last act is not Eros tearing a virtual object out of the pure past so that Leo can live it in the mode of go-between. The mythical object – Virgo, spooning, deadly nights, bi-cycling – falls away and in its place is made the face of the Thing, which is revealed only by affirmation; that is, only in being taken up. Thus, it is through the future that it will return, each time in a new act. Leo takes up his going between without compulsion or expectation of any mystical revelation or gratification. It is an act in the present time of his life which acknowledges the logic of his trajectory and represents nothing.

This end is thus not a dialectical resolution but a metamorphosis of the preceding order. By his affirmation, Leo enters time stretching ahead as a straight line and succumbs to living a life intensified by the presence of the death. He ceases trying to master the train of thought *nachtraglich* and embraces repetition as the emergence of the singular, without identity or resemblance to what is past, coming from the future. He puts his name to what was not thought. Would this not be a face or a making (*face/fasse*) of the knowledge of the psychoanalyst: that *jouissance*, living and present, has no complement? To ask why Leo turns in the gates of the south-west face would miss the point: he does it.

Notes

1 J. Lacan, *The Seminar of Jacques Lacan book XIX . . . ou Pire*, translated by C. Gallagher, 1971–1972, Unpublished manuscript.

2 G. Deleuze, *Difference & Repetition*, translated by P. Patton, Columbia University Press, New York, 1994 [1968].

3 Lesson of March 8, 1972, . . . *ou Pire* (1971–1972).

4 Deleuze, *Difference & Repetition*. Op. cit., pp. 71–74.

5 Ibid. pp. 102–103.

6 In the lesson of February 9, 1972, . . . *ou Pire* (1971–1972), Lacan asks "What indeed can be transferred from 0 to 1?"

7 Deleuze, *Difference & Repetition*. Op. cit., pp. 79–85.

8 Lesson of March 8, 1972, . . . *ou Pire* (1971–1972). *Queue* can be translated as either "queue" or "tail" (as of an animal), and the latter meaning lends it to being used as slang for "cock".
9 Lesson of February 9, 1972, . . . *ou Pire* (1971–1972).
10 Deleuze, *Difference & Repetition*. Op. cit., p. 107.
11 See, for example, lesson June 21, 1972, . . . *ou Pire* (1971–1972).
12 Deleuze, *Difference & Repetition*. Op. cit., pp. 85–86.
13 L. Lacan, *The Seminar, Book X, Anguish*, translated by C. Gallagher, 1962–1963, Unpublished manuscript.
14 Lesson of June 21, 1972, . . . *ou Pire* (1971–1972).
15 L. P. Hartley, *The Go-Between*, Readers Union, Hamish Hamilton, London, 1954.
16 Ibid., p. 13.
17 Ibid., p. 16.
18 P. Sloterdijk, *Spheres Volume I: Bubbles. Microspherology*, translated by W. Hoban, Semiotext(e), South Pasadena, CA, 2011, p. 12.
19 Lessons of March 15, May 17 and June 14, 1972, . . . *ou Pire* (1971–1972).
20 L. P. Hartley, *The Go-Between*. Op. cit., p. 3.
21 Ibid., pp. 4–5.
22 Ibid., p. 33.
23 Ibid., p. 261.
24 Deleuze, *Difference & Repetition*. Op. cit., pp. 88–89.
25 L. P. Hartley, *The Go-Between*. Op. cit., p. 264.
26 *Seminar X, Anguish*.
27 Deleuze, *Difference & Repetition*. Op. cit., p. 85.
28 G. Le Gaufey, (Text 2) Père, ne voit-tu pas donc que tu brûles? www.legaufey.fr/Textes/Attention_files/27.rtf.
29 S. Freud, *Totem and Taboo*. Standard Ed., XIII, 1913 [1912–13], The Hogarth Press and the Institute of Psycho-Analysis, London.
30 Lesson of March 15, 1972, . . . *ou Pire* (1971–1972).
31 G. Le Gaufey, (Text 1) On Fatherness, www.legaufey.fr/Textes/Attention_files/40.rtf.
32 Deleuze, *Difference & Repetition*. Op. cit., pp. 85–86.
33 Lesson of May 17, 1972, . . . *ou Pire* (1971–1972).
34 Deleuze, *Difference & Repetition*. Op. cit., p. 90.
35 Ibid., p. 280.
36 Ibid.
37 Lesson of June 21, 1972, . . . *ou Pire* (1971–1972).
38 R. Harari, Lacan Seminar of the Australian Centre for Psychoanalysis, 2006.
39 Lesson of March 8, 1972, . . . *ou Pire* (1971–1972).
40 See lesson of April 19, 1972, . . . *ou Pire* (1971–1972) for Lacan's discussion of the emergence of the One without co-respondent.

Chapter 17

The painter's saying

Michael Currie

There is a painting in the National Gallery of Victoria, titled the Garden of Love.[1] The painting depicts five people arranged around a fountain in an early renaissance garden. It was painted around 1465. A curator's note that used to hang next to the painting read:

> Few paintings in the collection present the number of questions posed by "The Garden of Love". This painting has been attributed to nine artists or studios since 1939. Today the attribution has settled on the artist known as the Master of the Stories of Helen, who worked in the studio of Antonio Vivarini, a fifteenth century Venetian artist. Although the painting represents a Garden of Love, the exact symbolism of some elements in the composition is still not well understood.

Figure 17.1

DOI: 10.4324/9781003212720-22

150   Michael Currie

This curator's note brims with reticence, a reticence to understand, which is unusual amongst such scholars in front of a public thirsty to understand. I found reticence to understand a painting that depicts love to be almost analytic. There is a resistance to finding a series of saids to explain the painting.

The curator's note encouraged me to pause in front of this image. For some months, drawn to the enigma, I returned regularly to look at the painting. Rather than filling me with an understanding, the reticence of the curator pointed to a question. What is the saying that is hidden in this painting? One day, this saying burst out of the painting as I stood gazing at it. This paper is my attempt to impart this moment to you.

Taken as a whole, for this is the painting's value as an image – presenting synchronically what can only be taken diachronically in speech or writing – the painting problematizes love. Its value, with a few drops of supposition, is to show the relation between various problems or aporias to do with love. There is no representation of Love, but rather of some sort of mysterious enactment. This is what makes the painting amenable to an analytic reading, rather than simply a contribution to the history or popular conception of love.

This painting is a Venetian variant of a tradition depicting gardens of love that flourished in Florence and Tuscany for the 100 years prior to this painting and then abruptly disappeared. There is agreement amongst scholars that this painting relies on "direct pithy symbolism" (i.e. signification) rather than the allegorical tendencies that came to infest art later (Watson, 1979). That the painting is depicting a garden of earthly, sexual love there is little question: the scrotal grapes on the base of the fountain, a pair of eagles, the dog (a familiar erotic symbol of the time), dragons (symbolizing lust and greed), the five figures dressed in an aristocratic manner (an uneven number of actors suggesting that some change in love relations is to occur); the syringe (a medieval contraceptive); the garlands (a symbol of progress or achievement of love and sexual union). The one exception appears to be the odd-looking but classically conceived statue that looks to the heavens. Most scholars agree that the painting was most likely commissioned as a wedding gift that was hung in the walls of a Venetian palace of the couple to whom it was given, although there is not a provenance proving this. The gift to the wedding couple appears to concern love and its embodiment and intertwining in the erotics of the sexual act (Anderson, 2005; Watson, 1979).

First reading

On the right of the painting there is a couple – a man and a woman. My supposition is to ask whether they are visiting the garden because something has failed between them. Their proximity suggests no problem with unity. Eros is not lacking here. The woman on the right appears to be in the process of dampening the towel she holds with water from the fountain of love and is about to daub her man's forehead with it. She touches the rear of his head in an intimate gesture. There is a supposition of love, a belief in the power of the fountain of love. Here

The painter's saying   151

they are, humble supplicants, asking Love to make up for, repair the failure. Their faces are serene and peaceful, despite the problem that has bought them here. The couple, like Aristophanes in the Symposium, are taken in by the power of love.

Love arises in the garden of the treatment as an effect of transference. After Freud's testimony, the psychoanalyst, like the supplicants of the painting, is tempted to trust in the love that his presence provokes to inspire the patient to do the difficult work of analysis. Love in analysis reduced to a metaphysical force, to a utility of the cure. The analyst allows his presence to be only a means, however large it looms as an end for the patient.

In his book Lacan Love, Allouch (2007) argues that any theory of love ends up being metaphysical, a definition of metaphysical here being the ascription of agency or force to abstract concepts. Love becomes a subject in a subject. If the statue on the top of the fountain is taken as Eros, we become tied up in an affair of representation rather than a subject constituting itself, as we find in Lacan.

The problem with attributing such powers to love is the inducement to passivity it offers to both actors in the arrangement: to the analysand (why should I do anything now I have you?); and to the analyst, who allows himself the stoical retreat of the process-cure by love, like water dripping on a stone.

Here are cogent, urgent reasons as to why Allouch is at pains to point out that there is no theory of love in Lacan. We also start to gain further respect for the stance of erotic aphasia shown by the curators in their note to the "Garden of Love".

A problem pointed to by Lacan is that it was not Freud, but his followers that were torn to shreds by their own hounds for their reductive use of love in analysis. The erotic bursts out unexpectedly on the analyst-who-relies-on-love, devoured by the hounds of love after he is taken for a rutting stag. For Freud, it is more a matter of working to keep the hounds in pursuit.[2] Far from being a trusty vehicle that delivers the cure each time, love surprises and destroys.

Second concern: love is reduced to a technique. Love draws on a universal from outside the patient rather than something from the particular, that gives a singular of the analysand.

For Freud, the question of the singularity played out in the shadow of love that his patient was ensnared within. Think Dora as an item of exchange within her father's quartet; Little Hans as a boy petting too much with his mother against his father's word and requiring his own phobic invention; The homosexual woman's love interest against the wishes of her parents; the Wolfman's erotics which Freud pins against his reconstruction of coitus a tergo; the Ratman struggling with his own amorous interests in the shadow of the debt of his father; Schreber's state of voluptuousness and invention of his system trailing after his unbearable ascension in the legal hierarchy. Freud's interest was not in the indispensable fact of love. Rather, Freud's interest (with the exception of Schreber, there it was a matter of Freud's transference to him) was in harnessing love in the service of the unpredictable set of erotics played out in the surrounds, that is, in the garden, where love emerged in the subject to whom he was listening, which, as for Actaeon, might only be glimpsed.

Second reading: fortune

The woman on the far left of the picture carries a dog, a sign of fidelity and carnality. Fidelity to what? The answer is given by her gaze, directed to the man standing next to her. The dog tells us that there is something that works in sexual love between the woman and the man on the left. This is in contrast to the passivity I have supposed on the other side of the fountain. The man on the left, of all the figures in the painting, is the only one looking at the viewer. His gaze, full of knowledge about love, draws the viewer into the painting. His right forefinger points to the statue on top of the fountain. Who is this statue, if not Eros?

That she is a woman, has a forelock and is standing on a globe indicates this is Fortune. The encounter with love is an encounter, the gentleman of the painting is indicating, with chance. Fortune's globe, which initially symbolized her chaotic nature, by the renaissance came to signify her dominion over the entire world (Watson, 1979). Fortune's chaos is tempered by a pair of eagles, one either side, giving the appearance of stability via the natural sexual relation, but this appearance is deceptive.

In the logic of the painting put forward by the web of gazes I have discussed already, the woman's loyalty to her man is given by his submission to Fortune. His submission is to a figure who is unconcerned by the goings on in the garden below. Fortune looks elsewhere, to another reality that man cannot hope to understand; to something inhuman. Nonetheless, this figure is crucial to love; one hand supports the whole frame of representation of the painting; the other hand holds the garlands of love worn by lovers following success in love making.

If one bends to look at the painting closely, the lion's head on the front of the fountain is shedding a tear. The lion's position at the base of the fountain close to the scrotal grapes leads us to suspect a link with sexual conquest. The lion's tear gives the futility and loss involved in the reliance on the transience of such acts.

In the end, the painting's message is that despite the appearance of stability of love, there is neither a god nor a master of love.

And now we come to the fifth human figure in the painting, the woman standing at the left of the fountain with her syringe. Her fingers are arranged so it appears she is not drawing water from the fountain, but adding something to it. Here is the position of the analyst, appropriately designated by a feminine figure.

At a point in seminar XX, Lacan gives us a start on the relation between love and saying. He raises several problems. He says there:

> We are confronted with a saying, the saying of another person . . . what is it that we must read therein? Nothing but the effects of those instances of saying. We see in what sense these effects bother speaking beings. For that to lead to something, it must serve them and it does serve them, by god in working things out, accommodating themselves, and managing all the same – in a bumbling, stumbling sort of way – *to give a shadow of life to the feeling known as love.*
>
> (p. 46)

The painter's saying   153

Here are the settings put forward at some sort of primary level for the (Lacanian) analyst. Reading the effects of a saying I take as hearing the bumbling, stumbling effects of a signifier free from the bindings of meaning at the moment of its utterance. The utterance returns to reverberate and shape meaning in the moments after the utterance. This saying serves the speaking being: but only by the speaking being's submission to the saying. It is via a submission to the effects of this saying through speech, a submission the analyst hears and enhances, that we make a "shadow of life" of love. In the end, this is a submission to something inhuman.

Lacan's final statement in the quote about love leads *a contrario*, back to the idea that there is the light of death (shadow) in love. Love and its deathly light are on the side of the human. The paired assertion is just as half-true: through love, we make something of speech. Through the clash of human love and inhuman saying, something can be produced. This is the site of psychoanalysis.

To put this in a similar way, Fortune (un)links the saying and the said. It is via loving submission to this (un)linking that something is produced.

This is the challenge for each analyst, to find a method in each instance that gives life to the feeling known as love; a method that takes love to give life to mere words. In this method, it is not a matter of love assisting the analyst. The importance of Lacan's quoted intervention in seminar XX is that the analyst gives something to love. This is what the woman at the left of the fountain embodies via her wielding the syringe in the manner she does.

Third reading: postscript

After my encounter with the painting that afternoon, I went home well satisfied that I had solved the problem of the painting after quite a few visits. In the weeks following this visit, I read what I could about the painting. There was a further surprise.

The painting itself has been subject to transformation by Fortune since the last drops of the painter's intent dried on its boards. In a paper given by John Payne following the painting's extended restoration, he writes of x-ray evidence that the painting originally depicted a sixth, male figure on the far right hand side. This figure wears a hat similar to the man on the left, and has been painted over. This modification was done presumably at the time of a renovation that required that the lower right hand corner of the painting be cut out to accommodate a doorway in the palace in Venice where the painting was originally installed. This piece of interior decorating probably happened a few hundred years ago. The top of the picture was also trimmed, presumably at the same time.

Fortune is represented not only by the goddess in the picture, but by the bumbling, stumbling of the painting's fate, random to the painter's original intention. With the sixth figure, the moiety (three men and three women) of the painting has been restored. This gives us an original, more commonplace meaning of the painting as a wedding gift. Two parental couples appear to be releasing their children into the encounter of sexual love. Despite the legality, Fortune still rules human relations.

My love of this painting gave life to the enactment that is this paper. Whatever satisfactions come to us, Fortune always has something she keeps prisoner in the toils of the pleasure principle.

I hear your sigh of disappointment that my interpretation of the painting could not have been within the intention of the painter. If you are left with only that, you have not received what I have written about the problem of love in this essay.

Notes

1 www.ngv.vic.gov.au/explore/collection/work/4440/
2 Jacques Lacan, *Ecrits*, translated by Alan Sheridan, Routledge, London, 1977, p. 124.

References

Allouch, J. (2007) *Lacan Love: Melbourne Seminars and Other Works*. Edited by María-Inés Rotmiler de Zentner and Oscar Zentner. Ourimbah: Bookbound Publishing.
Anderson, J. (2005) Gardens of Love in Venetian Paintings of the Quattrocentro. In: *Rituals, Images, and Words: Varieties of Cultural Expression in Late Medieval and Early Modern*. Edited by F. W. Kent & C. Zika. Turnhout, Belgium: Brepols Publishers.
Watson, P. F. (1979) *The Garden of Love in Tuscan Art of the Early Renaissance*. Philadelphia, PA: Art Alliance Press.

Chapter 18

The image that binds

Tine Nørregaard

The Danish journalist Morten Sabroe is in New York to write a book about Hilary Clinton. One night he wakes up after having fainted on the street, full of anxiety about his own impending death, having suffered a blood clot in the brain the year before. This crisis also leaves him touched by another death, his mother's, having thought 11 years earlier at her death bed, "*Then die, Goddamn, die*" (2007, p. 222, my translation). *Thou Who Art in Heaven* is a book written after this crisis in New York, a story that evolves around the image of Hillary Clinton, but which reflects the image of Sabroe's own mother. The crisis then also reflects the image of death in the mirror, his own as well as his mother's, a reflection that conjures up a story about difficult ties within a family; as Sabroe writes:

> It was a tough family to free oneself of. It would not let go. She was my family, the only family I had. My father was not family, he was just there.
>
> (Ibid, p. 187, my translation)

The family for Sabroe is defined by this close tie which binds him to his mother. This is a mother who became Nordic Champion of high diving in her youth and who shared the financial responsibilities of the family on equal terms with the father. It is an image of a mother who always asserted her right, a mother who in a manner of speaking "wore the trousers in the family". The father, on the other hand, did not care if he was right or wrong and as a result of this, according to Sabroe, "he did not bind anyone".

Sabroe's picture of Hillary Clinton acts as a mirror to the image of his own mother. It is a picture of two aspiring women who both swayed from their own career paths in order to follow their husbands' ambition, and whose images have both become tainted by the public eye on their marriage and speculations about extramarital affairs. Sabroe considers that Hillary Clinton's mission, to be the first female American president, is the act of a woman scorned by the allegations concerning a possible affair between Bill Clinton and Monica Lewinsky, hence he designates her as "Mrs Frigidaire" (Ibid, p. 59). This image of *Mrs Frigidaire* blends into Sabroe's image of his own mother: an image of a woman whose mission in life is to punish her husband for his affairs. Sabroe's mother was initially

DOI: 10.4324/9781003212720-23

one of his father's many lovers when he was still married to his first wife, and when they later married, she made him promise to end all his affairs. Yet Sabroe remembers his mother's words full of irritation and contempt for his father: "*Your father always wanted it*" (Ibid, p. 62, my translation), leading him to assume that she punished her husband for his sexual crimes by letting him wait lustfully in the bed every night while she scrubbed and cleaned the kitchen.

This sexual knowledge of the pre-history of the encounter between the parents is nevertheless also what pertains to a crisis with an image; something breaks the mirror. Beyond the image of Hillary Clinton, Sabroe encounters an image of his mother swept in a *jouissance* of her own, an image he looked for, but which in the mirror reflects his own shadow:

> I conjured up an image which only had something to do with me and nothing to do with Hillary Clinton. And neither with my mother. The way I served her on a platter to complete strangers, was, even though she was dead, a violation.
>
> (Ibid, p. 59, my translation)

It is a shadow that persists and makes Sabroe write in his notebook:

> "I spoke of something you cannot speak about in this way". How you can speak about it, I didn't know. The matter was that one could not speak about it to others, and not at all in a book. But, the matter was also that I had already decided to do so. I had known all along that I would go through the image of Hillary Clinton in order to reach my mother.
>
> (Ibid, p. 59, my translation)

Going through this image is also a way of confronting the shadow that dims the light of the pictures presented in the family album. It is a light that his mother wanted to shine on their family. This was a family of a certain public stature. Sabroe's father was a well-known director of the famous Circus Revue and his maternal grandfather was a recognised social reform figure with a statue erected in his name. Sabroe himself is also a public figure, an acknowledged journalist and writer, rewarded for his ability to touch on the truth of the subjects he writes about. So, what is this crisis which stifles him with anxiety and with obstacles in his writing about Hillary Clinton? Something insists of this shadow that falls on the image in the mirror, something that pushes him to reopen his family album to look beyond the images, beyond the imaginary tie that binds him with his mother.

We may then ask how it is possible to move beyond such a tie with an image, a tie which we in the clinic of psychoanalysis encounter as a bind with *jouissance*?

The family complex is founded on a crisis of weaning

In 1938, in his *Family Complexes in the Formation of the Individual* Lacan expands on Freud's notion of the Oedipus complex as a series of family complexes which constitute the subject from the ties that are formed with the object. Even though Lacan had at this stage not yet developed his conceptualisation of the symbolic, the imaginary and the real we can see the effects of this thinking already in his work. We hear the prevalence of the imaginary in the symbolic formation of the family complex as "an unconscious representation that is known as the imago" and in the sense that "family sentiments in particular are often the inverted image of unconscious complexes" (1938, p. 14). Nevertheless, the process of symbolisation of the object is at this stage considered in the Hegelian sense, as a series of crises that occur in the encounter with the real:

> As for the individual's integration of objectifying forms, this is the work of a dialectical process that makes each new form arise from the conflicts between the preceding one and the real.[1]
>
> (1984[1938], p. 23, my translation)

The initial crisis of weaning results in a difficulty with forming a symbolic representation of the mother in which the presence and absence, the fort-da of language, perpetuates the imaginary form of the imago of the maternal breast. There is already a discordance inscribed in this tie with the object which is anticipated by the earlier separation of birth:

> The latter – which is weaning in its strictest sense – gives the first and also the most adequate psychic expression to the more obscure imago of an earlier, more painful weaning that is of greater vital importance: that which, at birth, separates the infant from the womb, a premature separation from which comes a malaise that no maternal care can compensate for.
>
> (1938, pp. 19–20)

According to Lacan, we suffer from this prematurity of birth because we are born into language, the symbolic, without at this stage being able to master either speech or motor control of the body. This leaves a trace of a fundamental lack in relation to the first Other, the mother, which Lacan calls a *malaise*, an uneasiness, a longing for a return to the maternal womb; a return which in essence is death. Lacan asserts this as "a fusional and ineffable cannibalism" which is the manifestation of the death drive in the fusion of the child with the mother's body (1984[1938], p. 30, my translation). There is an eroticisation at this point of the mother's body with that of the child's, which opens the child to an encounter with a primordial *jouissance*. The sublimation of the imago of the maternal breast keeps a tie with the real which in essence is a tie with *jouissance* and death.[2] Elsewhere, Lacan considers this difficulty with tolerating the mother's desire like "being caught in the jaws of a huge crocodile" (1969–1970, lesson March 11, 1970). Being caught in the phantasy at this place of the mother's desire is being at the mercy of the *Jouissance of the Other*. It is this *jouissance* as an "appetite for death" which we find, persisting as a refusal of weaning, in the various symptoms associated with the oral forms of the complex, for example the starvation of the anorexic or the poisoning of the oral addictions.

The longing for the imago of the maternal womb, a form that is difficult to sublimate, becomes the sentiment of the family tie, the bond that Lacan refers to as the "domestic unity of the family group" (1938, p. 22). This primordial *malaise* of the weaning complex is reproduced as a crisis at every phase of development and each one has to pass through this crisis with a family tie in order to become a subject in his own right. Lacan refers to Hegel in this passage from the family to civilisation:

> Hegel proposed that the individual who does not struggle to be recognised outside the family group goes to his death without having achieved a personality[...]. As regards personal dignity, the family can only promote the individual to that of a name-bearing entity and it can only do this at the hour of its burial.
>
> (Ibid, p. 22)

We see that Hegel in his *Elements of the Philosophy of Right* claims that we are not in the family as persons, and that we are only recognised as persons when the family begins to dissolve:

> Thus, the disposition (appropriate to the family) is to have self-consciousness of one's own individuality *within this unity* as essentiality which has being in and for itself, so that one is present in it not as an independent person (*eine Person für sich*) but as a *member*.
>
> (2014[1821], p. 199)

In Hegel's *Phenomenology of Spirit*, we see that he considers the ethical action of the individual as central to being a citizen, which separates him from the membership of the family:

> But because it is only as a citizen that he is actual and substantial, the individual, so far as he is not a citizen but belongs to the Family, is only an unreal impotent shadow.
>
> (1977[1807], pp. 269–270)

Even though it is the Family as institution that is referred to here, we can nevertheless discern the maternal sentiment as a longing that binds one at this threshold of the family and society. In 1938, Lacan considers this as a crisis perpetuated by the decline of the paternal function of authority in the social structure of the conjugal family. This leaves a difficulty with the paternal imago that sustains the symbolic function of intervening in the close tie with the mother, leading to a crisis with the castration complex. As Lacan notes, this crisis affects the forms of the super ego and the ego ideal:

> Impotence and a Utopian spirit are the sinister Godmothers who watch over the cradle of the neurotic and imprison his ambition, either because he stifles in himself those creations expected of him by the world into which he comes, or because in the object against which he proposes to revolt he fails to recognise his own activity.
>
> (1938, p. 56)

In this difficulty with sustaining the symbolic function, the shadow of the maternal imago persists and haunts the subject as a narcissistic bind which procures an impotence at the level of one's own aspirations. In Sabroe's story, he refers to his family as a kind of flesh that he needs to cut himself out of; the flesh that he later witnesses in the decay of his mother's body when caring for her in the time of her approaching death. It is a crisis with the imaginary and the real, a haunting through the image that binds one in a struggle to death like the Hegelian master-slave dialectic. This difficulty with a shadow of death reflects a tie with a mythical *jouissance*, the bind with the *Jouissance of the Other*.

The creative subversion of the subject

For Lacan in 1938, it is a "creative subversion" which offers a possibility in regard to this bind with *jouissance* at the threshold of the family and society (1984[1938], p. 70, my translation). In 1960, in *Subversion of the Subject in the Dialectics of Desire* he reworks this "creative subversion" in relation to the symbolic phallus as what provides the bridge between *jouissance* and desire. Lacan denotes this symbolic phallus as "the signifier of jouissance", the bar to the forbidden mythical *jouissance* which is refused through castration, only to "be reached on the inverted ladder of the Law of desire" (1977[1960], p. 324) This phallus offers each one the possibility of moving around in the world according to the particular phantasm, that is, the articulation of desire as desire of the Other (1977[1960], p. 321).

At the end of his life, Freud considered the difficulties of overcoming the castration complex from the point of angst caused by the encounter with the lack of the penis in the mother. This point marks a conflict for the child between the demand of the drive and the prohibition of reality which requires a sacrifice of sexual enjoyment in order to accede to the cultural demands of society. However, as Freud underlines, this sacrifice at the same time leaves "a rift in the ego that never heals" (1940[1938], p. 462) We understand this rift as the split in the subject that is the effect of the lack circumscribed by the signifier of the phallus.

Lacan says the following about the symbolic castration which sacrifices *jouissance* through the choice of the phallus:

> This choice is allowed because the phallus, that is, the image of the penis, is negativity in its place in the specular image. It is what predestines the phallus to embody *jouissance* in the dialectic of desire.
>
> (1977[1960], p. 319)

The law of desire is inscribed through the paternal metaphor as it has intervened in the desire of the mother, which speaks of how this signifier of the symbolic phallus works both for the mother and for the child. For the child, the game of being and having the phallus is introduced by the symbolic anticipation of the law of the prohibition of incest as it has posed a limit to the mother's *jouissance*. This symbolic anticipation circumscribes the absence or lack in the mother's discourse which is designated by the Name of the Father. As Lacan stresses, in the myth of the mother and the child as one, there is already an elision, the object *a* having fallen from the body of the mother (1984[1967], p. 264). It is in regard to how the child's body is taken to respond to this place of lack for the mother that we may see the possibility of the object *a* also coming to function as object cause of desire for the child. This underlines the structural aspect of the super ego at two levels for each one, castration of the subject and castration of the Other.

We can say that the angst that grips the subject in the phantasy of castration is at once both imaginary, in regard to the mirror image, and real in regard to sexuality and the body, but it is also already symbolic, as the bar raised of primary repression which also bars the lack in the Other. Being at the mercy of the *Jouissance of the Other* is then already an articulation of the phantasm. As Benjamin Domb underlines, it is not the *jouissance* of the mother, but the "*jouissance* of the supposed primordial Other", the Other who enjoys (*jouit*) me (1998, p. 95). This is a struggle with being trapped as the instrument of the *Jouissance of the Other*, which one can only escape from by making use of the symbolic phallus. This symbolic phallus is the wedge that one has to grab hold of to keep "the jaws of the crocodile's mouth open", the metaphor which, as mentioned earlier, Lacan makes use of to describe the trap of the mother's desire (1969–1970, lesson March 11, 1970). The angst that grips one in relation to this wedge concerns the truth that is revealed of the lack in the Other, the implication that there is no Other of the Other. According to Domb, this implication for the subject entails the knowledge that this wedge of the symbolic phallus is also the only way out for the Other (1998, p. 91).

In his closing remarks to a conference on childhood psychoses in 1967, Lacan considers Freud's ethical concern around the death drive as central to the proposition of his own ethics which he asserts rather as a "curbing of *jouissance*" (1984[1967], p. 260, my translation). He follows Freud's concerns about the

The image that binds 161

identification with the father through religion and other ideals, an identification which assumes the Other as existing, not inscribed by lack. For Lacan, the question is rather in what manner the pleasure principle has acted as a "brake" to *jouissance* so as to promulgate the Other also as castrated.

In his seminar *RSI*, Lacan asserts that our only means of interpreting the *jouissance* of the symptom is through "the effects of the symbolic in the real" (1974–1975, lesson December 10, 1974). From this, we can surmise that it is through the symbolic function that *jouissance* is "curbed". It is through the symbolic phallus that something of this *jouissance* is metaphorised by accommodating it as "*Phallic Jouissance*" (Ibid, lesson December 17, 1974). The *Phallic Jouissance* traces this bar to the forbidden *jouissance*, the *Jouissance* of the Other. As Lacan notes, one ex-sist from this forbidden jouissance which is the primal scene of the parents' sexual encounter, the scene one is at once implicated in and removed from. . We can say that it is through the writing for each one of this *Phallic Jouissance* that the border is traced of this ex-sistence, the untenable *jouissance* as real. Could the creative subversion be such a writing that evokes the real through making the object *a* exterior to the body as a way of curbing *jouissance*; the writing of one's desire beyond the image?

Let us return to the writing of the journalist Sabroe.

Writing beyond an image

In his mid-20s, Sabroe wrote an autobiographical novel about his family in which he let moments of truth slip through the fiction of the story he told. In this book, he described his mother as a woman with fat dripping down her chin while eating, because she could not control her mouth and tongue due to a paralysis on one side of her face. Sabroe knew that this would be one of the family secrets revealed, the paralysis being a stain on the image of his mother, who always claimed that her restrained movement was caused by a draft while sleeping in front of an open window. Yet, his mother was the first one he presented the manuscript of the book to, the first one he asked to read it; an incident that leads to his mother writing him a letter signed "your former mother".

Sabroe is aware that this book is a writing carried by an image in the style of Freud's family romance, the fictitious story a child creates in order to untie himself from the close bond with the parents:

> I had romanticised my break away from my family as a story of emancipation, but when I had put the final full stop, I had not become free of anything other than the text. Inside the romantic text of a young man's rebellion with his pampered upbringing, was a more dramatic one: The fight between me and my mother. It was a fight which did not move out of place. It was conducted with the same violence each time. It had one and only aim: You have to die! Only when you are dead, I will be free.
>
> (2007, p. 167, my translation)

The crisis that had landed Sabroe back into his family ties that fateful night in New York had made real this tie with his mother in an imaginary fight to death. The moment of panic which procures a writing is not dissimilar to the one J. Allouch[3] refers to in relation to Lacan's invention of the object *a*, a state of urgency that introduces the impossible (1998, p. 50). For Sabroe, this urgency arrives with the confrontation of an image in the mirror: "*The mirror turns, it shows the same images again and again, but one day it must cease. One day one must change the old images with new ones*" (2007, p. 242, my translation). Eleven years after having sat at his mother's death bed, Sabroe realised that there is no forgiving possible at this moment, not from his mother, who, while he tried to assist in her in the struggle with death by offering calming and soothing words, summoned up her last strength to shout at him: "*Would you please stop that!*" (Ibid p. 241, my translation). It was not his forgiveness of her either, this former mother, who in that moment had installed the following thoughts in his mind: *Then die, Goddamn, die*. As Sabroe writes, this forgiveness is one that lies outside of reach for either of them. Yet what is not possible to say may be written, and it is from this gap, this lack, that the writing occurs as a *real-isation* of Sabroe's own story. The writing in New York of another book is a rewriting of the truth of his family romance, producing another way to bind the tie with his mother. In this story, Sabroe literally writes his mother into death, in the sense that he fictionalises himself in the night carrying her skeletal body to the River Styx, and sends her off on the biggest high dive of her life, to the stars.

Sabroe writes the following about the crisis which landed him in this writing, the one that was precipitated by the shock of the blood clot which he refers to in terms of being "hit by the paintball gun from the insect man":

> I would never have tried to change the image, if the insect man with the paintball gun had not hit me. I went through the picture of another, Hillary Clinton, to find my mother, but maybe it was the contours of myself I found. Just like my father sits at a desk in me and whispers and tiskers while he is writing, my mother walks around in me, but she does not walk around like a bitter marching former mother, she also walks around as the nineteen-year-old woman you can see on the cover of this book. I never had a chance to meet her, but I know that I would have liked her. I saw her in some happy moments, when we fought together on the grass when I was a child, and she overpowered me and drilled her knees into my arms so I couldn't move, and let some spit hang so far out of the mouth I was sure that it would hit me – after which she sucked it back into the mouth again.
>
> (Ibid, p. 243, my translation)

For Sabroe, the father is already in him, reflected in his own style of writing, which he acknowledges is very much like the pieces of writing that his father used to prepare for the newspaper, or for the Circus Revue. So, this writing, in which Sabroe encounters another image of his mother, is already a writing that moves beyond the image; it is already a writing tied with the symbolic. The spit that falls from the body of his mother, the spit full of grease and fat left hanging on her cheek in the image painted of her in his earlier book, is like the object *a* that has fallen out of the frame of the imaginary and is written into the real. It is a fictionalisation made possible through death.

It is through a writing, which is always a rewriting, that a residue, the shadow in the image of the family traits, may be accounted for. This is the *real*-ising which occurs for Sabroe through the writing as an effect of writing. Moving through the mirror Sabroe encounters a shadow: *I spoke of something that you cannot speak about in this way*. Could this something that you cannot speak about be an encounter with the impossible, the real of the parents' sexual union, an encounter with an untenable *jouissance*, the bind with the *Jouissance of the Other* – in which the child is included and from which he is also excluded at the same time? Perhaps, we can say that the angst which hit Sabroe that night in New York and which leaves him in bind with a tie of the image of his mother is an encounter which traces the *Jouissance of the Other*. It is something that at once falls out of the phantasm and at the same time can only be accounted for by moving through the phantasm, that is, through a writing that procures from *Phallic Jouissance*. It is at this crossing point that Sabroe through the symbolic function of writing effects a fictionalising of the real of his family tie. This is a tie of writing beyond the bind with an image in the mirror.

Notes

1 In the French version of Lacan's work, the term is "*le réel*" which I have chosen to translate as "the real" and not "reality" as it is rendered in the English version by Cormac Gallagher Lacan (1938).
2 According to Lacan, this tie with jouissance "*always survives in games and in symbolic words, which, in the most developed love recalls the desire of the larva*" (1984[1938], p. 30, my translation)
3 Allouch speaks about this moment that occurs in the lesson January 9, 1963, of Lacan's Seminar on *Anxiety* as a necessary moment of crisis that leads him to invent the "object *a*" as a theoretical concept. Allouch theorises this moment as reflecting what Lacan himself refers to as "a passage to the act" (1998, p. 50).

References

Allouch, J. (1998) How Lacan invented the Object (a). In: *The Lacanian Discourse, Papers of The Freudian School of Melbourne*. Edited by D. Pereira. Melbourne: Freudian School of Melbourne. Vol. 19.

Domb, B. (1998) The True Hole. In: *The Lacanian Discourse, Papers of The Freudian School of Melbourne*. Edited by D. Pereira. Melbourne: Freudian School of Melbourne. Vol. 19.

Freud, S. (1940[1938]) The Splitting of the Ego in the Process of Defence. In: *On Metapsychology: The Theory of Psychoanalysis. The Pelican Freud Library*. Translated by J. Strachey. London: Penguin Books. Vol. 11, 1991.

Hegel, G. W. F. (1977[1807]) *Phenomenology of Spirit*. Translated by A. V. Miller. Oxford: Oxford University Press, 1977.

Hegel, G. W. F. (2014[1821]) *Elements of the Philosophy of Right*. Edited by A. Wood. Translated by H. B. Nisbet. Cambridge: Cambridge University Press.

Lacan, J. (1938) *Family Complexes in the Formation of the Individual*. Translated by C. Gallagher. St. Vincent Hospital, Dublin 4. Unpublished version. www.lacaninireland.com

Lacan, J. (1969–1970) *The Seminar of Jacques Lacan. Book XVII. Psychoanalysis Upside Down. The Reverse Side of Psychoanalysis*. Translated by C. Gallagher. Unpublished version www.lacaninireland.com

Lacan, J. (1974–1975) *The Seminar of Jacques Lacan. Book XXII. R.S.I. 1974–1975*. Translated by C. Gallagher. Unpublished version www.lacaninireland.com

Lacan, J. (1977[1960]) Subversion of the Subject and Dialectic of Desire. In *Ècrits. A Selection*. Translated by A. Sheridan. New York: W.W. Norton & Company, Tavistock Publications.

Lacan, J. (1984[1938]) *Les complexes familiaux dans la formation de l'individu: essai d'analayse d'une fonction en psychologie*. Paris: Bibliothèque des Analytica. Navarin Èditeur.

Lacan, J. (1984[1967]) Discours de clôture des journées sur les psychoses chez l'enfant. In *Enfance aliénée: L'enfant, la psychose et l'institution*. Présentation de Maud: Mannoni. Paris: L'Espace Analytique. Denoë.

Sabroe, M. (2007) *Du som er i himlen*. Denmark: Politikens Forlag.

Chapter 19

On the edge of the abyss

Helen Dell

This essay is an attempt to find a way to talk about creativity, death and the mother "as she occupies the place of *Das Ding*". It is on the very edge of what it is possible for me to say. The 11th century Jewish poet, Samuel NaHagid (that is, Samuel the Prince) wrote of such a moment of creativity. Samuel was a spectacular figure in 11th century Granada (one of the Ta'ifa states of Andalusia after the fall of the Caliphate). This poem is called "The moment":

> She said: "Rejoice, for God has brought you to your fiftieth year in the world!" but she had no inkling that, for my part, there is no difference at all between my own days which have gone by and the distant days of Noah in the rumoured past. I have nothing in the world but the hour in which I am: it pauses for a moment, and then, like a cloud, moves on.
>
> (Samuel NaHagid, 285)

Samuel's poem captures for me something of the moment of creativity: an instantaneous flash of light, a moment suspended in the void. I associate that void with death, out of which the brief flash of life emerges and is quickly reabsorbed. In Samuel's poem history is erased, all sense of the continued existence of the speaker through time is erased. All that is left is this "hour in which I am" which "pauses but a moment", as all that anyone can have: now! An instant out of time – an instant in the face of death. Creativity feels like an attempt to snatch that now! To pull the chestnuts out of the fire with burnt fingers! To drag something (you don't know what) kicking and screaming into art in the face of death! To grasp the forelock of the naked Kairos as he dashes past![1]

Since this is a writing, I will speak of writing as that snatching. It isn't until the fingers hit the keyboard that something happens. It's that touch that sparks the flash. Like the match flaring in the darkness of the trenches, and the gunfire that comes swiftly to meet it. An explosive mating! That's when a kind of knowledge emerges in that ambiguous place – touch and go, smash and grab, hit and run. There's a violence in these words and images that flash up and a sense of extreme risk; also a theft – or a gift perhaps, with the words raining down, too many to capture. And something which I'm not sure whether to call fusion or fission.

DOI: 10.4324/9781003212720-24

Where the family comes in is with the mother, that which Lacan (1991b) called in *Ethics* "the maternal thing, the mother insofar as she occupies the place of that thing, of *das Ding*" (67). In Lacan's earlier writing, *the* mother is not clearly distinguished from *a* mother, any mother. In "The Family Complexes" (published in 1938), he puts in a claim for the modern patriarchal family, in the form which he called "the conjugal family", as the most productive structure for the harnessing of creativity via sublimation: "So, although in the mental conditions for creativeness psychoanalysis uncovers a revolutionary ferment that can only be grasped in a concrete analysis, it recognises that the family structure has a power to produce it". This is because

> it realises in the most human way the conflict of man with his most archaic anxieties . . . because it puts the most complete triumph over his original slavery within reach of his individual existence, the complex of the conjugal family succeeds in creating superior forms of character, happiness and creativity.
>
> ("Family Complexes", 54)

"This effect is produced by the transmission of the ego-ideal which in its purest form, as we have seen, is transmitted from father to son". Lacan continues:

> To the extent that the imago of the father is dominant, it polarises in both sexes the most perfect forms of the ego-ideal. It is enough to indicate that these forms produce the ideal of virility in the boy, and in the girl the ideal of virginity. On the other hand in the diminished forms of this imago we can emphasise physical lesions, especially those that present this imago as disabled or blind, as diverting the energy of sublimation from its creative direction and favouring its withdrawal into an ideal of narcissistic integrity.
>
> ("Family Complexes" 49)

There is a flavour here of the hand and the glove – two complementary ideals. The girl finds her place as the reverse of the boy's, raising a question of how her own creativity might find expression. Lacan speaks of a decline in creativity due to a decline in the social status of the father which he attributes to changes in contemporary matrimonial conditions:

> This decline is even more closely linked to the dialectic of the conjugal family, since it is the result of a relative growth in matrimonial demands – something that is very obvious, for example, in American life.
>
> ("Family Complexes" 55)

In relation to those archaic anxieties mentioned earlier, he remarks:

> If they [that is, psychoanalysts and sociologists – he aligns the two here] examine the sacrificial rites by which primitive cultures . . . with the

cruelest rigour reproduced phantasies of a primary relationship with the mother (human victims dismembered or entombed alive), they will read in many of the myths that the advent of paternal authority brought with it a tempering of primitive social suppression. . . . It appears . . . in the myth of Oedipus, provided we do not neglect the episode of the Sphinx, which offers a . . . representation of the emancipation from matriarchal tyranny . . . all these myths are situated at the dawn of history, a long way from the birth of humanity from which they are separated by the immemorial duration of matriarchal cultures and by the stagnation of primitive groups.

("Family Complexes" 51)

The Sphinx, with the body of a lion, the head of a woman and the wings of an eagle, devours those who cannot answer its riddle. Bested by Oedipus, it throws itself off the cliff; in other variants, it devours itself. Lacan's account here looks like an earlier, more sociological approach to what he later spoke of as *das Ding*.

Putting all this together, in "The Family Complexes" it appears that creativity is, ideally, the boy's domain, transmitted from father to son, but only if he can escape the smothering maternal tyranny represented by the Sphinx. In that escape, Oedipus is his saviour and guide. In this early account, the prohibition against incest and the promise it offers is what allows speech, movement, creation of the new. It is clear that Lacan, throughout his work, is no stranger to those "archaic anxieties", the horror associated with the mother's desire, witness the crocodile mother passage in Seminar XVII: "A big crocodile in whose mouth you are – this is the mother. One never knows whether she will suddenly decide to snap her trap shut" (*Other Side* 112).

Associations between the mother and destruction do not go away in Lacan's later writings. The return to something maternal is still associated with a silencing, a stagnation, an entombment, a tearing asunder – all very visceral associations. The body is present in *das Ding* in its most violent form – as the dumb flesh from which language is torn. But the Mother, "as she occupies the place of *Das Ding*", is raised to a different level. The sociological tone of "The family complexes" has gone. She is now *the* Mother, no longer *any* mother although mothers, and all women by extension, bear the weight of that association with *das Ding* in their lives.

In Seminar II, *The Ego* (1954–55), Lacan writes, not of *das Ding* by name, but of something that sounds like it. It is

the primitive object *par excellence*, the abyss of the feminine organ from which all life emerges, this gulf of the mouth, in which everything is swallowed up, and no less the image of death in which everything comes to its end . . . the ultimate real, the essential object which isn't an object any longer . . . the object of anxiety.

(*The Ego* 164)

Lacan is speaking here of the back of Irma's throat in Freud's dream – "the terrifying anxiety-provoking image . . . this real Medusa's head . . . the revelation of this something which properly speaking is unnameable". It is an "object" which isn't an object, something which devours all existence.

I am reminded of a James Thurber's story, *The Thirteen Clocks*, in which there is a terrifying creature not unlike the mother as *das Ding*. Named the Todal, it is made of lip, it cannot be killed and it gleeps (*Thirteen Clocks* 11). The Todal – interestingly named as it is a near homophone for "total" – swallows you up completely. The lip is also strange – a rim – half inside, half outside, and the gleeping. We are never told what gleeping is but it is safe to say that when you've been gleeped, nothing is left of you. The Todal is like a mouth, or a vagina, or a womb turned inside out – a negative made positive which, like the Medusa's head of snakes (the throat or vagina turned inside out), must never be seen. If you see it, you die.

All these are words and images, but words and images are how something of the experience (if it can be called an experience) of *das Ding* makes it into art. Art is an attempt to enclose the enclosing – to objectify it in some way before it devours you. Art, like the paintings in the cave, encircles a void and, treading a fine line, escapes being encircled by it.[2] But in doing so, by giving it form and substance, artists acknowledge it, even pay it a kind of homage. On the other hand, you could say that the encircling zero *creates* what is not, making nothing a something: "Fullness and emptiness", says Lacan – brought into a world that knew them not by the "fabricated signifier" of the potter's vase (*Ethics* 120) – are the terms by which *das Ding* comes into being as "that which in the real suffers from the signifier". The struggle to distinguish emptiness from fullness arises with that suffering and is not resolved.

In trying to speak of the creative moment, I find myself wanting to reverse everything – turn it inside out. *Das Ding* is a negative positive, an empty fullness. I dive into oxymoron in an attempt to indicate what language forbids. Lacan is making the same reversal with his reference to the Medusa's head in connection with Irma's throat. The glove becomes the hand, disturbing the neat complementarity he posited in his early writing, of the ideal of virility in the boy and of virginity in the girl – a brand new glove to fit the hand, a sheath for the sword – in fact the sexual relation.

In Lacan's *Ethics* seminar (Seminar VII), after his encounter with Claude Levi-Strauss and Ferdinand de Saussure, there is a shift away from the brute facts of dismemberment and live entombment to *das Ding* as the beyond-of-the-signifier, as "that which in the real suffers from the signifier". That suffering is the condition of speech (patriarchal intervention on a different level, that of "the name of the father") (*Écrits: A Selection* 67). The association remains, on a less sociological or historical plane, with a maternal darkness to which the idea of a return evokes both desire and horror:

What we find in the incest law is located as such at the level of the unconscious in relation to *das Ding*, the Thing. The desire for the mother cannot be satisfied because it is the end, the terminal point, the abolition of the whole world of demand, which is the one that at its deepest level structures man's unconscious.

(*Ethics* 68)

The function of the pleasure principle is to "make man always search for what he has to find again, but which he will never attain" (68). There is both an imperative to keep on searching and an imperative never to find, because to find is to be found and swallowed – to be gleeped. The "abyss of the feminine organ from which all life emerges" is also "the image of death in which everything comes to its end". The return is death. What is not clear and cannot be made clear is whether the prohibition against incest with the mother is in place as a curb to that dangerous desire of the child's or whether in fact it operates to spare the child from the mother's desire or the fear of the mother's desire.

The abyss of *das Ding* and the lack on which language is founded are the same vast and irreparable injury. But who desires whom? Who threatens whom? Who is active, who passive? It is not possible to say. It seems to erupt from a moment when those oppositions do not operate. The dialectic of language fails here, the chain of signification ruptures; it is "this something [the Real] faced with which all words cease and all categories fail" (*The Ego* 164).

The question is how to understand a creative act in terms of this chasm. As it is not possible to say whose desire is in question, one also cannot say whether, in Lacan's writing, the strangeness of *das Ding* is inside or outside the subject. *Das Ding* is "the first outside" but also "the strangeness at the heart of me". It is extimate. But there is something about the *unheimlich* moment when the inside is outside, the enclosed enclosing, the empty full, which speaks to that sudden creative flash, that combustible moment. Lacan speaks, in relation to Sade, of "a centre of incandescence or of an absolute zero that is physically unbearable" (*Ethics* 201). I wonder if he is recalling the passage from Sade to which he later refers in Seminar X, *Anxiety*:

> "I had", cries the tormentor, "I had the skin of the cunt". This is not a feature which is obvious along the track of the imaginable, and the privileged character, the moment of enthusiasm, the character of supreme trophy brandished at the high point of the chapter is something which, I believe, is sufficiently indicative of the following: it is that something is sought which is in a way the reverse (l'envers) of the subject, which takes on here its signification from this feature of the glove turned inside-out which underlines the feminine essence of the victim. It is the passage to the outside of what is most hidden that is involved.
>
> (*Anxiety* 114)

Here is the terror and ecstasy of the inside turned out. Again, in *Ethics* Lacan speaks of the function of the beautiful "to reveal to us the site of man's relationship to his own death, and to reveal it to us only in a blinding flash" (295). And of a will to destruction which is also a will to create from zero, a will to begin again (212). I think that zero from which one creates is the circle that outlines the empty fullness of *das Ding*.

In these passages, Lacan is speaking from that moment of the blinding flash. He is speaking as a poet, or, as he once said, a poem – on that edge, both and neither active nor passive. That is the major difference from the speaker of "The family complexes". This is the work he has done, the art he has made, with those archaic anxieties. There is no historical past in this moment; this is the time of Kairos. You cannot say what was there *before* – any more than Samuel can say what was there before "this hour in which I am"; the blinding flash tears apart (creates) the temporal chain as it disrupts (inaugurates) the chain of signifiers. But in that moment one does not flee the snapping jaws of the mother as *das Ding*. That is not the place where desire circles; desire hides behind the barrier erected by the pleasure principle. Nor is it a suicidal plunge into the abyss. It is not a return. The sudden strangeness is what alerts one to the opening of that impossible moment. It is the place where one grapples with *das Ding* on the very edge of the abyss and calls something forth – or tears it out.

That last sentence carries a reference to another Andalusian poet who lived 900 years after Samuel, Federico Garcia Lorca. He is speaking of fighting hand to hand on the rim of the well with the "duende". The duende was traditionally a kind of hobgoblin, a figure from popular Spanish culture, which Lorca brought into play to speak of the arts, particularly the performing arts and their effects on an audience. Lorca said, in "Play and Theory of the Duende": "The great artists of the south of Spain . . . whether they sing, dance, or play, know that no emotion is possible unless the duende comes" ("Play" 60). But if the duende brings the possibility of emotion, what brings the duende? It is death. The duende

> does not come at all unless he sees that death is possible. The duende must know beforehand that he can serenade's death's house and rock those branches we all wear, branches that do not have, will never have, any consolation. With idea, sound or gesture, the duende enjoys fighting the creator on the very rim of the well.
>
> (Federico Garcia Lorca, "Play of the *Duende*" 67)

That is the risk the artist takes, the risk of death, but without it nothing can be made.

Afterwards, after the moment of Kairos, one has to come back to chronological time and mop up, fill in the gaps, the ands and the buts, restore the linguistic logic that makes that impossible Thing speakable, although mutilated in speech. The difficulty – the impossibility – then is in recovering what it was that was known in that moment or who it was who knew it.

Notes

1 "Kairos is an ancient Greek word meaning the right or opportune moment (the supreme moment). The ancient Greeks had two words for time, chromos and kairos. While the

former refers to chronological or sequential time, the latter signifies a time between, a moment of indeterminate time in which something special happens. What the special something is depends on who is using the word. While chronos is quantitative, kairos has a qualitative nature" ("Kairos").

2 See Lacan on the cave art of Altamira (*Ethics* 139).

References

Lacan, J. (1938) *Family Complexes in the Formation of the Individual.* Translated by C. Gallagher. Unpublished. www.lacaninireland.com/web/wp-content/uploads/2010/06/FAMILY-COMPLEXES-IN-THE-FORMATION-OF-THE-INDIVIDUAL2.pdf

Lacan, J. (1962–1963) *The Seminar of Jacques Lacan Book X Anxiety 1962–1963.* Translated by C. Gallagher. Unpublished. www.lacaninireland.com/web/wp-content/uploads/2010/06/Seminar-X-Revised-by-Mary-Cherou-Lagreze.pdf

Lacan, J. (1977) *Écrits: A selection.* Translated by A. Sheridan. London: Tavistock Publications.

Lacan, J. (1991a) *The seminar of Jacques Lacan. Book 2, the Ego in Freud's Theory and in the Technique of Psychoanalysis, 1954–1955.* Edited by J.A. Miller. Translated by S. Tomaselli. Notes by J. Forrester. New York and London: W.W. Norton & Company.

Lacan, J. (1991b). *The Seminar of Jacques Lacan: The Ethics of Psychoanalysis, 1954–1955.* Edited by J.A. Miller. Translated by D. Porter. New York: W.W. Norton & Company. Vol. VII.

Lacan, J. (2007) *The Seminar of Jacques Lacan the Other Side of Psychoanalysis: Other Side of Psychoanalysis.* BK. XVII Translated by R. Grigg. New York: W.W. Norton & Company.

Lorca, F. G. (2010) *In Search of Duende. Prose Selections.* Edited by C. Maurer. Poems translated by N. di Giovanni, E. Honig, L. Hughes, L. Kemp, W. S. Merwin, S. Spender, J. L. Gili, & C. Maurer. New York: New Directions

NaHagid, S. (1981) The Moment. In: *The Penguin Book of Hebrew Verse.* Edited and Translated by T. Carmi. London: Penguin.

Project Gutenberg (2015a) *Kairos.* Gutenberg.org. http://self.gutenberg.org/article/whebn0000311973/kairos

Thurber, J. (1950) *The Thirteen Clocks.* http://img1.tapuz.co.il/forums/34104327.pdf

Part VI

Spaces of madness

Chapter 20

A speaker's corner

Jonathan Kettle

"Do you know what this means . . ."
A man, outpatient psychiatric clinic, Melbourne, Australia.

These words were screamed at us. The man was seething with fury and, as he clenched his fists, he paced around the room. He had attended, without notice, the psychiatric clinic in which I worked and had not passed through the usual, although not mandatory, channel of telephone contact and then an interview scheduled via an appointment. Patients may attend this clinic without an appointment and must be seen by a "duty" clinician. In the waiting room, he was on the verge of irruption. When in the interview room, the screaming began. Duty had called us to him.

The man had no prior contact with the clinic nor with anybody who worked there. Clearly, however, the man recognised the clinic's existence. As he paced, he screamed repeatedly, "Do you know what this means . . .", and whilst he screamed, he began dealing tarot cards onto the table and pointing at them. He pointed at tattoos, written in a foreign script, on his arms, and began to remove his t-shirt, bursting out of his skin. As he raged, I told him that I did not know what the tarot cards or the tattoos meant. He persisted screaming. He screamed at me about the chip that had been implanted behind his eye and that he might remove it. His final words before storming out of the clinic were, "I'm going to make Peyton pay".

The man requested to speak to anybody from the multitude at the clinic. I was called because I was "on duty". He was provided with two bodies – not one – as I instinctively enlisted the company of a colleague after I noticed his irruptive presence in the waiting room. The more he screamed, the more colleagues within the clinic thronged the interview room. These colleagues were visible from the interview room through the rectangular window in the interview room door.

"Do you know what this means . . .". Such words are normally a question but there was nothing normal about this encounter. These words were not a question. The man came to the clinic, without appointment or invitation, and only tore himself away after screaming these words, repeatedly, at those within the clinic. Why? Let us begin with transference.

DOI: 10.4324/9781003212720-26

In Freud's oeuvre, transference was predominantly, though not exclusively, developed and reworked in relation to neurosis. The first overt discussion of transference in Freud's published writings is in Chapter IV, Psychotherapy of Hysteria, in *Studies on Hysteria*.[1] At the point of his pressure technique failing, Freud postulated that the content of an unconscious wish, but not memories of its surrounding circumstances, became conscious and the content of this wish was transferred onto the analyst. This was transference. Freud nominated this as a *"mésalliance"*.[2] He used the French word in the original German text yet, in an attempt at explanation, he also described the process with the German *"falsche Verknüpfung"*,[3] which was translated by Strachey as "false connection".[4] *Mésalliance* speaks where false connection is silent.

Mésalliance historically connotes a marriage of one to another who is out of place due to the latter's inferior social status. Crucially, and this is crucial, the other is out of place because he or she is where someone else is supposed to be. Transference, as *mésalliance*, is deception. It is no accident that the example that furnished Freud's theorisation in *Studies on Hysteria* was a female patient who was apprehensive that Freud might kiss her – no better way for him to be taken as another! Freud was not like someone else, nor was he as someone else, but he was someone else, supposed.

Freud recognised the deception of the transference, thereby not dissolving the deception but permitting him to work with it through speech. On the other hand, at least at the beginning of an analysis, the analysand is deceived by the deception itself in the *mésalliance* (such that it is not recognised).[5] The principle that in neurosis transference is deception persists in Freud's writings in the subsequent two decades, including in such seminal papers as *Fragment of an Analysis of a Case of Hysteria*,[6] *The Dynamics of Transference*[7] and *Observations of Transference Love*.[8]

Freud did attempt to theorise transference in relation to psychosis, albeit in a manner that was neither as clearly articulated as it was in neurosis, nor formulated to a point of praxis.

How does transference function in Freud's major clinical and theoretical working of psychosis, *Psychoanalytical Notes on a Case of Paranoia (Dementia Paranoides)*?[9] Freud's analysis of this text was predicated upon a working of transference that established the psychological conditions that necessitated *Wahnbildung*[10] – the "delusion formation" – to thus produce Schreber's madness. Freud's interpretation of Schreber's delusion was that it developed in relation to alterations in the investment of his libido. He proposed that Schreber's delusion was built not only from the withdrawal of Schreber's libido from the external world but from the reinvestment of libido to Professor Fleschig and God. Freud proposed that *Wahnbildung* operated as a compromise formation in relation to his struggle against the homosexual investment of libido, itself intertwined in the operation of transference. Crucially, Freud interpreted that God and Fleschig were Schreber's father and brother, whom Schreber loved. Freud argued that Schreber's libido was subject to a process of transference[11] through his brother, father,

Fleschig and God. Thus, Freud interpreted Schreber's madness as neurotic by using the principle of transference as *mésalliance*. His interpretation relied upon deception as the mechanism that effected a metaphorical substitution,[12] in his madness, amongst Schreber's father, brother, Fleschig and God.[13]

Freud's analysis of Schreber's text yields a tension when read in conjunction with his attempt to theorise transference in psychosis in his other papers in the years immediately following: *The Dynamics of Transference* and *On Narcissism: An Introduction*. In these two papers, Freud grappled with the perplexing relation of psychotic patients to others in their worlds after their psychotic breaks, and by extension whether deception might occur in a psychotic patient's transference to an analyst. He traversed positions that either there was no relation to others and thus no transference, or there was a secondary or partial relation to others (Freud did not clarify in the text what this was), or that there was such negativity in the transference that it precluded psychoanalysis.[14] All three possibilities do not tally with Freud's analysis of Schreber's madness, imbued as the analysis was with a transference brimming with deception and eroticism.

Let us return to my encounter with the man. Remember his repeated scream: "Do you know what this means . . .". These words were not a question, which would have implied that that which was before him was instead something else – deception. Deception did not operate in the encounter with this man. It was the truth that operated.

What differentiates psychosis from neurosis? It is language and, by extension, truth. Fundamentally, as Lacan extensively developed in *Seminar III: The Psychoses*, whereas "the neurotic inhabits language, the psychotic is inhabited, possessed, by language".[15] A consequence of the neurotic inhabiting language is that the neurotic "to a greater or lesser extent speaks out in language with all his being, that is, in part unknowingly".[16] The neurotic thinks that by speaking he will say what he wants to say. However, he is prey to the trap that one must then infer that something else is said.[17] Truth is only ever half-said. The neurotic, as soon as he opens his mouth, is under the sway of *mésalliance*, deception and a half-said truth.

And for the psychotic? The psychotic is used by language. He does not labour, with his speech, under the illusion of using language in order to say what he wants to say. The psychotic becomes a vehicle through which language itself speaks, inhabiting him, parasitic. The man's tarot cards, tattoos, the "this" of "Do you know what this means . . .", they were not links in a chain of deception that produces a half-said truth – they were not something else, which was something else, which was something else, which. . .

What was it that language was speaking, with this man as its vehicle? It was speaking not a metaphorical chain of deception, not a half-said truth, but the truth, upon which the tarot cards, tattoos, the "this" converged. This was the essence of the man's transference.

Such transference has been recognised before. Oscar Zentner, in a paper published in 1996, *Connaissance and Psychosis*,[18] proposed a reworking of the psychotic transference, in which the analyst, in the transference, is not the subject-supposed-to-know but the subject-supposed-*connaissance*. Zentner argued that there indeed is a transference in psychosis and that it is marked by the fusion of knowledge and truth. In my reading, the fusion of knowledge and truth yields a certainty of the truth, quite in distinction to the doubt that impels the neurotic to seek the truth but to forever come up short, plagued by the realisation that it is only ever a half-said truth that he speaks and receives. Antecedents of Zentner's proposition exist in his paper, *Psychoanalysis*, published 16 years prior, in which, being an examination of the nature of psychoanalysis itself, Zentner proposed that "psychoanalysis deals with the truth insofar as it does not reach it".[19] He additionally proposed the truth as being a "logical truth . . . that is to say, without any division between knowledge and truth".[20]

Returning to my question: why, then, did this man come to the clinic, without invitation or schedule, scream these words, and leave? I propose that he did so in an attempt to alter his relation to the truth; that is to say, to do something to the transference in which he was encapsulated. How did the man attempt this?

What the man received at the clinic was a crowd – first two in the interview room, and then many peering through the window inset in the door. I propose that this mass of bodies served a function for him in his attempt to alter his relation to the truth.

My encounter holds some important similarities to and differences from the presentation of patients, another encounter in which a patient and a mass of bodies is involved. In the presentation of patients in the Freudian School of Melbourne, it has been the analyst who interviews the patient, often supposed psychotic. The analyst initially sustains the interview through his own transference with the patient as the subject-supposed-to-know.[21] Without such a supposition by the analyst, the interview will collapse. The clinic in which I worked, by supplying, out of duty, a clinician in this fashion, supposes that any person, regardless of psychiatric diagnosis or structure, holds a knowledge that can be articulated and heard. Such a supposition operated in my encounter with this man.

However, and crucially, the collection of others[22] in this encounter came to exist through a different process than that which convokes the audience in the presentation of patients. In the presentation of patients, the audience convokes because, in conjunction with their transference to the patient as a subject-supposed-to-know, a demand is made upon the patient by another, often an employee of the psychiatric facility in which the patient resides, to attend to speak to an analyst, with the others in the room as an audience.

On the contrary, in this encounter from the clinic, it was the man who convoked the others through the barrage of language that bore the truth. Furthermore, there was no demand made upon this man by an employee of the clinic that he attend the clinic. The demand, and there absolutely was one, residing in this barrage of language, came from the man. The sheer force of his language, bearing the truth, convoked the others around the interview room.

I propose that this mass of bodies, this collection of little others, functioned to provide this man with the possibility of effecting a space beyond the place of the

A speaker's corner   179

fusion of knowledge and truth. This could occur through the literal substantiation, composed of a mass of bodies, of a beyond that was a place not of deception, nor of the truth, but a place in which nothing of the truth was known.[23] The screaming, "Do you know what this means . . ." was insistent precisely to enforce that in the place of the flesh that substantiated the beyond, "this" was not known.

In such a fashion, the clinic can function as a speaker's corner and a space, located outside a fusion of truth and knowledge, in which "this", which is not known, can exist.[24]

Notes

1 Joseph Breuer & Sigmund Freud, Studies on Hysteria, in *The Standard Edition of the Complete Psychological Works of Sigmund Freud,* edited by Anna Freud & James Strachey, translated by James Strachey, Hogarth Press, London, 1955, Vol. II, pp. 1–309, 302. The discussion of the relation between "*mésalliance*", "*falsche Verknüpfung*" and "false connection" that follows is in relation to Freud also introducing transference at this point in *Studies on Hysteria* with the term that he came to use consistently in his work to denote this concept: *Übertragung*.

2 Joseph Breuer & Sigmund Freud, Studies on Hysteria, in *The Standard Edition of the Complete Psychological Works of Sigmund Freud,* edited by Anna Freud & James Strachey, translated by James Strachey, Hogarth Press, London, 1955, Vol. II, pp. 1–309, 303.

3 Joseph Breuer & Sigmund Freud, Studien über Hysterie, in *Gesammelte Werke, Erster Band, Werke Aus Den Jahren 1892–1899,* Imago Publishing, London, 1952, pp. 1–311, 309. An edition of *Studies on Hysteria* that provides the original German text and the English translation alongside has been compiled by Richard G. Stern and is available at www.freud2lacan.com/docs/Studies_on_Hysteria.pdf

4 Joseph Breuer & Sigmund Freud, Studies on Hysteria, in *The Standard Edition of the Complete Psychological Works of Sigmund Freud,* edited by Anna Freud & James Strachey, translated by James Strachey, Hogarth Press, London, 1955, Vol. II, pp. 1–309, 303.

5 Freud wrote of this deception by the deception itself regarding his patient with an erotic transference: "strangely enough, the patient is deceived afresh every time this [a transference and a false connection] is repeated". In Joseph Breuer & Sigmund Freud, Studies on Hysteria, in *The Standard Edition of the Complete Psychological Works of Sigmund Freud,* edited by Anna Freud & James Strachey, translated by James Strachey, Hogarth Press, London, 1955, Vol. II, pp. 1–309, 303.

6 Sigmund Freud, Fragment of an Analysis of a Case of Hysteria, in *The Standard Edition of the Complete Psychological Works of Sigmund Freud,* edited by Anna Freud & James Strachey, translated by James Strachey, Hogarth Press, London, 1953, Vol. II, pp. 3–124.

7 Sigmund Freud, Fragment of an Analysis of a Case of Hysteria, in *The Standard Edition of the Complete Psychological Works of Sigmund Freud,* edited by Anna Freud & James Strachey, translated by James Strachey, Hogarth Press, London, 1958, Vol. II, pp. 97–108, 103.

8 Sigmund Freud, Observations on Transference Love, in *The Standard Edition of the Complete Psychological Works of Sigmund Freud,* edited by Anna Freud & James Strachey, translated by James Strachey, Hogarth Press, London, 1958, Vol. II, pp. 157–171.

9 Sigmund Freud, Psycho-analytical Notes on an Autobiographical Account of a Case of Paranoia (Dementia Paranoides), in *The Standard Edition of the Complete*

180   Jonathan Kettle

Psychological Works of Sigmund Freud, edited by Anna Freud & James Strachey, translated by James Strachey, Hogarth Press, London, 1958, Vol. XII, pp. 1–84.

10 Sigmund Freud, Psychoanalytische Bemerkungen über einen autobiographisch beschriebenen Fall von Paranoia (Dementia paranoides), in *Studienausgabe Band VII: Zwang, Paranoia und Perversion*, Fischer Verlag, Frankfurt am Main, 1973, pp. 135–203, 194.

11 The German text uses the word, "*Übertragung*", the noun that Freud used consistently since at least 1905, and introduced in 1895, in his writing to denote transference. Sigmund Freud, Psychoanalytische Bemerkungen über einen autobiographisch beschriebenen Fall von Paranoia (Dementia paranoides), in *Studienausgabe Band VII: Zwang, Paranoia und Perversion*, Fischer Verlag, Frankfurt am Main, 1973, pp. 135–203, 175. Whilst Freud did not retain writing *mésalliance* for transference in his work in his career, his usage of *Übertragung* retains the essence of *mésalliance*: deception.

12 I am not proposing that metaphor operated in Schreber's madness.

13 Lacan was able to extract, and develop, something other than deception from his reading of Freud's analysis of Schreber's text, in conjunction with his reading of Freud's case of the Wolfman. This was the mechanism in psychosis of foreclosure, not of deception, and hinged upon two German words: *Aufgehobene* and *Verwerfung*. In his analysis of Schreber's psychosis, Freud made an erudite comment about a mechanism of paranoia, distinct from projection, which was that "what was abolished internally returns from without" (Sigmund Freud, Psycho-analytical Notes on an Autobiographical Account of a Case of Paranoia (Dementia Paranoides), in *The Standard Edition of the Complete Psychological Works of Sigmund Freud*, edited by Anna Freud & James Strachey, translated by James Strachey, Hogarth Press, London, 1958, pp. 1–84, 71). The German that was translated as "abolished" was *Aufgehobene*, from *Aufheben*. In his analysis of the Wolfman's history, Freud proposed a period in which the Wolfman had rejected castration, which he inferred not only from the Wolfman's position on sexual knowledge but also from the manifestation of a hallucination. In relation to the Wolfman's position on sexual knowledge, Freud proposed that a fear of castration and an identification with the Wolfman's mother (Sigmund Freud, From The History of An Infantile Neurosis, in *The Standard Edition of the Complete Psychological Works of Sigmund Freud*, edited by Anna Freud & James Strachey, translated by James Strachey, Hogarth Press, London, 1955, Vol. XVII, pp. 3–122, 79–80), though contradictory, co-existed in the unconscious through *Verdrängung* because *Verdrängung* was not *Verwerfung* (Sigmund Freud, Aus der Geschichte einer infantilen Neurose ["Der Wolfsmann"], in *Studienausgabe Band VIII Zwei Kinderneurosen*, Fischer Wissenschaft, 1969, pp. 125–231, 195). In this instance, Strachey confusingly translated *Verwerfung* as "condemning judgement". This translation of *Verwerfung* as "condemning judgement" contradicts his translation of *verwarf*, three pages later (page 198 of the German text and page 84 of the English text), as "rejected", a passage in which Freud wrote *verwarf* to designate the process underpinning his clinical observation that, at times, it was not that castration was condemningly judged by the Wolfman but it was that castration did not exist for him. To be judged, something must first exist. Strachey's translation completely unravels an intricate thread in Freud's text (intricate in that he posited the operation of two different psychical mechanisms upon castration, *Verdrängung* and *Verwerfung*, at different moments for the Wolfman) that can only be rewoven if one consults the German! Lacan did so, and it was from these two gems in Freud's analyses of Schreber and the Wolfman that Lacan thrust *Verwerfung*, with considerable labour, into light as the central mechanism of psychosis in his *Seminar III: The Psychoses* (Jacques Lacan, *The Seminar of Jacques Lacan. Book III: The Psychoses. 1955–1956*, edited by Jacques-Alain Miller, translated by Russell Grigg, W. W. Norton, New York/London, 1993, see p. 46 and p. 12). Certainly, *Verwerfung*

was not the thrust of Freud's analysis of Schreber's psychosis; it was *mésalliance* and deception.

14 Sigmund Freud, The Dynamics of Transference, in *The Standard Edition of the Complete Psychological Works of Sigmund Freud*, edited by Anna Freud & James Strachey, translated by James Strachey, Hogarth Press, London, 1958, Vol. XII, pp. 97–108, 107. Sigmund Freud, On Narcissism: An Introduction, in *The Standard Edition of the Complete Psychological Works of Sigmund Freud*, edited by Anna Freud & James Strachey, translated by James Strachey, Hogarth Press, London, 1957, Vol. XIV, pp. 69–102, 86.

15 Jacques Lacan, *The Seminar of Jacques Lacan. Book III: The Psychoses. 1955–1956*, edited by Jacques-Alain Miller, translated by Russell Grigg, W. W. Norton, New York and London, 1993, p. 250.

16 Ibid., pp. 249–250.

17 Lacan had commented on this colloquialism itself in his paper *Variations on the Standard Treatment* (Jacques Lacan, Variations on the Standard Treatment, in *Ecrits*, translated by Bruce Fink, W. W. Norton, New York and London, 2006, pp. 269–302, 275), in that it speaks the disjunction between one's conscious intention and the articulation of the subject through speech itself, the gap between which is a logical necessity posed by the French, "*Il veut dire*".

18 O. Zentner, *Connaissance* and Psychosis, *Papers of the Freudian School of Melbourne*, 17 (1996): 127–140.

19 O. Zentner, Psychoanalysis, *Papers of the Freudian School of Melbourne*, 1 (1980): 59–72, 64.

20 Ibid., p. 64.

21 David Pereira & Luis Riebl, From Transference to Structure: The Presentation of Patients, *Papers of the Freudian School of Melbourne*, 14 (1993): 55–62. M. Plastow, The Presentation of Patients and the Question of Structure, *Écritique, Letters of the Freudian School of Melbourne*, 8 (2011), www.fsom.org.au/ecritique2011%20index. html

22 We were not an audience because, I for one, spoke back to him.

23 Erik Porge proposed an effect that was due to the composition of others as an audience during the presentation of patients. He proposed the audience afforded a third place to which, indirectly, both analyst and patient spoke at different times. This audience, beyond the boundary of the stage, was silent, not speaking of or to the patient, not duplicating the mental automatism of psychosis. Porge proposed this as the mechanism in which the presentation of patients, for a psychotic patient, has "a calming role on the suffering of the imposition of speech . . . because this elsewhere functions as a boundary". In E. Porge, The Presentation of Patients: Charcot, Freud, Lacan, Today, *Papers of the Freudian School of Melbourne*, 15 (1994): 163–175, 174. I am proposing not a boundary but the substantiation of a space, created, that is beyond the fusion of truth and knowledge.

24 Whilst I was writing this paper, I noticed two other men, in separate locations. One was standing atop a brick pillar on a corner thronged by people, as it was the intersection of two busy streets in the central business district of Melbourne. One hand brandished a megaphone, the other some papers; a torrent of exhortation, admonition and biblical quotations spewed forth. He looked at the ground and never made eye contact with anyone. The other man, Howard, wore a placard emblazoned with, "I have discovered the secret of eternal youth", as he wandered around Speaker's Corner in Hyde Park, England, ready to speak to any members of the crowd who would listen about his immortality. His comment was, "I'm not there to convince them that I'm right. They can go away and think I'm a complete lunatic, for all that matters". Exactly. Available at www.youtube.com/watch?v=syNx6xnCcEw

Chapter 21

Close to the wild child[¶]

Peter Gunn

What is it about madness that we should want to get close to it? Putting the question of our engagement with madness in this way might suggest that it is akin to pursuing a wild animal. If so, this is an animal which, though it might leave some trace of its passing, remains always beyond our range.

That is, in tracking this beast, we can get no further than the outskirts. But can we even locate these outskirts? Are they the outskirts which mark the boundary of our own domain, or are they the outskirts of the territory of the animal itself? Not only that. Given our disorientation, is it possible that the animal could break through and take a piece out of us? Even more confusing than that, might we find, if we dare to go on, that, not only are these boundaries rather fluid, but that, paradoxically, it is this same piece, that is, the one taken out of us, which has been leading us astray all along?

Certainly, these are questions which have come to pose themselves to me through my own pursuit of madness. In recent years, I have conducted this pursuit primarily by way of my clinical and theoretical work as a psychoanalyst, but I have taken my lead from the work of artists. I should say, however, that I am using the term "artist" here in a way that takes it well outside its usual domain of reference.

It's not by chance that, in 1945, in an attempt to categorise the productions of mad people who were outside the stereotype of artist, Jean Dubuffet came up with the term "*art brut*".[1] The French word *brut* has connotations of the savage or bestial. But, as was the case with the word *fauve*, which, in an earlier period, came to refer to certain French post-impressionist painters whose work was seen as placing them outside the accepted canon, the reference of the word *brut* can easily slip from the art to the one who has produced the art; it is now the artist who is the wild beast. More worryingly, it can also come to refer what might be let loose in those exposed to it; this, we might say, is the beast within.[2]

In this vein, the "art" which has drawn me along in the present project is that of Fernand Deligny. Deligny has been categorised as an educator and social worker, and sometimes, in an acknowledgement of his productivity, as a writer; he was also a film-maker. But perhaps only the appellation "artist" goes some way to encompassing the aberrancy of his work.

DOI: 10.4324/9781003212720-27

Certainly, one way or another, Deligny did spend all of his adult life with children and adolescents. Many of these young people were regarded by mainstream institutions as refractory and uncontrollable.[3] They included those deemed psychotic, as well as recidivist juvenile offenders.[4] In the years straddling World War II, he did so whilst formally employed in roles which more or less approximated that of a teacher, including 4 years as a specialist teacher at the asylum of Armentières.[5] After World War II, Deligny created the Grande Cordée, an experiment which was originally designed to keep delinquent adolescents out of institutions, including psychiatric hospitals.[6]

In a continuation of that experiment, Deligny and his associates, along with his then partner Huguette Dumoulin and their young daughter, lived for several years with a number of such young people in the Cévennes region, a remote and unforgiving mountainous environment in the south of France.[7] Following the collapse of that experiment due to a lack of financial support, Deligny spent 2 years at La Borde, the clinic run by Jean Oury and Félix Guattari.

My interest in Deligny's work is, however, focused on the period beginning in the summer of 1967 when Deligny left La Borde to return to the Cévennes, where he remained for the rest of his life. It was there that he established what he called, in an allusion to the way the French resistance organised itself during World War II, a "network". Here he, in company with a few other adults, lived in close proximity with the children who came to be placed in his care.

With this sequestered experiment, or, to use his term, *tentative*,[8] Deligny seems to have embraced the position of outsider artist. As for the children, it seems that what "troubled" them had already placed them outside. Most did not speak and some were seen as so uncontrollable that they needed to be institutionalised; in medical terms they would now be described as profoundly autistic.

He himself described his *tentative* as a work of art.[9] In doing so, he rejected any categorisation, either of the children or the adults. The children were not social defects, but defectors from the social function as such.[10] The adults too had defected. In committing themselves to living without pay and in close proximity, but yet, necessarily, at a distance, to these children, they were neither teachers, psychologists, educators, nurses, social workers, or even researchers.

The primary motivation of Deligny's *tentative* was not therapeutic. Nor, on the other hand, was it intended to be rehabilitative for the adults. If there was some effect which might be judged, retrospectively, to be either therapeutic or rehabilitative, this was by chance. Deligny's *tentative* was an always-in-becoming, and thus also never-ending, project.

If his *tentative* could be said to have a purpose, it was to attempt to evoke, or activate, what he called the "common". This common is the conjunction of the living-space inhabited by the adults and the outside space inhabited by the autistic children.[11] For us, domesticated "humans-that-we-are",[12] this space is not just *liminary* but *pre-liminary*, or, to go beyond Deligny, even *ex-liminary*.[13] If we might think of this space as being on the margins of our world, it is also beyond it. There is no way of making a bridge between it and the all-too-well-symbolised world which we inhabit, including the intentional, doing-the-job, space of therapeutics. In other words, as Deligny puts it, the common never shows itself to us in the light of day.[14]

And yet, given the close, intensely interested, yet purposeless, proximity which Deligny and his collaborators maintained with the children over many years, when they children were "activated", that is, when they seemed to take the initiative in their wanderings, this common did come to manifest itself topographically. Deligny and his company made maps of the children's "wander-lines", and also of the associated "customary"[15] journeys of the "close presences"[16] who lived with them in close proximity in the living areas. By comparing these maps, various points of overlap and intersection, or, as Deligny puts it, "cross-beams" (*chevêtres*)[17] or points of *here* (*là*), could be discerned. For the children, these seemed to be points of attraction, sometimes to water, and also to some repeated gesture on the part of one or other of the adults.

The child who accompanied Deligny at the outset to the Cévennes was Jean-Marie J., a 12-year-old entrusted to him by his mother. Deligny met him at the end of 1966 when he was at La Borde.[18] He was mute; he had never spoken a word. In 1965 he had been diagnosed by a psychiatrist at the Salpêtrière psychiatric hospital in Paris as having "acute encephalopathy" with psychotic traits. In a voice over to the film *Ce Gamin, là*, which takes the boy as its focus, Deligny describes the place to which society had assigned him as "incurable, unbearable [and] unlivable".[19]

Later, Deligny "rebaptised" Jean-Marie as Janmari, saying that in doing this he was acknowledging that, in the same way as Victor, the so-called wild boy of Aveyron, he had always been outside all the usual rituals, both civil and sexual.[20] In 1968 Deligny wrote to the film-maker François Truffaut about Janmari. In a striking coincidence, it seems that Deligny was trying to interest him in a film which would take Janmari as its focus.[21] Unbeknown to him, Truffaut had already begun work on *L'Enfant Sauvage* (The Wild Child), his film based on the story of the wild boy of Aveyron.

In describing Janmari to Truffaut, Deligny already drew on images of the child-as-animal. He implicitly compares Janmari to Mowgli, the village boy in Rudyard Kipling's *Jungle Book*. By extension, in its animality, Deligny seems to see the life of his community as akin to that of the pack of wolves which raises Mowgli as its own:

> A kid 12 years old who hasn't said a word his whole life. He is neither deaf nor dumb, agile as a chimpanzee. . . . Here [in the Cévennes] he goes naked when he can in the sun; you could say that he knows by heart all those passages from *The Jungle Book*. He dances in front of the fire . . . he sniffs for a long time what he eats. He's beautiful, except when he scowls, just like a young orangutan.[22]

Deligny's *tentative* seems to have been an attempt to both *accommodate* and *activate* this animal-outside which he takes children such as Janmari to inhabit. But this works both ways. He says at one point that at the outset, in 1967, that he was "in search of a mode of being that allowed them to exist even if that meant changing our own mode . . .".[23]

In reflecting on one moment of intersection or overlap of the paths of the adults and the children, in this case involving him and Janmari, Deligny provides a glimpse of the wildness of this animal-territory beyond the "self" into which this change in "our" mode might lead "us":

> Fortunately, there are some, the de-voted, the un-avowed, even if they are rare, even if they are autistic, to remind us of an "order" other than the law, and which would be that of the very nature of this "animal" itself before the vow, it being understood that that "before" persists as prelude despite the predominance, which seeks to be absolute and exclusive, of the SELF without which there might be some tracing, perhaps, but no writing at all.[24]

Certainly, the prospect of this outside seems already to have been activating for Deligny himself. His relationship to the asylum gives some indication of this. In the early 1930s, when he was still a young man living at home in Lille, he and two friends would pay regular visits to the asylum at Armentières.[25] Deligny says of this time, "I loved the asylum. Take the word as you will: I loved it . . .".[26] What this confinement afforded him, somewhat paradoxically, was proximity to the outside. This, I suggest, is what he loved in the asylum.

It is not surprising to learn, therefore, that, in 1983, in the midst of a debate in France on the "sectorisation" of mental health services and the associated closing down of psychiatric hospitals, Deligny wrote a little book titled *Éloge de l'asile* (*In Praise of the Asylum*).[27] According to L'inactualité de Fernand Deligny. Op. cit., p. 21, "[t]he asylum became his island, both the place for a second birth and for a definitive inner exile, the condition for writing, the institutional and spatial model for his future *tentatives*".[28]

I propose however that for Deligny the asylum was not a passive cloistering from the outside world. As the institutional structure *par excellence* which attempts to encompass what is always radically outside, the asylum was not just the condition for Deligny's future *tentatives* but was itself a *tentative*. It enabled Deligny to bring the outside as such into proximity. As such, the asylum can be considered as providing the imaginary structure for his later *tentatives*. My corollary proposition is that the extremity of Deligny's *tentative* is such that it must be located beyond any debating position, however radical, on the question of the psychiatric institution.

These propositions are not however the primary concern of this paper, and I will not be making an explicit case for them. I want to focus not on individual psychology or the history of the institution, but on the logic of Deligny's practice in his *tentative*. It may be that what I am putting forward will provide support for my propositions, but I will leave it to the reader to make that assessment.

In order, as it were, to set the scene for this, I want to consider the site of another *tentative*. This one is also located in the south of France, and although it too is imaginary, it has the advantage of being expressly fictional.

The narrator of Edgar Allen Poe's short story "The System of Doctor Tarr and Professor Fether"[29] is an American tourist who has been travelling, with a companion, through what is described as "the extreme southern provinces of France". It so happens that his route takes him to within a few miles of a *Maison de Santé*, or private madhouse, which had been set up in an isolated chateau.

This establishment has adopted what Poe calls the "system of soothing". This is an allusion to what came to be known, following initiatives taken more or less contemporaneously at the end of the 18C by the English Quaker philanthropist William Tuke and the French secular physician Philippe Pinel, as "moral treatment" of the insane.[30]

This soothing system is of great interest to the narrator's medical friends back in Paris and, on an impulse, he decides to take leave of his companion and make an inspection. Fearing however that he might have difficulty in gaining access, and learning that his companion had previously made the acquaintance of the superintendent, a Monsieur Maillard, he accepts his offer to take him as far as the gate in order to introduce him.

Characteristically, in describing the narrator's approach to the world of this asylum, Poe begins to draw the reader himself into a domain which, in an echo of Deligny's description of the place to which society has relegated Janmari, is not just down a by-path, but "scarcely tenantable":

> I thanked [my companion], and, turning from the main road, we entered a grass-grown by-path, which, in half an hour, nearly lost itself in a dense forest, clothing the base of a mountain. Through this dank and gloomy wood we rode some two miles, when the *Maison de Santé* came in view. It was a fantastic *château*, much dilapidated, and indeed scarcely tenantable through age and neglect. Its aspect inspired me with absolute dread, and, checking my horse, I half resolved to turn back. I soon, however, grew ashamed of my weakness, and proceeded.[31]

At first glance, the narrator finds that, in keeping with the moral treatment reforms, the inmates of this institution, who would previously have been treated like wild beasts and kept in irons, have been allowed to roam about the house and grounds and wear ordinary clothing. In addition, both punishments and confinements are avoided.

By the end of his visit however the narrator comes to the realisation that he has been duped. In the world of this "fantastic" chateau the tables have been turned. Monsieur Maillard has himself gone mad and led the other inmates in a revolt. It is now the keepers who are the kept, and with no consideration of moral treatment. Pinioned hand and foot and thrown into the old confinement cells, they have been reduced to occasionally howling like a pack of wild dogs.

Doubling this twist, Monsieur Maillard reveals this "revolution" to the narrator in the course of an apparently rational discussion of the consequences of allowing lunatics too much liberty. But this revelation is itself hidden within a deception. Maillard speaks as if these events had happened sometime in the past. On the contrary, they are happening as he speaks. The head rebel (that is, Maillard himself, masquerading as the superintendent) has only been prepared to allow the narrator into the asylum on the basis that he is a "very stupid-looking young gentleman" and presents no threat. He does this, furthermore, "just by way of variety, – to have a little fun with him".[32]

One critic has suggested that Poe's innocent narrator is a satire directed at Charles Dickens' naiveté in relation to his enthusiastic support for the moral treatment of the insane.[33] Certainly, in the account in *American Notes* of the visits he made in 1842 to two New England asylums, Dickens does indicate his support for institutions run according to "those enlightened principles of conciliation and kindness . . .".[34]

There is a further parallel with the Poe story. Of one of these visits Dickens comments that

> I very much questioned within myself, as I walked through the Insane Asylum, whether I should have known the attendants from the patients, but for the few words which passed between the former, and the Doctor, in reference to the persons under their charge.[35]

What is in play in all of this is of the order of appearances, appearances which can, when it comes to differentiating between who is mad and who is not, be deceptive. Monsieur Maillard himself warns the narrator, ironically, that it is "[w] hen a madman *appears* thoroughly sane. . . [that] it is high time to put him in a straitjacket".[36] Dickens himself qualifies his remarks by acknowledging that they are limited to the looks of the inmates. When it came to conversation, he judged this to be mad enough.

The emphasis on the deceptiveness, and concealed menace, of appearances in Poe's story recalls Michel Foucault's famous account of the part which moral treatment played in the birth of the insane asylum. If, in classical confinement, the gaze of the keeper went "no deeper than the monstrous surface of [the inmate's] visible bestiality", there was at least a recognition of that bestiality: "healthy men could read there, as in a mirror, the imminent movement of their own fall".[37]

By contrast, the new regime was directed precisely at house-training this bestiality and, at the same time, paradoxically, removing it to the dungeons. In an asylum run according to these principles, madness, in being constantly corrected by reference to the codes of good behaviour, is made to dissimulate probity and, at the same time, to keep silent about that dissimulation. If there is closeness between keeper and kept, there is no reciprocity:

> [Madness] is judged on its actions alone; its intentions are not put on trial, and no attempt is made to plumb its secret depths. It is only answerable for

the part of itself that is visible. All the rest is reduced to silence. Madness no longer exists except as that which is seen. The proximity that comes into being in the asylum, in the absence of chains and bars, does not encourage reciprocal interaction. It is simply that of a piercing gaze, observing, scrutinizing, moving pitilessly close the better to see, while remaining sufficiently distant to avoid any contamination by the values of the Stranger.[38]

But Poe's fiction, as I read it in this context, takes us beyond any such critique of the moral treatment of the insane, including of the more recent, "de-institutionalised" variants of that model. Poe creates a phantasmagoric world where nothing is at it appears, and where, as a result, the unboundedness of madness can at any moment erupt and turn the tables. Indeed, this turning of the tables can go so far as to put in doubt not only what is being seen, but the solidity of the "self" who is supposed to be speaking.

Even in the course of an apparently sane "conversation", what appears, at the beginning, to be a humorous but otherwise disinterested report, given in the third person and in the past tense, about the madness of another, can turn into an act of madness by the speaker. More than that, it can turn out that what the speaker is enacting, and not only in speech but also in gesture, is his own madness.

The person the narrator first encounters on entering the asylum provides a good example of this. Supposedly Monsieur Maillard's niece, and also supposedly his assistant at the asylum, this "young and very beautiful woman" is seen accompanying herself in the parlour singing an aria from an opera by Bellini. Already, the narrator is drawn in, describing her as follows:

> Her voice was low, and her whole manner subdued. I thought too that I perceived the traces of sorrow in her countenance, which was excessively, although to my taste, not unpleasantly pale. She was attired in deep mourning, and excited in my bosom a feeling of mingled respect, interest, and admiration.[39]

The narrator's next encounter upends this whole performance, including the part played in it by the narrator himself. On this occasion this same young woman begins by apparently reporting on the madness of one of the inmates, one called Eugénie Salsafette, ". . . a very beautiful and painfully modest young lady, who thought the ordinary mode of habiliment indecent, and wished to dress herself, always, by getting outside instead of inside her clothes". But so saying, and to exclamations of horror from all present, the young woman, who we now see is this same Eugénie Salsafette, promptly "dresses herself": "It is a thing very easily done, after all. You have only to do so – and then so – so – so – and then so – so – so – and then – . . .".[40]

If Poe's story carries an insistence which brings the innocent narrator, and, by identification, the innocent reader, into proximity with madness, this is not for the purpose of making an assessment of such behaviour. As Mlle. Eugénie Salsafette's two performances indicate, this is a world where oppositions, such as that between surface and depth, self and other and mad and not-mad, are overturned.

On the basis of Mlle. Salsafette's first performance, our narrator, with his refined and discrete eroticism, discerns "secret depths". But his discernment is given a kick in the teeth by her second display. So relentlessly inhuman is the logic of her action on this occasion that, even though she might end up getting outside her clothes, what is revealed is that she herself is beyond any such "self"-oriented appraisal. What is also revealed, as an effect of this "out-becoming", is that the surveying and sovereign "self" of the narrator has no clothes.

With Poe's upending in mind, I would now like to return to Deligny's *tentative* in order give further consideration to its logic.

It needs to be remembered that the autistic children with whom Deligny and his companions lived in close proximity were mute; for the most part they did not speak. From the perspective of the adults who inhabit language, their world was radically outside. From that perspective also, the world which they inhabited was silent. However, as Deligny points out with reference to Janmari, if it was just a question of breaking that silence, "an autistic being can easily make himself or herself heard. On occasion, the autistic being close to whom I have lived for quite a long time barks by yelping . . .".[41]

In writing about the children's supposed lack of voice, Deligny plays on the homophony, in French, between the word for "path" (*voie*) and that for "voice" (*voix*).[42] What Deligny proposes here, as I read him, is that, by following, and mapping, the wander-lines of these children, their *voix* (voice) can be read in the "writing" of their *voies* (paths). Putting aside any attempt to make the children speak "like us", by mapping this "silent" world, Deligny and his companions acknowledged the children's voice. But, respecting the radical lack of reciprocity between "us" and "them", their voice (*voix*) was acknowledged as path (*voie*).

If, then, there was close proximity to the children, this was not proximity in the expectation of direct communion. Before any proximity to another, this was proximity to the outside, that being the unmapped "territory" which the children inhabited. They themselves inhabited this "territory" without question; there was, in particular, no question of their mapping it. For us, on the other hand, just because we already approach it as not yet mapped, it is already-mapped or, at least, symbolised, as territory. Paradoxically, just because of our capacity to prefigure it as territory, we can have no direct access to it as the outside.

For the close presences this meant that there was a need to abandon any perspective based on "looking". "Looking" is the perspective of the "humans-that-we-are". This looking is a looking for, and what it looks for is the self in the other. This looking is to be differentiated from the way the children "see", or "eye", the world:

> It is well known that an "autistic child" does not look (at us); one should say "eying" to evoke the way they have of seeing without looking. There is *that* [*CE*] way of seeing and there is the seeing the SELF [*SE*] or an OTHER [*SE*].

190 Peter Gunn

It takes just one character (S), one that is a little twisted, to evoke what I call the fissure between our viewpoint – which is capable of seeing itself – and the "seeing point" of an "autistic child".[43]

What Poe's narrator demonstrates is that for us, when it comes to the outside, looking is always seduced into a self-aggrandising looking-for; it becomes a looking which looks for what is like us. Taking Janmari as his reference, Deligny describes this looking-for as follows:

> And it is that, watching Janmari live, there's no question, he does turn around us, and we need only rely on what we can feel in order to suppose that he wanders like a soul in pain deprived of the ability to identify someONE. But this way of feeling can come from the fact that each one of us is someONE, and that this ONE of the existing subject has an undeniable propensity for self-projection, as we say, as if every ONE of us were a soul having a hard time identifying, and then the charade comes from us, and not from the autistic individual. . .[44]

Deligny's mapping was a way of disciplining such looking. Rather than being a looking *at* the children, mapping was confined to "eying". If this took the form of an interested mapping, it was not, and could not be, directed towards communalising the children as others like us.

"Eying" did not, in particular, take the perspective of seeing the children as errant. Rather, by tracing "their" "detouring" wander-lines and noting "their" "pointless" gestures, it followed them in "their" errancy.[45] Furthermore, if, as Deligny says, even if it was around "us" that Janmari turned, this did not make this errancy *from* us; being always also outside, his errancy remained errancy in-itself, in act, here-and-now.

By re-positioning itself as an attempt at mapping this outside errancy, Deligny's *tentative* had itself to be open to being constantly re-positioned at the very limits of the mapped. In studying the children's wander-lines and noting cross-beams, a "detour" into the wild became, in some instances, an opening onto new territory. Mapping that detour as a cross-beam, that is, a structure which supports an opening onto elsewhere,[46] led to the noting of a threshold or doorstep, and even before there was any actual door.

This is what was surprising here: "[t]hat there is a *crossbeam* even before the door is there and before the customary paths have been established . . .".[47] And what Deligny and his companions found equally surprising was the fact that, once mapped, these detours into the wild sometimes led to the "re"-discovery of not-known mappings; they coincided "more often than they ought to with old paths and trajectories of which we were unaware".[48]

In further remarks Deligny seems to imply that, in this search, the cross-beams provided support for envisaging the "supposed", whether in the form of the human

Close to the wild child 191

foot or the door. As I read him here, in looking to find traces of these supposeds at these limit-points, he and his fellow close presences lost them-*selves*. Faced with the persistence of such cross-beams at those limits, and of the *theres* which they designate, it was only by losing themselves *there* that they could catch language "completing our surprise":

> If I lose myself as much as I like in the dictionary, it is to find traces of the supposed: the foot, the door. Since the door is not there yet, we would be dealing with an expectation; any *crossbeam* is sturdy enough. And we see how language ends up completing our surprise in front of the persistence of these crossbeams, which, I remember, are merely the traces from the *theres* where the wander lines converge, crisscross, and sometimes stop, all of them, *there*.[49]

For the children, not inhabiting language, there can be no such surprise. The *theres* are simply there as they always are; it is these *theres* which constitute what is, for them, the immutable nature of the customary. Deligny takes the example of the children's peremptory insistence on acting to re-close doors immediately after they have been opened. He hypothesises that for them a door is, in its immutability, completely real; it is never, therefore, *a* door, but always *that* (closed) door *there*. In other words, for the children, the thing and the place of the thing are the same; if there is a *there*, there is already always some *thing*.[50]

For us, faced with the unexpected persistence of a cross-beam on the borders of no-man's-land, language acts to "complete" [*combler*][51] our surprise by *creating* something *there*, albeit out of, what is for us, nothing. And if such an act of creation occurs at the very limits of the mapped, it occurs, necessarily for us, also at the very limits of language.

It is here that we catch language "in the act of exerting itself". The nothing out of which language creates takes the form of the opening or hole for which the cross-beam lends support. Language creates out of that nothing *there* in the only way it can. It completes our surprise by filling that hole *there*. Usually, and as was the case with the "re-discovery of old paths and trajectories", this immediately takes on the form of something familiar. But it occurs, first of all, not by way of an imaginary in-fill, but by way of the logical function of negation.

Deligny puts it as follows:

> The *pas de porte* (doorstep) is then the passage, or the fact that, there is not – yet – a door. Either the *pas* (step) is the action of allowing the support of the body to pass from one foot to another, or the *pas* (not) is an auxiliary of negation.[52]

It was with the formal proximity to the children which the mapping afforded the close presences, that the logic of this operation of filling-in was caught and, furthermore, suspended. The effect of this was to confront those adults with a doorway, but not just any doorway; this is the doorway which leads to the passage-to-the-act,[53] that act being one of stepping out into what is not only *un*-familiar and *un*-named, but radically outside. It is, nevertheless, *there*.

In their proximity to the children, it was in this way that, at the risk of getting lost, that is, of getting lost as subjects, Deligny and his companions arrived at the borders of this most foreign territory. In keeping with the etymological trajectory of the word "pilgrim", if the children remained strangers, they were now also pilgrims.[54] For the close presences, it was the children, now fully *there* for them, though remaining distant, who showed the way. If, as Deligny says, they are strangers for *us*, that, now, is "the least we can say about them. The least and perhaps the best".[55]

The texts which are assembled in *The Arachnean and Other Texts* seem in some cases to have been written out of a somewhat ambivalent engagement with Lacanian psychoanalysis. Despite this I have, with one exception,[56] made no explicit connections with psychoanalysis. I have done this partly for reasons of time and space but also, more importantly, because as I worked on this paper, I began to realise the importance of allowing Deligny's work to have its own voice. In this respect, just as Deligny did with his autistic children, I do him the honour of regarding him as a pilgrim.

That said, two further things need to be said. Firstly, like Lacan, Deligny's work resists any attempt at exegesis; whilst he undoubtedly has a voice, it is not one which is there waiting to be declaimed; his voice, you could say, is one which has to be drawn out and articulated. And yet, as a psychoanalyst I cannot avoid bringing my own voice to that articulation. And that voice is, in turn, inflected, if not infected, by psychoanalysis.

Secondly, and as a psychoanalytic postscript, I would also now like to explicitly draw out one Lacanian connection.

In one of the lessons of his seminar *The Ethics of Psychoanalysis* Jacques Lacan talks about creation *ex nihilo* (out of nothing). Drawing on Heidegger's essay "Das Ding", he takes the vase as an example of what he calls a "fabricated signifier".[57] If such a signifier is fabricated, it itself has the power to create. The vase, "creates the void and thereby induces the possibility of filling it. Emptiness and fullness are introduced into a world that by itself knows not of them".[58]

As signifier the vase represents the existence of the Thing, the Thing being, as Lacan puts it, the "outside-of-the-signified".[59] That is, the vase stands in for that outside, that being the emptiness or nothing at the centre of what Lacan calls the real. For that reason, "[t]he fashioning of the signifier and the introduction of a gap or a hole in the real is identical".[60]

We can contrast this last assertion with what I said earlier in relation to Deligny's mute children. For them, what is indistinguishable is the place or *there* of the thing and the thing itself. With Lacan we can now say that the effect of the children's muteness on us is to make the Thing present.

And it is not coincidental that, earlier in the *Ethics* seminar, we find Lacan talking about a mute, in this case Harpo, the silent brother of the four Marx brothers:

> Is there anything which can pose a question which is more pressing [*pressante*], more present [*présente*], more captivating [*prenante*], more disruptive, more nauseating, more calculated to throw into the abyss and nothingness everything that takes place before us, than the figure of Harpo Marx, marked with that smile of which one does not know whether it is that of the most extreme perversity or foolishness. This mute on his own is sufficient to sustain the atmosphere of placing-in-question and radical annihilation that is the stuff of the formidable farce of the Marx Brothers, of the uninterrupted play of *jokes* [in English in original] that makes their activity so valuable.[61]

By his silent and enigmatic insistence, Lacan's Harpo makes present the Thing.[62] This has particular relevance for the practice of psychoanalysis. Sometimes, the analyst, by remaining mute, can also make present the Thing, thereby calling into question the only thing which stands before that outside: the analysand's own, subjective existence.[63]

The act of stepping over into that outside would be, as Lacan puts it in his seminar on anxiety, a "vagabond departure into the pure world, where the subject sets off to search for, to encounter something that's been rejected and everywhere refused".[64] But, as the narrator of Poe's story demonstrates, both as the narrator and also as the character in that story with whom we identify, our world is inescapably one which has the structure of a fiction. It is on this stage that "man as subject has to be constituted, to take up his place as he who bears speech . . .".[65]

If then, being the humans-that-we-are, we have no alternative but to draw back from taking that step, that rejected something might nevertheless be encountered, but with horror. This is because it turns us inside out. Though most intimately part of us, just because we inhabit language rather than the real, it has been rejected. This piece is what Lacan calls *object a*,[66] and it is this which continues to lead us astray.

Notes

¶ I would like to acknowledge the origins of this paper. It was written in response to a call for papers from my colleague Trudy Clutterbok. This was in the context of her project *Notes from the Outskirts: Spaces of Madness*. She précised this project as follows: "Madness speaks. But how to speak in return? Whatever madness charges us with, some of us love to be nearby it". Although Trudy's project did not result in a publication, it continued to provide direction for this paper.

1 For the history of Art Brut and of outsider art more generally, see Lucienne Peiry, *Art Brut: The origins of Outsider Art*, tr. James Frank, Flammarion, Paris, 2001.

2 See Jack Flam, 'Taming the Beasts', *The New York Review of Books*, April 25, 1991.

3 Deligny's patron, the psychiatrist Henri Wallon, also had an interest in such children. He wrote his PhD thesis on this topic, later (in 1925) published as a book entitled *L'enfant turbulent* [*The Troublesome Child*].

4 Fernand Deligny, Fernand Deligny, *The Arachnean and Other Texts*, Univocal Publishing, Minneapolis, 2015, p. 47.
5 See «Chronologie», in Fernand Deligny, *Oeuvres*, L'Arachnéen, Paris, 2007, pp. 1821–1824.
6 François Dosse, *Gilles Deleuze & Félix Guattari – Intersecting Lives*, tr. Deborah Glassman, Columbia University Press, 2011, p. 72.
7 «Chronologie», in Fernand Deligny, *Oeuvres*. Op. cit., pp. 1825–1826.
8 The French word *tentative* can be translated as "attempt".
9 Fernand Deligny, «Au défaut du langage», *Cahiers de l'Immuable/3, Recherches* No. 24, November 1976, p. 66.
10 Ibid., p. 65.
11 What I am providing here is my own summary account of both Deligny's "common", and of his *tentative* more broadly. I make no claim to definitiveness, my excuse being the poetic and lapidary nature of Deligny's writings. Eschewing academic punctiliousness, I invite the reader to produce their own account, an account which will, undoubtedly, be different to mine. The primary text on which I am drawing for this paper is Fernand Deligny, *The Arachnean and Other Texts*. Op. cit. For the "common", perhaps the most relevant sections of this book are the ones entitled "The Fulfilled Child" and "When the-Human-that-We-Are Is Not There". Also important are the photographs of Janmari reproduced in the middle of the book, and the maps at the end.
12 Deligny's holophrase "humans-that-we-are" questions "our" arrogant assumption that to be human any other must be like "us": "But 'like us' implies a necessary belief in the validity of this 'us', of the humans-that-we-are as we think and conceive ourselves, after millennia of domestication, and Lord knows what advantages humanity has drawn from this". Fernand Deligny, Au défaut du langage. Op. cit., p. 206.
13 Cf., Fernand Deligny, Au défaut du langage. Op. cit., p. 224.
14 Ibid., p. 225.
15 The French is *le coutumier*. The translators of *The Arachnean and Other Texts* point out that, 'Deligny uses *le coutumier* to refer to the customary practices developed within the living spaces . . .' Fernand Deligny, Ibid., p. 68, n. 9. Sandra Alvarez de Toledo expands on this when she comments that the customary 'is distinguished from the day-to-day by the respect for the notion of usage, in other words the imperious need of immutability [*immuable*] that characterizes autism . . .' (Sandra Alvarez de Toledo (ed.), *Cartes et lignes d'erre / Maps and Wander Lines: Traces du réseau de Fernand Deligny, 1969–1979*, p. 12).
16 "Close presence" (*présence proche*) is Deligny's term for the adults who live in close proximity to the children. Sandra Alvarez de Toledo comments that the term was chosen by Deligny to emphasise "the necessary distance between the adult and the child: 'close' is not 'near' the child, not is it 'for' him". (Sandra Alvarez de Toledo (ed.), *Cartes et lignes d'erre / Maps and Wander Lines: Traces du réseau de Fernand Deligny, 1969–1979*. Op. cit., p. 12).
17 Fernand Deligny, Oeuvres. Op. cit., p. 156. Sandra Alvarez de Toledo comments that in Deligny's vocabulary a "binding joist" (her translation of *chevêtre*) is a "point in space where the adults' journeys and the children's *wander lines* cross each other (are 'entangled'); a specific spot they tend to go, and where their *acts* coincide"' (Sandra Alvarez de Toledo (ed.), *Cartes et lignes d'erre / Maps and Wander Lines: Traces du réseau de Fernand Deligny, 1969–1979*. Op. cit., p. 12).
18 «Chronologie», in Fernand Deligny, Oeuvres. Op. cit., p. 1826.
19 The film *Ce Gamin, là*, directed by Renaud Victor, was made in 1975. A video version is available on YouTube at www.youtube.com/watch?v=i20VWKO9Sdk. A transcription of the voice-over of this section of the film is available in Fernand Deligny, *Oeuvres, op. cit.*, p. 1040.

20 Even before meeting Janmari, Deligny had already read Jean Marc Gaspard Itard's *The Wild Boy of Aveyron* (see Louis-Pierre Jouvenet et al, Fernand Deligny, *50 ans d'asile*, p. 17). In notes which he made in 1972, and which were later published in his book *Nous et l'innocent*, Deligny makes reference to this as a renaming in which Jean-Marie's original, sexually 'concocted' name, is replaced with one which respects his identity as being so singular as to be outside any such sexual conjunction:

> And we concoct ourselves [*nous nous conjuguons*] from the ones and the others, outdoing each other, and yet here we have one *gamine* [kid, feminine] who is called Marie which is not concocted. And then this other who is a gamin [kid, masculine] and who is called Marie, the same, except that for the *gamine* [girl], it's Marie which appears first and, after a little dash, it's Pierre, and yet for the *garçon* [boy] it's Jean which is said first, then a dash and then Marie.
>
> This Janmari, I've doctored the actual spelling of his first name, definitely comfortable in making that his religion, which for him comes to gestures without the least borrowing from any rituals in use. His remarkable identity - it is obvious that he cannot be in the register of births – identical in his ways of being to Victor of Aveyron, the wild child observed by Itard.
>
> (Fernand Deligny, *Nous et l'innocent*, reprinted in, Oeuvres, op. cit., pp. 781–782)

21 Dudley Andrew, 'Every Teacher Needs a Truant: Bazin and L'Enfant sauvage', in Dudley Andrew and Anne Gillain (eds.), *A Companion to François Truffaut*, Wiley-Blackwell, Oxford, 2013, p. 231.

22 Quoted in Dudley Andrew, Ibid., p. 231. The quote is taken from a letter to Truffaut written by Deligny. Their correspondence has been published: Bernard Bastide (ed.), 'Correspondance François Truffaut-Fernand Deligny', *Mille huit cent quatre-vingt-quinze*, 2004, 1, number 42. It is available online at https://1895.revues.org/281.

23 Fernand Deligny, *The Arachnean and Other Texts*. Op. cit., p. 79.

24 Ibid., p. 144, translation modified.

25 See «Chronologie», in Fernand Deligny, *Oeuvres*. Op. cit., p. 1821.

26 Quoted in Sandra Alvarez de Toledo, «L'inactualité de Fernand Deligny», in Fernand Deligny, Oeuvres, Op cit., p. 21. This text has been translated into English with the title "The untopicality of Fernand Deligny". It is available online at http://www.editions-arachneen.fr/?p=2460.

27 Fernand Deligny, *Élogie de l'asile*, Dunod, Paris, 1983; the text was later included in Fernand Deligny, *A comme asile, suivi de 'Nous et l'innocent'*, Dunod, Paris, 1999. Unfortunately, I have not had access to this text; both of these publications are out of print and are now, it seems, unobtainable.

As part of the move to the deinstitutionalisation of psychiatric services, beginning in 1960 France moved to a system of 'sectorisation' based on local catchment areas. It took another twenty-five years for the system to be fully implemented. For a brief history of psychiatric sectorisation in France, see, F. Petitjean, D. Leguay, «Sectorisation psychiatrique: évolution et perspectives/Psychiatric sectorization. Evolution and perspectives», *Annales Médico-psychologiques, revue psychiatrique*, Volume 160, Issue 10, December 2002, pp. 786–793, and also V. Kovess, B. Boisguerin, D. Antoine, M. Reynauld, 'Has the sectorization of psychiatric services in France really been effective', in *Social Psychiatry and Psychiatric Epidemiology*, Volume 30, Issue 3, 1995, pp. 132–138.

28 Quoted in Sandra Alvarez de Toledo, *L'inactualité de Fernand Deligny*. Op. cit., p. 21.

29 Poe's story 'The System of Doctor Tarr and Professor Fether' can be found online and in many anthologies, including, Edgar Allan Poe, *The Complete Tales and Poems*, Vintage Books, New York, 1975, pp. 307–321.

30 The term 'moral treatment' is a translation of Pinel's traitement moral. For a discussion of the complex issues, both linguistic and practical, surrounding this usage, see Louis

196 Peter Gunn

C. Charland, "Benevolent Theory: Moral Treatment at the York Retreat", in *History of Psychiatry*, Volume 18, Issue 1, 2007, pp. 61–80. For an overview of the initiatives of both Pinel and Tuke, see Michel Foucault, "Birth of the Asylum", paper 4 of *History of Madness*, tr. Jonathan Murphy and Jean Khalfa, Routledge, London, 2006, pp. 463–511. For an account specifically of Pinel's traitement moral, see Jan Goldstein, "The Transformation of Charlatanism, or the Moral Treatmen", chapter three of *Console and Classify: The French Psychiatric Profession in the Nineteenth Century*, Cambridge University Press, Cambridge, 1987, pp. 64–119.

31 Edgar Allan Poe, The System of Doctor Tarr and Professor Fether. Op. cit., p. 307.

32 Ibid., p. 319. As Daniela Fargione points out, the refusal of the narrator's companion to go any further than the gate of the asylum may be due to the fact he himself is a former inmate (Daniela Fargione, "The Irony of E.A. Poe's Lunatick Asylum", in *Merely a Madness? Defining, Treating and Celebrating the Unreasonable*, ed. Daniela Fargione and Johnathan Sunley, Inter-Disciplinary Press, Oxford, 2012, pp. 51–72). It is worth noting here also that *colin-maillard* is the French term for blind man's buff, a game in which a blindfolded player tries to catch others while being pushed about by them.

33 William Whipple, "Poe's Two-Edged Satiric Tale", *Nineteenth Century Fiction*, Vol. 9, No. 2 (Sep, 1954), pp. 121–133.

34 Charles Dickens, *American Notes: For General Circulation*, Penguin Classics, London, 1972, p. 95.

35 Ibid., p. 122.

36 Edgar Allen Poe, The System of Doctor Tarr and Professor Fether. Op. cit., p. 318, my emphasis.

37 Michel Foucault, Birth of the Asylum. Op. cit., p. 486.

38 Ibid., p. 487.

39 Edgar Allen Poe, The System of Doctor Tarr and Professor Fether. Op. cit., p. 308.

40 Ibid., p. 315.

41 Fernand Deligny, *The Arachnean and Other Texts*. Op. cit., p. 197.

42 Fernand Deligny, The Missing Voice. Op. cit., pp. 197–200.

43 Fernand Deligny, *The Arachnean and Other Texts*. Op. cit., p. 157.

44 Ibid., p. 173.

45 In putting several words in quotation marks here, I am wanting to draw attention to the fact that, for Deligny, the children, not being subjects like us, cannot be said to possess anything in their name, neither their wanderings as trajectory, nor their gestures as meaningful, nor even themselves as errant. As Deligny puts it at one point, "as autistic and mute individuals, although addressed directly, they have not responded to the call . . .". (Fernand Deligny, *The Arachnean and Other Texts*. Op. cit., p. 153)

46 I am translating *chevêtre* as cross-beam, but it can also be translated as "binding joist" or "trimmer joist". In architecture a trimmer joist is a crosspiece fixed between full-length joists (and often across the end of truncated joists) to form part of the frame which supports an opening in a floor or roof.

47 Fernand Deligny, *The Arachnean and Other Texts*. Op. cit., p. 210.

48 Ibid., p. 198.

49 Ibid., p. 211, translation modified.

50 Ibid., p. 208–209.

51 The primary sense of the French verb *combler* is to fill in.

52 Fernand Deligny, *The Arachnean and Other Texts*. Op. cit., p. 211. The translators make the following observation: "The French noun *pas*, 'step', has a homonym in the negative particle *pas*; thus *pas de porte* can mean 'doorstep' or 'no door'". I should stress that what I am offering here is very much my own reading of Deligny's more than usually lapidary statements.

53 I am using this phrasing deliberately. For Lacan, the passage à l'acte (passage-to-the-act) is, as he puts it in one of his formulations in his seminar on anxiety, a moment

when the subject passes into the real. It amounts to what, in psychiatry, is called a "fugue state" (Jacques Lacan, *Anxiety: The Seminar of Jacques Lacan Book X*, p. 116).

54 "Here the autistic being becomes a pilgrim – a word that used to mean 'stranger' before coming to mean 'traveler'". Fernand Deligny, *The Arachnean and Other Texts*. Op. cit., p. 198. It should be noted that the English word "pilgrim" has the same etymology as the French word *pélerin*.

55 Fernand Deligny, *The Arachnean and Other Texts*. Op. cit., p. 198.

56 See footnote 52 above.

57 Jacques Lacan, *The Ethics of Psychoanalysis 1959–1960*. Op. cit., p. 120.

58 Ibid., p. 120.

59 Ibid., p. 54.

60 Ibid., p. 121.

61 Cf. Jacques Lacan, Ibid., p. 55. Instead of the published translation, I am using a slightly modified version of the translation of this passage which appears in Simon Critchley, *Ethics, Politics, Subjectivity: Essays on Derrida, Levinas*, Verso, London, 1999, p. 231.

62 In the passage immediately preceding the reference to Harpo, Lacan plays on the homophony between the phrases *faire mouche* (to hit the bull's eye) and faire mot (to become word): 'the Thing only presents itself to the extent that it becomes word [*fait mot*], hits the bull's eye [*faire mouche*], as one says.' (Jacques Lacan, Ibid., p. 55, translation modified).

In Clarice Lispector's novel *Near to the Wild Heart*, the character Joana makes the following observation about vision: "To have a vision, the thing didn't have to be sad or happy or manifest itself. All it had to do was exist, preferably still and silent, in order to feel the mark in it."(Clarice Lispector, *Near to the Wild Heart* [*Perto do coração selvagem*], tr. Alison Entrekin, Penguin Books, London, 2012, p. 37.) In other words, Lispector's Vision (I take the liberty of making it hers, and capitalising it) also makes present the Thing.

63 In Lispector's novel, Joana goes on to say something which comes close to being a summary of Deligny's own project: "You see, vision consisted of surprising the symbol of the thing in the thing itself". (Clarice Lispector, *Near to the Wild Heart* [*Perto do coração selvagem*]. Op. cit., p. 38). In recognition of this, I have appropriated Lispector's title as my own. I note, in doing so, that the Portuguese word *perto* can also be translated as "close".

64 Jacques Lacan, *The Ethics of Psychoanalysis 1959–1960*. Op. cit., p. 116, translation modified.

65 Jacques Lacan, The Cause of Desire Lesson of 16 January 1963. *Anxiety: The Seminar of Jacques Lacan Book X*. Op. cit., p. 116.

66 Lacan introduced *objet a* in his seminar on anxiety. See Jacques Lacan, 'The Cause of Desire', lesson of 16 January 1963, in Ibid., pp. 100–113.

References

Alvarez de Toledo, S. (2007a) Chronologie. In: *Oeuvres*. Edited by Fernand Deligny. Paris: Éditions L'Arachnéean, 1820–1831.

Alvarez de Toledo, S. (2007b) L'inactualité de Fernand Deligny. In *Oeuvres*. Edited by Fernand Deligny. Paris: Éditions L'Arachnéean, 21–37.

Alvarez de Toledo, S. (Ed.) (2013) *Cartes et lignes d'erre / Maps and Wander Lines: Traces du réseau de Fernand Deligny, 1969–1979*. Paris: L'Arachnéen.

Andrew, D. (2013) Every Teacher Needs a Truant: Bazin and *L'Enfant sauvage*. In: *A Companion to François Truffaut*. Edited by D. Andrew & A. Gillain. Oxford: Wiley-Blackwell.

Antoine, D., Boisguerin, B., Kovess, V., & Reynauld, M. (1995) Has the Sectorization of Psychiatric Services in France Really Been Effective. *Social Psychiatry and Psychiatric Epidemiology*, 30(3): 132–138.

Bastide, B. (Ed.) (2004) Correspondence François Truffaut-Fernand Deligny. *Mille huit cent quatre-vingt-quinze*, 1(42).

Charland, L. C. (2007) Benevolent Theory: Moral Treatment at the York Retreat. *History of Psychiatry*, 18(1): 61–80.

Critchley, S. (1999) *Ethics, Politics, Subjectivity: Essays on Derrida, Levinas*. London: Verso.

Deligny, F. (1976) Au défaut du langage. *Cahiers de l'Immuable/3, Recherches* No. 24, November.

Deligny, F. (1983) *Élogie de l'asile*. Paris: Dunod.

Deligny, F. (1999) *A comme asile, suivi de 'Nous et l'innocent'*. Paris: Dunod.

Deligny, F. (2007a) *Nous et l'innocent*, reprinted in *Oeuvres*. Paris: L'Arachnéen, 685–794.

Deligny, F. (2007b) *Oeuvres*. Paris: L'Arachnéen.

Deligny, F. (2015a) *The Arachnean and Other Texts*. Translated by D. S. Burk & C. Porter. Minneapolis: Univocal Publishing.

Deligny, F. (2015b) The Missing Voice. In: *The Arachnean and Other Texts*. Translated by D. S. Burk & C. Porter. Minneapolis: Univocal Publishing, 197–200.

Deligny, F. (Producer) & Victor, R. (Director) (1975) *Ce Gamin, Là*. www.youtube.com/watch?v=i20VWKO9Sdk

Dickens, C. (1972) *American Notes: For General Circulation*. London: Penguin Classics.

Dosse, F. (2011) *Gilles Deleuze & Félix Guattari – Intersecting Lives*. Translated by D. Glassman. New York: Columbia University Press.

Fargione, D. (2012) The Irony of E.A. Poe's Lunatick Asylum. In: *Merely a Madness? Defining, Treating and Celebrating the Unreasonable*. Edited by D. Fargione & J. Sunley. Oxford: Inter-Disciplinary Press, 51–72.

Flam, J. (1991) Taming the Beasts. *The New York Review of Books*, 38(8) (April 25).

Foucault, M. (2006) *Birth of the Asylum, Paper 4 of History of Madness*. Translated by J. Murphy & J. Khalfa. London: Routledge, 463–511.

Goldstein, J. (1987) The Transformation of Charlatanism, or the Moral Treatment. In: *Console and Classify: The French Psychiatric Profession in the Nineteenth Century*. Cambridge: Cambridge University Press, 64–119.

Jouvenet, L. P. et al. (1988) *Fernand Deligny, 50 ans d'asile*. Toulouse: Privat.

Lacan, J. (1992) *The Ethics of Psychoanalysis 1959–1960*. Edited by J. A. Miller. London: Tavistock and Routledge.

Lacan, J. (2014a) *Anxiety: The Seminar of Jacques Lacan Book X*. Edited by J. A. Miller. London: Polity.

Lacan, J. (2014b) The Cause of Desire Lesson of 16 January 1963. In: *Anxiety: The Seminar of Jacques Lacan Book X*. Edited by J. A. Miller. London: Polity, 100–113.

Leguay, D., & Petitjean, F. (2002) Sectorisation psychiatrique: évolution et perspectives/Psychiatric sectorization. Evolution and perspectives. *Annales Médico-psychologiques, revue psychiatrique*, 160(10) (December): 786–793.

Lispector, C. (2012) *Near to the Wild Heart*. Translated by A. Entrekin. London: Penguin Books.

Peiry, L. (2001) *Art Brut: The origins of Outsider Art*. Translated by J. Frank. Paris: Flammarion.

Poe, E. A. (1975) The System of Doctor Tarr and Professor Fether. In: *The Complete Tales and Poems*. New York: Vintage Books, 307–321.

Wallon, H. (1984) *L'enfant turbulent*. Paris: Presses Universitaires de France.

Whipple, W. (1954) Poe's Two-Edged Satiric Tale. *Nineteenth Century Fiction*, 9(2) (September): 121–133.

Index

Note: Page numbers in *italics* indicate a figure and page numbers in **bold** indicate a table on the corresponding page. Page numbers followed by "n" indicate a note.

Abel, Karl 122
abstinence, principle of 30
abyss, edge of 165–170
academic discourse 38, *38*, 46
agent as knowledge (academic discourse) 42
agent as signifier (master discourse) 42
agent as subject (hysterical discourse) 42
Allouch, Jean 3–4, 7, 10n6, 11nn20, 23, 151, 163n3
anal object 36
analysand 38, 40, 43–45, 47–48
analyst 38–40, 43–44, 47–48
Andrew, Dudley 195n21
antigonality, ethics of 106–108
antigonal path 103–108; antigonal to the good 106; death, melancholia and the master 106–107; ethics of antigonality 106–108; the impossible 107–108; non-universality of the doll 107
Antigone 104, 106–108
Anti-Oedipus 12, 15
Anxiety 169
Arachnean and Other Texts, The 192
archaic anxieties 166–167, 170
Archilochus 112
Austin, John Langshaw 30
autistic language 118
auto-erotism 119
Autopsychography 132

Benjamin, Jessica 84–86
becoming, between destruction and 129–135

Beyond the Pleasure Principle 116
blank reality 40
Bleuler, E. 118–119
Borromean knot 68, 96
Breuer, Joseph 179nn1–4

capitalist discourse 44
carnality 152
Carotenuto, Aldo 135n4, 136nn10, 21, 23
castration 48, 55–57, 85, 144, 159–160, 180n13
Clinton, Hilary 155–156
Cogito and psychoanalytic discourse 38–49; *see also* Freudian cogito
common, the 183–184
Connaissance and Psychosis 177
contrasting signifiers 123
creative subversion of the subject 159–161
Cunningham, Valentine 5–8, 10nn3, 10, 14, 17, 19

Deleuze, Gilles 12–14, 17nn2, 9, 137–140, 143–146, 147nn2, 4, 7, 148nn10, 12, 24, 27, 32, 34
Deligny, Fernand 182–186, 189–192, 193n3, 194nn4–5, 7, 9, 11–13, 15–20, 195nn22–23, 25–28, 196nn25, 41–43, 47, 52, 54–55, 197n63
Desargues, Girard 96
destruction, between becoming and 129–135
de Toledo, Sandra Alvarez 195nn15–17, 26, 28

de Zentner, María-Inés Rotmiler 77, 80nn16, 19
Dickens, Charles 187, 196n34
Dickinson, Emily 6, 10n13
Difference and Repetition 137, 147nn2, 4, 7, 148nn10, 12, 24, 27, 32, 34
difference-in-itself 146
Ding, das 165–170
Dire Destiny, A 83
discourse of the analyst 38–40, *43*; academic discourse 38, *38*; agent as knowledge (academic discourse) 42, 46; agent as signifier (master discourse) 42, 46; agent as subject (hysterical discourse) 42, 46; capitalistic 44; discourse of the master 39, *39*; hysterical discourse 39, *39*; realistic 44; realistic stuff, or the matters of 42–44
discourse of the master 38–39, *39*
dissolute, meaning 83
dissolution 81–88; analyst, the dissolute 85–86; necessity of becoming dissolute 81–88; psychoanalyst knowledge, functions as particular truth 82–83; school 86–87; of transference 83–85
Domb, Benjamin 160
dreams 61–63, 65
drive, the 31–32, 34
drives 138
Dubuffet, Jean 182
Dynamics of Transference, The 176–177, 181n14

Ego 137–141, 143–145
Ego, The 167, 169
elaboration, principle of 94
Elements of the Philosophy of Right 158
Éloge de l'asile (*In Praise of the Asylum*) 185, 195n27
Enfant Sauvage, L' (The Wild Child) 184
equivocation 33–35, 65; accordance with reality or conflictual, question of 34; analysand or analyst, question of 34; Borromean knot, types linked in 68; exo or endo, question of 34; grammatical 65, 66; homophonic 65; living 35; logical 65, 66–67; same or different, question of 33–34; types of 33–35, 65–68
Eros 138, 150
Ethics of Psychoanalysis, The 192, 196n57, 197nn62, 64
Ethics seminar 166, 168–169

étourdit, L' 63–65
ex-sistence 68, 95, 161

failure of the phallus, The seminar (Fierens) 28, 50–59
family complex, foundation 156–159
Family Complexes and the Formation of the Individual ("Family Complexes, The") 14, 156, 166–167, 170
feminine formulae 56
fidelity 152
Fierens, Christian 27–37, 107–108
Figures of Heresy 5
Flying Dutchman 134
formula of impossibility 57
formal heresy 9, 10n3
Foucault, Michel 187, 196nn30, 37
Founding Act of 1964, *The* 94, 97, 99nn13, 23
Four Fundamental Concepts of Psychoanalysis, The 82–83
Freud, Sigmund 5, 7, 9, 12, 14–15, 28, 32–33, 47–48, 51, 59, 61, 63, 66, 84–85, 87, 98, 106–107, 111–113, 114nn7, 14, 116, 118–119, 122, 129–134, 135n2, 136n26, 137–138, 143–144, 148n29, 151, 157, 159–161, 168, 176–177, 179nn1–10, 180nn10–11, 13, 181nn14, 23
Freudian castration 55–56
Freudian cogito: I am as I think 40–41; I think as I am 40
Freudian School of Melbourne 90, 92, 94, 97–98

Gallagher, Cormac 91–92, 98n1, 99nn5, 9, 20, 22
gaze (regard) 36–37
go-between 140–147; *see also* unconscious
Go-Between, The 140, 145, 148nn15, 20, 25
grammatical equivocation 65–68
Grande Cordée experiment 183
Guattari, Felix 12–14, 17, 17nn2, 9, 18n25
Guibal, Michel 136nn8, 28
Guilet, Nicole 93

haeresis 6, 8, 10n16
Harari, Roberto 146, 148n38
Hartley, L. P. 140, 148nn15, 20, 25
Hayden, Josef 112

Hegel, G. W. F. 158
heresy 3–10, 10nn3, 10, 14, 17–19
heretics 5–6, 9, 10n3
Hölderlin, Friedrich 132, 136n20
Homer 115n19
homophonic equivocation 65, 68
How to do something with only the saying seminar (Fierens) 27
How to do Things with Words 30
hysterical discourse 39, *39*, 40, 42–43, 45–46

I am as I think 35, 40, *41*, 42
Id 137–138, 145
image that binds 155–163
Imago 116
impossibility 35–37; forms of 35–37; in sexuality 51; types 47
interpretation 43–44, 48, 61–69; characteristics 63; quotation and 62; with-out meaning 61–69
Interpretation of Dreams 61, 63
Interpretation with-out meaning seminar (Fierens) 28, 61–69
invocatory object 37
I think as I am 40
"I think" in the psychoanalytic discourse seminar (Fierens) 27, 38–49
I think: "therefore I am" 144

jouissance 96–97, 156–161, 163, 163n2
Jouissance of the Other 157, 159–161, 163
Journées 94–95
Joyce, James 6, 8, 10n16
Jung, Carl 129–135, 136nn7, 27
Jungle Book 184

Kafka, Franz 113–114, 115n20
Kipling, Rudyard 184
Klein, Melanie 123
Knowledge of the Psychoanalyst, The 83

Lacan Love 7, 10nn1, 6, 20, 23, 151
language 117–118; cave of 123–124; fields of 117–118; magical 119; melody or rhythm 117; spoken 116–119
Le Gaufey, Guy 144, 146, 148nn28, 31
Lévi-Strauss, Claude 110–111, 114nn2, 4
logical equivocation 65–67, 69
Look, Listen, Read 110
Lorca, Federico Garcia 170

love 149–154
Luther's Final Answer 10n18

madness 182–193; *L'Enfant Sauvage* (The Wild Child) 184, 195n21 ; *tentatives* 185
magical language 119
Maillard, Monsieur 186–188
Masson, Jeffrey Moussaieff 110–111, 113, 114n15
master discourse 39–40, 42–43, 45–47
material heresy 4, 9, 10n3
matheme, principle of 67
matheme of the impossible 45–48; academic discourse 46–47; accepting the possibility 47; hysterical discourse 46–47; impossibility, types 47; master discourse 46–47
McGuire, William 136n6
melancholic effacement 106
melody or rhythm language 117
mésalliance 176–177, 179n1, 180n11, 181n13
Miller, Jacques-Alain 8, 10, 10n2, 11nn21, 24
"moment, The" (NaHagid) 165
"moral treatment" 186–188; 195n30
Murnane, Gerald 85
My Barbaric Yawp 93, 97

NaHagid, Samuel 165
narcissistic self 138
Nasio, Juan-David 13–15, 17n3
Necessity of Heresy, The 5, 10, 10nn3, 14, 17, 19
neologism 7, 83, 139
neurosis 16, 30, 106, 137, 176–177
Nietzsche, Friedrich 17, 17n1, 98, 99nn25, 26
normativisation 112
Nunberg, Herman 136n32

object *a* 27, 35–37, 43–44, 46, 48, 63, 67–68, 82–85, 87–88, 108n1, 139–140, 143, 146, 160–163, 163n3
object-based libido 119
Object of Psychoanalysis, The 96, 99n20
oceanic feeling 111, 112
Oedipus complex 12–16, 18n15, 57, 62, 112, 156; belief in 12–17; dis-evangelism and 17; human relations notions and 14; invoked by Nasio 14;

as a key to *jouissance* 15–16; Lacan's approach to 14; myths operating in 15; reductive Oedipalism 14
Oedipus: The Most Crucial Concept in Psychoanalysis 13, 17n3
One 74–76; analyst-despite-himself 77–78; that Lacan encounters in Plato's *Parmenides* 76; *One* of absolute difference versus one of attribute 76; *Parmenides One* 75–77; of pure difference 77
On Narcissism: An Introduction 177, 181n14
oral object 36
Other, the 139, 144, 146
. . . *ou Pire* seminar 74, 75, 79nn1–2, 85, 137–138, 144, 146, 147nn1, 3, 6, 148nn 8–9, 11, 14, 19, 30, 33, 37, 39–40

painter's saying 149–154; first reading 150–151; second reading, fortune 152–153; third reading, postscript 153–154
Papa and Mama words 116–124; *see also* spoken language
paradoxes 67
"parasitic Real" 84
parlêtre (speaking-being) 92, 94–95
Parmenides One 75–77
Payne, John 153
Pereira, David 12–17, 73–79, 139–140, 181n21
perversion 22, 30
Pessoa, Fernando 132, 135
Petit Silence ("A Little Silence") 110–111
Phallic Jouissance 161, 163
phallus/phallic formulae 50–59; appearance and not a reality 52; characteristics 52; discourses versus 52; failure of 50–59; feminine formulae (third and fourth phallic formulae) 56; first phallic formulae 54; fourth formula (not all x phi of x) 58; must *fully* fill the gap of the absence 52; second phallic formulae 54; as a signifier 52; third formulae (formula of impossibility) 57
phantasy 123, 157, 160
Phenomenology of Spirit 158
Pinel, Philippe 186, 195n30
Plastow, Michael Gerard 27–28, 50, 79n8, 110–114, 129–135, 181n21
Plato 75–76, 79n9, 123–124

play 4, 104–105, 106, 108, 170
pleasure principle 112, 154, 161, 169–170
plus-one 94–95, 97
Poe, Edgar Allan 186–190, 193, 195nn29, 31–32, 196nn33, 36, 39
Porge, Erik 181n23
Psicanálise, Toro de 99n11
psychic reality 40, 44, 144
psychoanalysis 73–79; anal object 36; concepts of 31; the drive 31; Either I don't think or I am not 42; four fundamental points for 42; fundamental concepts of 36; I don't think and I am 42; I don't think and I am not 41–42; invocatory object 37; I think and I am not 42; oral object 36; *Psychoanalysis* 178; psychoanalyst or psychoanalyst*s* 74–75; repetition 31; school of 78–79; scopic object 36–37; transference 31; unconscious 31–32; *see also One*
psychoanalyst 16, 27, 33, 38–49, 52, 74–75, 82–83, 85, 86, 90, 151
psychoanalytical discourse 44–45; assurance of 49; empty space of the four loci of, sustaining 44–45; four places in 48–49; "I think" in 38–49; *see also* discourse of the analyst
Psychoanalytical Notes on a Case of Paranoia 176
psychosis 30, 176–178, 180n13, 181n23

Quignard, Pascal 111–112, 114, 114nn8, 12, 115nn18, 23

realistic discourse 43–45
reality 40
reductive Oedipalism 14
reminiscence 138, 140–143
repetition 31
Repetition 95
ritornello 104–105
Robinson, Thomas M. 135n3
Roustang, François 83–87

Sabroe, Morten 155–156, 159, 161–163
Safouan, Moustafa 107
saying 29–30; conditions of 29–31; doing something with only 29–30; functions of 30–31; silence, value of 29–30; *see also* equivocation
Schröter, Michael 115n16
scopic object 36–37

Seminar III: The Psychoses 177, 180n13, 181n14
Seminar X 121
Seminar XVII 123
S-exploitation 19–24
sexuality 12, 15–16, 50–54, 56–57, 59, 86, 118, 160
sexual relation, as subject matter 21
sexuation 50–59
Sibony, Daniel 94
signifier 7, 14, 23, 27–28, 31, 39, 42–46, 48, 51–55, 83, 85, 88, 91–92, 106, 116, 120–124, 131, 133, 137, 139, 146, 153, 159–160, 168, 170, 192
silence 29–37, 110–114
Sint'Home Rule 6, 8, 10n16
Sinthome, The 63
Sloterdijk, Peter 16–17, 18n23, 140, 148n18
Song of Myself 93
speaker's corner 175–179
Spielrein, Sabina 116–124, 129, 132–133, 135nn1, 4, 136nn23, 25, 28, 29, 31, 33, 34
spoken language 116–119
Studies on Hysteria 176, 179nn1–5
Subversion of the Subject in the Dialectics of Desire 159

tentatives 183–186, 189–190, 194nn8, 11
Then die, Goddamn, die 155, 162
Thirteen Clocks, The 168
Thou Who Art in Heaven 155
Three Essays on the Theory of Sexuality 118
Thurber, James 168
Totem and Taboo 15, 119
transference 31, 32; dissolution of 83–85; Oedipal view of 139; psychotic 177–178; in relation to neurosis 176; Sloterdijk's definition of 140; subject-supposed-*connaissance* 178
Traumdeutung (*Interpretation of Dreams*) 61
Tuke, William 186, 195n30

Ulysses 62
unconscious 31–32; first synthesis (passive contemplation) 138; logic for 67; second synthesis (from passive and involuntary contemplation of presence to the active and voluntary re-presentation of former) 138–139; syntheses of time in 138–139; third synthesis (determined in the image of a unique event) 142; timelessness of 144
unian (term) 140, 146

variety/varity of truth 7
verbal language *see* spoken language
Vivès, Jean-Michel 112–113, 114n1

Wagner, Richard 131–132, 134, 136n19
Wahnbildung (delusion formation) 176
Wharton, Barbara 116
Whipple, William 196n33
Whitman, Walt 93
Wunsch (wish) 61–63
Writer, The 93–95, 97
writing out of school 90–98
Wunschwort (wish word) 117, 120–121, 124

Yawp, The 93, 97–98

Zentner, Oscar 5, 8–10, 10nn1, 7, 8, 11nn26, 27, 30, 80n19, 90, 99nn2, 11, 177–178, 181nn18, 19

Printed in the United States
by Baker & Taylor Publisher Services